TRANSNATIONAL GOVERNANCE

Transnational Governance
Emerging Models of Global Legal Regulation

Edited by

MICHAEL HEAD, SCOTT MANN and SIMON KOZLINA
University of Western Sydney, Australia

Routledge
Taylor & Francis Group
LONDON AND NEW YORK

First published 2012 by Ashgate Publishing

2 Park Square, Milton Park, Abingdon, Oxon OX14 4RN
711 Third Avenue, New York, NY 10017, USA

Routledge is an imprint of the Taylor & Francis Group, an informa business

First issued in paperback 2016

British Library Cataloguing in Publication Data
Transnational governance:emerging models of global legal regulation.
1. Law and globalization. 2. International law. 3. Conflict of laws. 4. Law–International unification. 5. International organization.
I. Mann, Scott. II. Head, Michael, LL. B. III. Kozlina, Simon.
341–dc23

Library of Congress Cataloging-in-Publication Data
Transnational governance:emerging models of global legal regulation/by Scott Mann, Michael Head and Simon Kozlina.
p. cm.
Includes bibliographical references and index. ISBN 978-1-4094-1826-9 (hardback : alk. paper) 1. International law. 2. International cooperation.
3. International organization. 4. Corporate governance. 5. Globalization. I.
Mann, Scott. II. Head, Michael, LL. B. III. Kozlina, Simon.
KZ1321.T73 2011
341—dc23
2011042507

ISBN 978-1-4094-1826-9 (hbk)
ISBN 978-1-138-24933-2 (pbk)

Contents

List of Contributors

Editors

Dr Michael Head: Professor of Law, author of books on public law, legal theory and law and society
Dr Scott Mann: Associate Professor of Law, author of works on legal theory, economics and ethics
Simon Kozlina: Lecturer in Law, specialising in international trade law

Contributors

Professor Michael A. Adams: Professor of Law and author of texts on corporate law and management
Dr Simon Chapple: Barrister and Lecturer in Law, specialising in legal history
Professor Steven Freeland: Professor of Law, who has been Visiting Professional (Chambers) at the International Criminal Court
Dr Laura Horn: Senior Lecturer in Law, specialising in environmental law
John Juriansz: Lecturer in Law, with a background in public policy, governance and constitutional law
Dr Marina Nehme: Senior Lecturer in Law, specialising in corporate law
Dr Elfriede Sangkuhl: Lecturer in Law, author in the areas of tax and corporate reform
Dr Michelle Sanson: Senior Lecturer in Law and author of texts on international law, global governance, international trade and arbitration

Preface

The last century has seen the development of governance as a critical area of study for economics, politics, finance, accounting, law and regulation. Without doubt, hundreds of books and articles have been written on governance and, over the last 25 years, a particular focus has been on corporate governance. This book has uniquely put together a series of essays with a common theme of transnational governance. There are few books that have tried to connect the complexities of legal, ethical, political and economic paradigms in the way this volume has done.

It is a credit to the quality of authors in one law school that so many different points of view can be expressed with such analytical approach. The University of Western Sydney School of Law brings together a unique approach to the issues surrounding transnational governance. It attempts to grapple with large issues the twenty-first century will face in the coming decades. The authors each show a detailed analysis of the existing literature and topics, but also provide a wide range of solutions, commentaries and reforms for the problems outlined in each chapter.

As a professor of corporate law and an expert in national corporate governance, and some elements of international governance, for me this book really opens up the debates and the topics which impact many societies and nations around the world.

Scholars, students, lawyers, politicians, activists and reformers will all benefit from the insights shown in this collection of essays. The diversity of topics within the transnational governance umbrella reflects the continuing issues with the global move to transnational corporations that are much larger and have more influence than many sovereign nations. This book adds important value to the debates that are raging on these topics.

It is important to start in an historical context with the origins of transnational governance and then move to the economics and trade influences on global entities. Many forget the importance of taxation across borders and the impact on foreign currency in transactions. As we look forward, the planet is at risk in ways that could never have been imagined and the growth of environmental governance and its link to human rights is critical. A special emphasis of this collection of essays is that topics of governance over terrorism, international criminal governance and global regulation through the United Nations are left wanting in the twenty-first century.

The general editors (who are also contributors), Dr Michael Head, Dr Scott Mann and Simon Kozlina, have done an excellent job of balancing diverse views and adding to the independent research and analysis of transnational governance.

I can guarantee the reader will be left challenged, but stimulated, in examining the role of transnational governance across these many domains. The world has shrunk in many ways, but the underlying issues have not been appropriately resolved. This provides huge opportunities for exploitation and long-term damage to individuals, to regions, to nations. This book places these issues high on the global agenda.

Professor Michael A. Adams
Head, School of Law, University of Western Sydney

Introduction

Michael Head, Scott Mann and Simon Kozlina

Introduction: The Significance and Problems of Transnational Governance

This volume examines the challenges to traditional notions of regulation, governance and authority posed by the globalisation of economic and social life. Increasingly, vast financial, technological and corporate processes are eroding the capacities of national governments to meaningfully regulate society. At the same time – as the ongoing global financial crisis that erupted in 2007–08 and the breakdown of the 2009 Copenhagen climate change summit demonstrate – efforts at international coordination are proving highly problematic.

These developments and crises are themselves, to a significant extent, bound up with deep-seated changes in economic life. These are, in turn, reflected in shifts in ideologies and practices of national and international governance in the 1970s and 1980s. The three planks of the post-Second World War Keynesian Bretton Woods system – capital controls, demand management and full employment – have given way to what has been called the 'Washington Consensus' system of free trade, deregulation and 'shareholder value'. These developments accentuate the changing ways in which authority and sovereignty can be exercised in such a globalised political context (Stiglitz 2008). As globalisation continues to extend and change, it has become increasingly important to understanding the institutional and transnational means by which nation states and others have attempted to govern international phenomena such as financialisation, tax evasion, corruption, terrorism, civil and military conflicts, environmental dangers, social polarisation, and the challenges in human rights implementation.

Scope and Focus

While much has been written on the emerging forms of transnational governance in the early years of the twenty-first century (for a review, see Djelic and Sahlin-Andersson 2006), this book brings together differing legal perspectives on the issues of corporate governance, environmental regulation, human rights, humanitarian intervention, international trade, global corruption, international taxation, international peace and security, international crime, terrorism and civil liberties. Necessarily, these legal perspectives are bound up with economic, political and ethical approaches and analyses. The volume's scope highlights the challenges of governing human activity in an age of remarkable interconnectedness. The combined contributions are an attempt to continue understanding of the competing models of transnational governance in this era. While the studies in this volume are predominantly legal in approach, they incorporate a broad range of policy areas and analyse these emerging governance structures from a range of frameworks, from liberal to critical and Marxist. Contemporary financial, environmental and strategic developments pose tremendous challenges for transnational governance in the first half of the twenty-first century. They have profound implications for the viability of economic regulation, as well as legal responses to social unrest, human rights violations, climate change and military interventions. Arguably, the future of the planet itself is threatened unless the environmental and economic contradictions are resolved. This volume is another contribution to the growing study of the emergent forms of authority, coordination and power developing in response to today's challenges.

The Idea of 'Transnational Governance'

This book adopts a broad approach to the concept of transnational governance. While not exhaustive, the understanding of governance in this work is consistent with Sanson (2008) in its focus on outcomes, rules, practices and actions of actors, including but not limited to national governments, which remain important but not the sole sources of authority and power. In this view, transnational governance is a multi-layered system of rules, practices, procedures, customs, values and activities through which influence is exercised and resources deployed to address issues and achieve objectives at a level beyond a single state.

In the context of this volume, a simple definition of 'transnational' means to be beyond the boundaries of any one nation-state, and embodies a less grandiose aim than to assume a 'global' or world-wide application of all regimes. While there may be legitimate distinctions to be drawn between 'global' and 'transnational', the distinction is not emphasised in this volume. For various reasons, transnational governance may fall short of being truly global. To be precise, 'transnational' in this book is most consistent with Djelic and Sahlin-Anderson's idea of 'entanglement and blurred boundaries' (2006: 4) – in that 'transnational' is a term that upsets traditional understandings of power and government rather than clearly establishing an alternative. The contributions to this volume examine some quite different aspects of the 'transnational', but they all share this notion of a shifting balance between nation-states, individuals and other international actors in exercising authority and power.

In that sense, transnational governance recognises and seeks to reinforce the role of the state in the exercise of domestic and international authority but it also enhances the relevance of non-state actors such as international organisations, non-government organisations and trans-national corporations, and implies a restriction of nation-states' assumed independence and sovereignty.

The dual focus of the volume is the practical problems of transnational governance and an evaluation of the paradigms and theoretical frameworks that exist to solve transnational problems. There are compelling reasons supporting the invention and growth of transnational institutions and regulations, but there are concomitant concerns and risks to these developments. The concept behind this collection is that, through a diverse range of perspectives, useful insights can be obtained on transnational governance in three key areas: first, the effectiveness of coordination between nation-states and other actors when engaging in transnational governance, secondly, the viability of transnational regulation, and third, the implications for democracy and sovereignty. These perspectives provide the organising themes of the book and are explored below.

The Role of Law

Law is implicit in the notion of transnational governance examined in this book. The rule of law, the use of legality, the adoption of standards, principles and coercion all point to the 'law-centred' method of exercising power. Governance need not be limited to law, but the works in this collection all recognise the ubiquitous role of law in the exercise of power and authority. This is not the same as a traditional legal approach that assumes the centrality of law. An expanding body of writers are reconceptualising the role of law internationally, especially in relation to governance. Goldstein and others (2001) laid the groundwork for a rigorous study programme in the 'legalisation' of international governance. Byers (2000) reconsidered the role of law in international relations to expand the notion of what is law, but also to examine more closely the significance of institutions and actors in the creation, interpretation and application of law. The collection of works by Simmons and Steinberg (2006) re-imagines the ways in which law is now deployed in international governance.

Underlying the works in this volume is a broad conception of law that recognises legality in the language, structure and practices by which governance is often exercised or legitimated. Most of these works do not explore in depth the 'lawyer' distinctions between 'hard' and 'soft' law, nor do they directly deal with the changing conception of 'rules' in the transnational system of regulation (Byers 1999). However, they examine and analyse the role and effect of emerging structures that define themselves as 'legal' or clearly are so in manner or form.

The Effective Coordination of Nation-states

The changing role of nation-states in the regulation of transnational activity has already been examined from many perspectives. Chayes and Chayes (1995) emphasise the role of international regulatory compliance in determining state action on transnational issues. Slaughter (2004) highlights the increasingly important role of governmental and non-governmental networks for the transnational implementation of rules and principles. Barnett and Finnemore (2004) examine the 'bureaucratisation' of transnational governance through the increasing scope and operation of international organisations. These writers are examples of a growing body of researchers examining governance by studying the changes in the ways nation-states and other actors coordinate international and domestic action, usually with a growing emphasis on the role of non-state actors. With this approach, sovereignty is maintained or pooled and the exercise of power becomes more diffuse, but nation-states remain the main agents for action and accountability. In some ways, most of the studies in this volume directly or indirectly examine this theme, whether that is the role of international organisations like the United Nations, World Trade Organization, or the International Criminal Court, or the coordinated actions of states in dealing with corruption of public officials and terrorism.

But in all respects, the contributors to this volume are interested in whether this coordination is effective: can humanity rely on improved coordination to address fundamental global problems and how effective can these emerging forms of governance be? In most respects, the writers are optimistic that coordination is possible, that there are sufficiently shared interests between nation-states (and citizens of nation-states) to believe that a negotiated outcome is possible. However, several contributions in this volume question this belief. Even if there is coordination, and even if it is effective, is that necessarily good? Do the coordinated actions of nation-states protect the interests of the global citizenry or do they deliver outcomes that serve only partisan interests?

The Viability of Transnational Economic Regulation

Economic regulation provides some of the greatest challenges and opportunities for 'transnational governance'. Braithwaite and Drahos (2000) comprehensively re-examined the role of nation-states and other actors in regulating global business activity. They identified as a key challenge the mismatch between the transnational scale of some commercial practices and the often sub-national scale of domestic regulatory enforcement by nation-states, such as in consumer goods where manufacturing processes are transnational in operation but consumer protection is often carried out on a local or regional basis. At one level, as economic activity has become more globalised, so then the regulation of that economic activity must occur at a global (or transnational) level. However, at another level and at the same time, legitimacy in economic regulation is still tied very much to the nation-state. Currencies, stock exchanges, competition agencies, trade barriers (and trade facilitation) remain primarily under the aegis of nation-states. As outlined by Braithwaite and Drahos, the difficulty is in aligning the two levels of activity and regulation – transnational business practice and nation-state governance. Braithwaite and Drahos also emphasised the role of non-state actors and non-legal forms of persuasion and modelling as some of the most effective and novel means by which economic activity is regulated beyond the national sphere.

Many of the contributions in this volume examine the issue of economic regulation and ask whether such transnational regulation is at all possible. An important aspect of this book is the extent to which the writers evaluate the effectiveness of transnational governance structures and diagnose what failures exist in current transnational practices. Several writers in this collection point to the question: if there are successful examples of transnational regulation, whom does this benefit and how do we determine whether the outcomes are desirable?

The Maintenance of Democracy and Sovereignty

The third theme in the book is the concern that the methods of transnational regulation result in the diminution in the involvement of domestic citizenries in their own government. Sometimes called the 'democratic deficit' of international institutions, the delegation of authority to foreign ministers and other international negotiations – often in the context of deliberations and treaty negotiations that are necessarily private or opaque – means that decisions made at a global level do not reflect popular concerns and are not subject to democratic accountability. This theme challenges the assumption that states act as agents of their citizens, rather than on behalf of powerful elites.

Related to this is the broader notion of sovereignty and the population's right to participate in their own governance. An aspect of the global changes and problems that frame this volume is that the traditional understanding of sovereignty is being undermined. Climate change, for example, may remove a state's ability to act in its own defence. Economic liberalisation may deny democratic participation in traditional areas of economic activity.

In framing the theme in these terms, there is an explicit recognition that there is often a difference between sovereignty and democracy. Sovereignty – recognition of a nation-state by other nation-states of their independence and legal authority – is not necessarily based on democratic processes and institutions. In most of the studies in this volume, sovereignty and democracy coexist but that need not be the case and, even where that does occur, may not remain that way in the future.

Governance and Power

Underlying much of the analysis in this book is a keen awareness of the relationship between governance, law and power. Underpinning the exercise of law is power and often, when examining method of governance, the manifestation of power is framed in legal terms. As Simpson (2004) has suggested, the global reality may be better described as legalised hegemony, with the most powerful states exercising greater influence internationally.

The adoption of law in many forms of governance is not neutral. As examined in several chapters of this book, legality privileges some interests over others. Legalism presents barriers and opportunities to different actors competing against each other in a transnational space for governance. More importantly, law is imbued with ideas and assumptions that find their source outside of the law, especially in the area of economic regulation. Critiques of theories such as neoliberalism by critical and Marxist writers add depth to the reappraisal of law's function and purpose in transnational governance.

Apart from their engagement with the three themes of the volume, a common question to all the contributions is whether the extension of the 'transnational governance project' is 'good' or 'bad'. The writers fall into several different but sometimes overlapping camps in responding to this question. Some express scepticism toward the transnational governance project, in particular in its ability to extend inequality and power imbalances, both nationally and internationally. Others believe that the current forms of exercising transnational power can be changed to achieve better outcomes. Others still espouse that the project is essentially good, is generally heading in the correct direction and only requires some modification to minimise adverse consequences that have emerged in implementation.

Another assumption underlying many, but not all, of the works in this volume is that the rules we analyse through the framework of transnational governance are a product of rational development and consultation; in other words, the legal frameworks of transnational governance are a rational output of a rational and deliberative law/policy development process. However, other authors question whether this is true, and suggest that the rules might result from unintended consequences of a system of compromise and negotiation, or from the direct or indirect exercise of power.

Outline of the Book

This volume begins with historical and economic examinations of transnational governance. Further chapters then turn to trade, corporate and taxation dimensions, before widening the survey to issues of climate change, conflict, terrorism and international criminal justice. Finally, proposals are considered for a humanitarian law paradigm shift from state sovereignty to an international responsibility to protect.

Origins of Transnational Governance

In Chapter 1, Simon Chapple provides some important and thought-provoking historical context. He argues that the origins of transnational governance may be found in the interconnectedness of the legal regimes of developed countries in the nineteenth century. This chapter examines the evolution and development of transnational governance in the areas of commerce, property and human rights by considering the legal legacy of colonialism, the exchange of legal ideas among developed nations, the influence of moral norms and economic networks on the development of law, and the role of non-government organisations. The chapter is an examination of the history and context of coordination amongst nation-states, in particular the circumstances that allowed such coordination to develop.

By considering the connections between national legal regimes and the shared influences that cut across national borders, this chapter explains how transnational laws developed within national legal frameworks and laid the foundation for the development of more formal examples of transnational governance in the twentieth century.

Economic Governance: Challenging Neoliberal Ideology in a Global Financial Crisis

In Chapter 2, Scott Mann examines more recent historical settings. He considers the ways in which, over the past quarter-century, the theory and practice of governance has been profoundly influenced by neoliberal ideas, espousing the benefits of free trade and free investment, financial deregulation and privatisation, welfare cut-backs for the poor and tax cuts for the rich, accompanied by huge rewards concentrated at the top of corporate hierarchies and unrestricted corporate lobbying and funding of political parties. Mann argues that the policies of major developed-world 'governments' and the operations of the World Bank, International Monetary Fund and World Trade Organisation have been built around these ideas and policies throughout this period. Mann argues that neoliberal ideas have served to facilitate and justify the thoroughgoing subordination of government to the interests of big capital and the expansion of corporate globalisation. He suggests that the policies directed by such ideas paved the way for the global financial crisis, as well as producing a range of increasingly deleterious consequences at every level of contemporary society. In particular, the chapter focuses upon increasing inequality within and between nations, increasing instability and lack of real and sustainable growth in the world economy, and accelerating pollution and climate change. It argues the case for radical changes in structures, practices and policies of governance at all levels of society to begin to reverse these developments. Mann points to the benefits of re-regulated trade, investment, and financial operations and of re-nationalised banks and infrastructure. He argues for protection of political democracy from the business world by the extension of democracy within the business world.

Trade Governance: Legal Institutionalism as a Magnet for Non-trade Issues

In Chapter 3, Simon Kozlina probes the 'mixed benefits' of seeking to tackle wider issues through one of the most pervasive institutions of international trade regulation. He examines the evident attraction of making human rights, environment and labour standards enforceable through the dispute settlement system of the World Trade Organization. The chapter probes the limits and barriers that emerge to effective coordination and enforcement due to the nature of particular institutional forms – in this case, highly legalised dispute settlement. He argues that the 'turn to law' and legal institutionalism through strict enforcement of trade obligations creates a magnet for non-trade issues in a transnational legal vacuum for enforcement of those rights, but that it is unlikely that this form of transnational governance will be effective for the enforcement of these rights. In that sense, the chapter is a study of the use of a heavily legalised international organisation to improve nation-state coordination in both economic and non-economic spheres.

Taxation Governance: Would the Tobin Tax Democratise Globalisation?

In Chapter 4, Elfriede Sangkuhl explores the implications of the unprecedented growth in daily currency trading in largely unregulated world currency markets. She examines the potential role of a Tobin Tax, which could be levied on currency exchange transactions with the intended purpose of curbing the massive rate of currency speculation. In examining this proposed method of transnational economic regulation, she argues that regulation of speculative foreign currency trading is necessary because it primarily affects people living in countries with vulnerable currencies. Although many advocates of the Tobin Tax support the development of a supranational body to levy, collect and distribute the tax, she argues that this would reduce its effectiveness through exposure to political manipulation, unless power were distributed in such a manner that the needs and desires of members could be balanced against those of other affected parties. This chapter suggests the changing ways in which transnational economic regulation can be re-imagined and the potential problems with this form of institutional nation-state coordination.

Corruption, International Business Transactions and the OECD

In Chapter 5, John Juriansz and Marina Nehme examine corruption – a ubiquitous, complex, multifarious and seemingly intractable transnational concern. They ask why, 14 years after the adoption of the Convention on Combating Bribery of Foreign Public Officials in International Business Transactions by the OECD, member states have achieved only moderate success in their progressive goal of eradicating foreign bribery in international business transactions with their economic, legal and political jurisdictions. The lack of significant demonstrable success, attributable to both a flagging commitment to the ambitious goals of the Convention and to the considerable complexities of corruption, has effectively rendered the collective response of the member states unstable and in jeopardy of failure. The authors suggest that, given the transnational nature of the bribery of foreign officials, it is essential for any reform initiative to focus upon the international coordination of laws and enforcement systems. However, a lack of political will demonstrates itself in the lack of adequate funding and staffing of the various enforcement mechanisms as does the political obstruction of investigations and prosecutions.

Environmental Governance: Global Civil Society and Public Interest Advocacy

In Chapter 6, Laura Horn's key argument is that a new global environmental institution is needed that could operate in the interests of the common concern of humankind to ensure that the global environment is protected. This argument is founded upon the view that international environmental governance should be in a process of transformation through innovation. This perspective of innovative governance questions the present reliance upon states to develop effective international institutions to deal with global environmental protection, and raises the possibility of a new global environmental organisation that has a wider representation to include non-state actors. This change could take some time to occur, however, and the threat to the environment is becoming critical. So, it is argued that interim changes such as the development of a human 'right to a healthy environment' could assist to protect the global environment in the intervening period of time. Because of the lack of standing that non-government organisations have in prevailing international fora, Horn asks: who can speak on behalf of future generations? Along with a new human right to a healthy environment, she also suggests the creation of international dispute resolution institutions, with experts competent to deal with technical environmental questions, and appropriate enforcement mechanisms.

Governance Implications of Terrorism: Justifying Abuse of Due Process Rights

In Chapter 7, Michael Head questions the role of the United Nations in the 'war on terrorism'. He examines a tendency toward the selective use of international legal instruments on 'terrorism' to justify the imposition of far-reaching erosions of legal and civil rights. In looking at the relationship between international norms and domestic legislation, he considers how these instruments, supposedly expressing the collective will of states to respond to the problem of terrorism, sit with existing and widely accepted international human rights instruments such as the Geneva Conventions and the International Covenant on Civil and Political Rights (ICCPR). Head suggests that the UN Security Council, while apparently moving with unprecedented unity to require all member states to legislate against terrorist-related activity, became a conduit for the strategic and economic interests of the major powers, notably the United States. Indeed, Security Council resolutions effectively paved the way for military unilateralism, starting with the US invasion of Afghanistan, and for equally self-interested domestic responses, with governments seizing upon the declared 'war on terrorism' – and the lack of any definition of terrorism by the UN – to introduce repressive measures that served their own political purposes. Head considers the driving forces and implications of an indefinite 'war' and how various governments have used it to disorient and distract public opinion and introduce extensive police and military powers. He argues that the ramifications of these legislative abuses of due process rights will only become apparent in the longer term, which will make them more difficult to challenge.

International Criminal Governance: The ICC and Other International Justice Mechanisms

In Chapter 8, Steven Freeland reviews the significance of the establishment of the International Criminal Court, which is generally regarded as the most significant mechanism as of yet in international criminal governance and as representing an advance toward what is often referred to as the 'internationalisation of justice'. He explores the various governance structures and enforcement mechanisms created to invoke a system of international criminal justice for those serious crimes that represent gross violations of human rights. He argues that, as many of these crimes have been committed in the context of complex factual circumstances, often involving historical as well as diverse cultural, economic, political and religious considerations, it is appropriate that a range of structures, ranging from community-based localised justice mechanisms to supranational criminal tribunals, are used. There is no one simple formula, and the structures established to date have had mixed 'success' in dealing with gross violations of human rights. The internationalisation of justice remains very much a work in progress and highlights the challenge of seeking a coordinated response by nation-states to global problems.

Governing Humanitarian Intervention: Time for Change

In Chapter 9, Michelle Sanson explores one of the most recent and contentious issues in international law. She examines the crystallising customary international law principle whereby state sovereignty yields to an international responsibility to protect ('RTP' or 'R2P'). The development of a norm of humanitarian intervention has had a checkered history since the end of the Second World War and remains in an unacceptable situation where decisions on intervention are subject to the individual foreign policy objectives of the permanent five members of the United Nations Security Council. The question goes to the heart of what are the limits of transnational action and when domestic sovereignty should and should not be respected. In that sense, she explores the competing tensions between effective transnational governance and the protection of state sovereignty. Sanson argues that clear criteria need to be established not only for when intervention is justified but also for when inaction can be justified. If such criteria had been in place prior to the outbreak of tensions in Darfur, and the conflicts in Syria, interventions may have occurred and these situations resolved with less human suffering.

Conclusion

One of the challenges of writing and researching in the field of transnational governance is that there is the constant emergence and inspiration of new developments, new institutions and new technologies that can beguile the focus of the researcher and force our attention to turn to fresh issues, actors and regimes. Constant change and 'evolution' provide an ever-more demanding terrain with which to grapple with theoretical paradigms. At the same time, analysis always required asking whether phenomena are truly new, or rather a development of an existing structure/concept or the re-emergence of an earlier form of authority, governance and power. This book looks into the past, the present and the future and through a range of perspectives to gain a better appreciation of the scope, limitations and potential of transnational governance in the twenty-first century. The volume identifies important aspects of nineteenth- and twentieth-century history that provide the context, the theoretical underpinnings and ideological assumptions of existing forms of transnational governance. It examines some of the key existing and emerging contemporary governance issues – such as terrorism, trade, crime – and assesses the risks and opportunities they present. The volume looks to the future and makes bold statements about environmental governance, human rights and global inequality, with proposals that extend transparency and accountability, while also recognising the practical limitations and pitfalls of previous regulatory attempts. While making numbers of proposals for reform or restructuring, it does not present an overly optimistic, Pollyanna-ish view of transnational governance – there is a recognition of the exercise of power on behalf of particular interests in the current assumptions and frameworks of transnational governance.

References

Barnett, Michael and Finnemore, Martha 2004. *Rules for the World: International Organizations in Global Politics*. Ithaca, NY: Cornell University Press.

Braithwaite, John and Drahos, Peter 2000. *Global Business Regulation*. Cambridge: Cambridge University Press.

Byers, Michael (ed.) 2000. *The Role of Law in International Politics*. Oxford: Oxford University Press.

—— 1999. Custom, *Power and the Power of Rules: international relations and customary international law*. Cambridge: Cambridge University Press.

Chayes, Abram and Chayes, Antonia 1995. *The New Sovereignty: Compliance with International Regulatory Agreements*. Cambridge, MA: Harvard University Press.

Djelic, Marie-Laure and Sahlin-Andersson, Kerstin 2006. 'A world of governance: The rise of transnational regulation', in Djelic and Sahlin-Andersson (eds), Transnational governance: institutional dynamics of regulation. Cambridge: Cambridge University Press, pp. 1–28.

Goldstein, Judith, et al. 2001. *Legalization and World Politics*. Cambridge, MA: MIT Press.

Sanson, Michelle 2008. *International Law and Global Governance*. London: Cameron and May.

Simmons, Beth and Steinberg, Richard 2006. *International Law and International Relations*. Cambridge: Cambridge University Press.

Simpson, Gerry 2004. *Great Powers and Outlaw States: Unequal Sovereigns in the International Legal Order*. Cambridge: Cambridge University Press.

Slaughter, Anne-Marie 2004. A New World Order. Princeton, NJ: Princeton University Press.

Stiglitz, J.E. 2008. *The Washington Consensus Reconsidered: Towards a New Global Governance*. New York: Oxford University Press.

Chapter 1

Origins of Transnational Governance in the Nineteenth Century

Simon Chapple

The last century has seen the growth of an interconnected world. Diplomatic, economic and social conversations now take place across national borders to an unprecedented extent. Economic pressures, social and political movements, and military engagements are recognised as having both a local and also a global impact. Attempts to regulate and govern the effect of these movements and pressures are increasingly conducted on a global level, either led by international organisations that transcend nation states, or brought about through a coordinated international response. The fact that this trend has increased in pace over the past few decades is well-recognised. David Levi-Faur and Jacinta Jordana have noted that 'In recent decades, regulatory reforms have spread around the globe, accompanied by new institutions, technologies, and instruments of regulation that have had a profound impact on the social and economic fabric' (Levi-Faur and Jordana 2004: 6). Similarly, Marie-Laure Djelic and Kerstin Sahlin-Anderson discuss the 'rise' of transnational regulation and state that 'The proliferation of regulatory activities, actors, networks or constellations leads to an explosion of rules and to the profound re-ordering of our world' (Djelic and Sahlin-Andersson 2006:1). As the following chapters indicate, the increased importance and prevalence of transnational governance clearly raises unique challenges. However, the obvious, and growing, interconnectedness of the twentieth and twenty-first centuries should not mask the fact that transnational governance has a long history. That history provides an important context within which to consider the growth of transnational institutions and transnational governance in the twentieth and twenty-first centuries.

The history of transnational governance stretches back as far as ancient and mediaeval times. Communities of states were regulated by law in ancient Greece, and more recently by the modern 'law of nations' that developed in Europe in the sixteenth and seventeenth centuries. This history has been the subject of much academic discussion. Less explored, and more relevant to the rise of transnational governance over the last century, are the transnational connections and exchanges that occurred between nations throughout the nineteenth century. The transnational influence of the common law, the impact of various law reform movements that crossed international boundaries, and the adoption into national law of legal ideas that circulated internationally meant that regional and national legal systems in the nineteenth century converged towards certain legal norms and methods of governance. In many respects, this form of transnational governance was not 'self-conscious', but 'informal' in the sense that a sharing of legal norms resulted in systems of regulation that were shared across national borders. In this way, the nineteenth century saw the birth of some of the types of transnational governance that operate today. This history provides important context for two reasons. On one level, there are obvious similarities between the informal ways in which transnational systems of governance developed in the nineteenth century, and the way in which transnational governance has continued to develop in the twentieth and twenty-first centuries (as discussed in subsequent chapters). On another level, the 'interconnectedness' of the nineteenth century provided the bedrock on which more formal institutions of transnational governance were built in the following century.

Transnational systems of governance developed in different and varied ways during the nineteenth century. National or regional legal systems were part of wider transnational networks, but the nature of those networks and their international influences depended on the type of law (statute, common law, civil, criminal) and the subject matter of the law. This chapter illustrates some of the various systems of transnational governance that existed in the nineteenth century, such as the transnational application of the English common law, the international movement to reform the content and enforcement of the criminal law, and the development of a transnational commercial law. For ease of illustration, this chapter concentrates on the Anglo-American experience, drawing in particular on two legal regimes that were established in the middle of the nineteenth century: the American state of California, and the Australian colony of Queensland.

At the outset, it must be recognised that the examples provided in this chapter are certainly not the only ways in which legal regimes were connected across time and space during the nineteenth century, or provide an exhaustive overview of all the ways in which international legal norms were shared, exchanged and adopted. Rather, the examples have been chosen to illustrate the ways in which transnational governance operated in the nineteenth century to enable parallels to be drawn with the twentieth century, and to describe the legal and political context in which transnational governance in the twentieth century developed. Further, although there is still much work to do in order to provide a more synthesised account of the development of transnational governance in the nineteenth century (particularly in relation to the transnational connections and exchanges with and among Asia, Africa and South America), it is hoped that this analysis may contribute to the small but growing scholarship that considers the transnational reach of law and governance in the nineteenth century.

A Transnational Approach to Governance in the Nineteenth Century

Compared to the burgeoning literature that discusses internationalisation and globalisation in the twentieth century, scholars have neglected the systems of transnational governance that emerged in the nineteenth century. This is partly because nineteenth-century legal systems did not, of themselves, have a transnational dimension, and partly because their 'interconnectedness' is not immediately obvious. To a large extent, national legal systems operated within geographic boundaries that expanded and contracted depending on the subject matter of the law. Rarely did these boundaries expand beyond the nation-state. Consider, for example, the nineteenth-century legal regime of California in the United States of America and the legal regime that operated in the Australian colony of Queensland. In California, cases were decided in regional, state and federal courts, and legislation was drafted in local, state and national legislatures. In Queensland, cases were decided in regional and colonial courts, and legislation was drafted in the colonial legislature. For this reason, the story of law in California and Queensland is often told within particular regional and national boundaries. It is unsurprising, therefore, that legal historians tell stories that implicitly entrench the distinctive nature of regional and national legal regimes. Even the eminent American legal historian Lawrence Friedman, who has acknowledged the possibility and importance of highlighting connections between regions, argues that American law is a product of American culture that is peculiar to the United States (Friedman 2005: xi). This is not to say that all legal scholars fail to look beyond the nation-state; scholars such as Stuart Banner, Lauren Benton and John Weaver have published important transnational work.

The primacy of the nation-state does not mean that transnational governance did not exist in the nineteenth century. Instead, the story of transnational governance in the nineteenth century can be recovered by conceiving of law and its history simultaneously in different geographic scales in order to go outside the boundaries of any one national legal story. Such an approach involves consideration of the importance of international global pressures, such as international economics or immigration, the exchange of ideas across national boundaries, and the study of international organisations or movements (Saunier 2008: 163; Thelen 1999: 971; Tyrrell 1991: 1033). Put another way, the content of a particular law might appear to have had local origins, but it also derived its meaning from a range of local, regional, national and international sources. Laws were received into legal systems (by cession, settlement, or conquest), or adopted by legal systems (where a legislature chose to copy the law of another nation, or a local court chose to follow a decision of a foreign court). These legal principles sometimes flowed in only one direction (in the case of a direct transfer of legal ideas from one nation to another), but could also flow in multiple directions (in the case of an exchange of legal ideas between nations). Laws evolved organically in response to particular social, economic, or political conditions, and were also enacted in response to geographic or geologic conditions that were shared across national boundaries. In this way, any one particular law could be (and often was) part of a wider global circulation of legal ideas. Viewed globally, these laws formed part of (sometimes informal) systems of transnational governance.

Systems of Governance and the Hegemony of the Common Law

The spread of the English common law around the world, particularly during the eighteenth and nineteenth centuries, meant that not only did Anglo-American nations share important legal principles, but also that their similar legal histories facilitated the exchange of legal ideas across national boundaries. When the argument is put at its strongest, those legal regimes that were touched by the legal legacy of the British Empire formed part of an informal nineteenth-century common law hegemony. A more realistic statement perhaps is that each legal regime evolved independently (to varying degrees), but continued to apply fundamental common law rules, giving the common law the character of a tool of transnational governance.

The transnational influence of the common law is well illustrated by reference to the Californian and Queensland experiences. The legal systems of the American and Australian colonies were both moulded by the tentacles of the English common law that reached out from London and across the world's great oceans. Across these vast distances, the law floated in the pages of Blackstone, the English law reports, and the remembered legal experience of settlers themselves. The law that arrived in the English colonies was not an exact replica of the law that existed in London, nor did it operate the same way in every colony. Colonies inherited English law at different stages of the law's development and sophistication, and colonial law was moulded by the local circumstances, economics, politics, society and historical context. Nevertheless, despite differences in the process of the adoption of English law, the legal regimes of each colony shared substantial similarities.

The American legal system of the nineteenth century was constructed on a bedrock of English law. British authorities clearly contemplated that English law would apply in the first American colonies. Early colonial charters allowed the governing authority to make its own laws, but these were to mirror, as close as possible, the laws that existed in England (Hall 1950–51: 791). Nevertheless, the law in these colonies did not replicate English law directly. In 1829, Justice Joseph Story wrote that 'the common law of England is not to be taken in all respects to be that of America. Our ancestors brought with them its general principles, and claimed it as their birthright; but they brought with them and adopted only that portion which was applicable to their situation' (*Van Ness* v *Pacard*, 27 US (2 pet.) 137, 143–4 (1829)).

The American War of Independence represented a radical break with the old legal order. It marked the end of English royal authority and the development of a new political system (Handlin and Handlin 1947: 3). By the end of the eighteenth century, however, the common law had gained a strong enough foothold in America to withstand hostility to England, and Americans in the post-revolutionary period maintained a strong commitment to English law (Hall 1950–51: 797; Friedman 2005: 66–7). When the original colonies became states in their own right, their commitment to English law was reflected in the formal adoption of that law in their constitutions and early legislation. At the same time, American law continued to be anglicised by the absorption of English rules through English legal texts. Daniel Boorstin has argued that Blackstone's *Commentaries* provided 'ambitious young Americans' with all the tools that they needed in order to make a living from the law and noted that the *Commentaries* sold nearly as many copies in the American colonies as they did in England (Boorstin 1996: xiii). Lawrence Friedman suggests that 'only from England was there a source and supply of law that American lawyers could use without translation' (Friedman 2005: 3). Most legal literature was sourced from England and an early American lawyer's library was filled with English texts. American jurisprudence was nurtured by English precedent. The first American casebook on contracts by Christopher C. Langdell cited 310 English cases and only 22 from America (Kimball 2007: 353). In the late eighteenth century when Blackstone's *Commentaries* was published, 'Americans were among his most avid customers.' For American lawyers, 'England was the standard. English books, judges, ideas, were more available than the older colonial tradition' (Friedman 2005: 59).

At a more local level, the legal system of nineteenth-century California illustrates the pervasive influence of the English common law that linked California to a wider transnational story. It was not inevitable that English law would be adopted in California. In December 1849, in his first address to the legislature after California was ceded by Mexico to the United States, Governor Peter Burnett recommended that California adopt the English law of evidence, commerce, and crimes and misdemeanours, but adopt the civil code of Louisiana and the Louisiana Code of Practice. The governor argued that 'these codes, it is thought, would combine the best features of both the Civil and Common Law, and at the same time, omit the most objectionable portions of each' (Journal of the Senate of the State of California 1850: 33). Nevertheless, J.C. Brackett introduced the following resolution into the legislative assembly:

> That the Committee on the Judiciary be and they are instructed to report to this house a brief and comprehensive act, substantially enacting that the Common Law of England, and all statutes and acts of Parliament down to a certain reign, which are of a general nature … which common law and statutes are not repugnant to or inconsistent with the constitution of the United States, the constitution of this state, and statute laws that now are or hereafter may be enacted, shall henceforth be the rule of action and decision in the State of California. (Ibid.: 723)

On 27 February 1850, the Senate Judiciary Committee, chaired by Elisha Crosby and assisted by Nathaniel Bennett and Thomas Vermeule, reported that 'nowhere do all great branches of national wealth thrive as vigorously and prosper to so great an extent as they do under the countenance and protection of the Common Law' (Appendix to the Journal of the Senate of the State of California 1850: 469). The report referred to the political history of the United States, the fact that the common law operated in 29 of the 30 states in the Union, and the practical problem of obtaining the necessary texts if civil law was adopted in California. After the Senate and Assembly received the report, Brackett presented his common law bill to the house. It provided that 'the Common Law of England, so far as it is not repugnant to or inconsistent with the Constitution of the United States, or the Constitution or laws of the State of California, shall be the rule of decision in all the Courts of this State' (Act adopting the Common Law 1850). It was accepted and signed into law by the governor on 17 April 1850.

It is an oversimplification to suggest that the English common law was adopted in Anglo-American jurisdictions in its entirety, or reflected exactly the state of the law on the other side of the Atlantic. For example, the common law that operated in California was based on English precedent, but also paid homage to early American decisions. That is, the English common law provided the foundation of the legal regime, but did not define its precise content. In April 1854, for example, in a Supreme Court case dealing with the constitutionality of a retrospective law, Justice Alexander Wells applied the common law, ruling that 'we but concur with the great majority of the Judges in England and America, when we assert, that it is well established not only as a doctrine of the common law, but as a principle of general jurisprudence, that no Statute shall be so construed as to give it a retrospective effect.' However, in determining the precise content of the common law rule, Justice Wells found that it was not necessary to 'go to the civil law of Rome, the code of France, or the common law of England. The best authorities in American jurisprudence have approved of and maintained the doctrine we assert' (*The People ex rel. Isaac N. Thorne et al.* v *John C. Hayes, the City of San Francisco and P A Morse, D J Tallant, William Hooper, B C Saunders* 4 Cal 127, 1854 WL 669 (Cal.) (1854) at p. 6). Similarly, in January 1853, Chief Justice Murray, in a case of public nuisance, ruled that 'in the absence of any legislation on the subject, we are compelled to fall back upon the rules of the common law', but when determining the content of the law, held that 'this point has been so well settled in the courts of New York and New Jersey, that a reference to those authorities is all that is necessary to determine the present case' (*Pascal Surocco et al.* v *John W. Geary* 3 Cal 69, 1853 WL 639 (Cal.) (1853), p. 3). Thus, the reference to 'English' common law was interpreted as that system of unwritten law, developed through precedent that had English origins, that was applied in both England and the United States.

On the other side of the Pacific, English law played an equally important role in the development of law in the Australian colonies. International law recognised three ways of acquiring sovereignty over land: conquest, cession, and occupation of territory that was considered to belong to no one (the principle of *terra nullius*). Sovereignty over New South Wales by the English Crown was based on this last principle. In its purest form, this doctrine permitted the acquisition of land that was uninhabited, but its application was expanded to justify the acquisition of inhabited territory by occupation where the inhabitants were 'backward' or the lands were uncultivated. Thus, although New South Wales was occupied by aboriginal tribes at the time of settlement, these tribes were regarded in law as being 'so low in the scale of social organisation that their usages and conceptions of rights and duties are not to be reconciled with the institutions or the legal ideas of civilised society' (*Mabo* v *Queensland (No. 2)* [1992] HCA 23 per Brennan J at [41]). Put another way, the aboriginal occupation of the land was not recognised as being anything that amounted to ownership of the land, and English law was presumed to extend over the Colony of New South Wales from the moment of settlement. Alex Castles writes that the laws of the British Empire were 'honed and refined by the experiences involved in the regulation of colonial affairs'. If the early colonial experience in the American colonies was the first foray into empire, the experience of the colony of New South Wales and the later Australian colonies was a more sophisticated attempt, moulded by its American experience. Throughout the eighteenth century, British governments tightened their hold on their colonies (Castles 1982: 1–4).

Similar to the Californian experience, although English law was presumed to extend over the Colony of New South Wales from the moment of 'settlement', it was another matter entirely for that law to be applied uniformly and accurately. Alex Castles argued that 'the simple lack of authoritative legal texts and law reports in New South Wales, particularly in the first years after settlement, clearly affected the capacity even of conscientious legal officials to apply some laws along English lines' (ibid.: p. 382). As Bruce Kercher observes, the legal systems of England and New South Wales were only 'loosely connected'. Legal officials had 'a great deal of practical autonomy' as a result of the distance from London and 'a good deal of the day-to-day control of colonial affairs had to be left to the administrators on the spot.' New rules of law could be accepted in New South Wales 'regardless of Imperial views of legality' (Kercher 1995: 9).

As English law evolved through the nineteenth century, early Australian lawyers questioned the extent to which these legal developments should be incorporated automatically into colonial law. In an 1828 opinion, the Chief Justice of the NSW Supreme Court, Francis Forbes argued that '[w]ith respect to the application of English Statutes generally to this Colony, it has always been assumed by this Court that all statutes of a general character passed before the establishment of a local legislature in the Colony must be taken as a part of the Statute law which is imported into this Settlement' (*Brown* v *Mannix*). Of particular importance is that in forming this view, Chief Justice Forbes cited the American colonial experience, including a 1764 case from the Supreme Court of New York, and in the process illustrated the potential for the future exchange of legal principles across national borders. The controversy was resolved in 1828 when the Australian Courts Act 1828 (UK) was passed, which set the formal date of reception of English law as 25 July 1828. This Act provided that 'all laws and statutes in force within the Realm of England at the time of the passing of this Act … shall be applied in the administration of justice in the courts of New South Wales and Van Diemen's Land respectively, so far as the same can be applied within the said colonies.' As in the American colonies, English law provided the building blocks for law in New South Wales. However, the distance from London, and the presence of a local legislature from 1823, meant that in some respects New South Wales developed a type of indigenous jurisprudence. In an extensive review of colonial law in New South Wales, Bruce Kercher has cautioned not to exaggerate the distinctive nature of New South Wales law, but nevertheless discerned 'a genuinely innovative streak in the legal creations of the governors and judges of early New South Wales' (Kercher 1995: 216).

The reception of the English common law into the colony of Queensland is important because, like the equivalent process in California, it illustrates the way in which remote and newly settled regions were part of an informal transnational system of governance. Although the district of Moreton Bay was discovered by Europeans in May 1770, it was not until the 1820s that the area was 'colonised' by English settlers. In June 1859, Queen Victoria authorised the creation of the colony of Queensland and appointed Sir George Bowen as governor. The laws that applied in New South Wales continued to apply in the new colony of Queensland. The Letters Patent provided that on and from 6 June 1859 'such laws and ordinances as are now in force in our said colony of New South Wales and its dependencies … shall hereafter be in force in our said colony of Queensland.' Six months later, the colony of Queensland was proclaimed.

English law did not operate in Queensland in the same way as it did in London. Rather, English law was adopted, subject to modifications made by the New South Wales legislature and courts. Analogous to the Californian experience, the Queensland legal regime was a combination of English law, New South Wales law, and statute law that was passed in Queensland after 1859. When applying the law, Queensland judges applied a three-stage process: the first was to determine the English law that was received into New South Wales at 1828; the second step was to determine whether that law had been amended or altered by the passage of New South Wales legislation between 1828 and 1859, and the third step was to determine whether any laws of Queensland passed after 1859 had altered the New South Wales law (*Walsh* v *Kent* Queensland Supreme Court Reports 1 (1862) 44 per Lutwych J at 47).

It appears trite to conclude that the English common law was applied (to varying extents) in legal regimes across the globe. However, the similarities between legal regimes in the nineteenth century is something that is only beginning to be recognised in legal scholarship. Implicit (and sometimes explicit) in much of the work of legal historians in both Australia and the United States is the assumption that in each country there emerged a type of indigenous jurisprudence; a uniquely American or Australian version of law. To the extent that no legal regime is the same and that the precise content of the law is moulded to individual social, economic, political and historical situations, this statement is true. However, this shifts the focus away from the similar legal influences that transcended the nation state. As can be seen in both California and in Queensland, the common law provided a foundation for the development of a local legal regime.

This focus is important because it shows how the English common law was itself an important form of transnational governance in the nineteenth century, by causing similar legal principles to be applied across national borders. It also reveals how the common law facilitated legal exchanges between nations in the sense that laws enacted in one jurisdiction could be (and were) adopted easily in other jurisdictions that shared similar legal heritages. This form of transnational governance was not perhaps a 'self-conscious' process, but nevertheless the informal sharing of legal norms resulted in similar systems of regulation operating across national borders. The law of contract provides a good illustration. The cases heard by the Queensland Supreme Court reveal a strong adherence to decided English cases. In California, lawyers in argument before the Californian Supreme Court, including the future Supreme Court Justice Stephen J. Field, often referred to English texts, such as *Chitty on Contract* (*Cavillaud* v. *Yale* 3 Cal. 108 (1853); *Tyson* v. *Wells* 2 Cal. 122 (1852)). The Californian and Queensland experiences were far from being exceptional, but were part of a wider and more universal story of nineteenth-century frontier law and society. In Ghana, for example, English law governed court procedure, commercial claims, and criminal conduct (Asante 1987: 71). This process can be taken further by recognising that many of the jurisdictions that were not influenced by the English common law were often influenced by some other inherited legal tradition. John Schmidhauser has argued, for example, that the reception in various jurisdictions of what he classifies as the Romanistic family of law, the German family of law, the Nordic family of law, and the English common law was a sort of legal imperialism. Each jurisdiction that was influenced by such a received legal tradition was linked to other jurisdictions that had a similar inherited legal history.

Law Reform and the Emergence of a Transnational Criminal Law

The development of transnational systems of governance in the nineteenth century was not just the result of the reception of the common law (and other legal traditions). Although national law evolved and adapted to local circumstances, its evolution was also driven by international social, economic and political movements. In this sense, the 'exponential growth of international organizations' that took place in the twentieth century (Djelic and Sahlin-Andersson 2006: 1) had its origins in the nineteenth century. The nineteenth-century transnational movements were many and varied and included causes such as anti-slavery and temperance, and were associated with transnational organisations such as the Sons of Temperance and the Woman's Christian Temperance Union. One such intellectual movement that provides a convenient illustration of these transnational forces at work is the nineteenth-century movement to reform and modernise the criminal law.

The reform movement began with the work of European intellectuals such as Montesquieu in *Persian Letters* and *The Spirit of the Law*, and Cesare Beccaria in *Crimes and Punishment*. The work of these intellectuals in turn influenced the work of the English reformer, Jeremy Bentham, who is regarded by many scholars as the 'father' of the movement to codify the criminal law (Chapin 1989: 67).

These reformers supported the general propositions that retribution should not be the aim of the law, that penalties should be certain, and that the law should support and encourage the rehabilitation of the offender. Beccaria argued, for example, that punishment must be prompt, known, and proportionate to the crime (Beckman 1966: 150). The intellectual legacy of these reformers influenced the development of law in the United States and Australia such that their developing criminal regimes formed part of an emerging system of transnational criminal governance.

As discussed previously, the American colonies inherited the basic structure of the English criminal law. However, by the time that the colonial period was drawing to a close, this criminal law was increasingly being criticised by Americans on the basis of its brutality, and the fact that the law of crimes, derived from what were thought to be archaic English cases, was considered to be unintelligible. From the time of the American Revolution, therefore, the reform and codification of the common law of crime was a perennial issue (Banner 2002: 88–111). This codification and reform movement was in turn inspired by the work of reformers such as Beccaria and Bentham. One scholar has remarked that 'it would be difficult to find any other area where European thought had a more direct and demonstrable influence than the advocacy of humanizing the criminal law' (Chapin 1989: 165). Both Thomas Jefferson and George Washington owned copies of Beccaria's *Essay on Crimes and Punishments*, and its arguments were reported in newspapers and in the work of influential writers (Banner 2002: 91–2). Jefferson's draft penal code for Virginia was 'inspired by both European and English intellectuals' and incorporated the works of Montesquieu and Beccaria (Beckman 1966: 151). Although there was opposition to codification of the criminal law in some quarters (Herman 1996: 415), many American states in the nineteenth century moved to codify their criminal laws and, in the process, threw off 'many of the barbarities of the English criminal system' (Horwitz 1992: 117). It is impossible to classify the various American legal reformers under the one intellectual banner, but as a general principle they desired to simplify and demystify the common law of crime. These reformers drew variously on the *Code Napoléon*, and the work of Bentham and Beccaria. Edward Livingston, for example, who drafted a criminal code for Louisiana (ultimately never adopted), was in constant correspondence with Bentham (Beckman 1966: 162). Law reform in nineteenth-century America was in this way part of wider transnational criminal reform.

The practical effect of law reform in the United States is illustrated by the Californian experience. In creating a sophisticated legal regime from nothing, the first Californian legislators frequently borrowed legislation from other jurisdictions (Friedman 2005: 261). Governor Burnett initially recommended that the Louisiana Civil Code and Code of Civil Procedure be adopted in California. As discussed previously, this view did not prevail and instead the legislature adopted the English common law. Nevertheless, legislators believed that California's law should be contained in a readily ascertainable body of statute. The first legislature passed comprehensive statutes concerning crimes, criminal procedure, civil and probate procedure, and corporations. The result was that 'substantial portions of the law were in effect codified' (Kleps 1954, p. 766). The intellectual influence of the American codifiers in California can be seen most clearly in the work of Stephen J. Field, who drafted the Californian code of civil procedure, which was based on the work of his brother David Dudley Field, the father of an equivalent code for New York. David Dudley Field was, in turn, influenced by Livingston, Sampson and Bentham (Subrin 1988: 317).

The Californian criminal legislation itself (An Act concerning Crimes and Punishments 1850) was not an original invention of legislators. Instead, it was almost an exact replica of an equivalent criminal statute, passed in Illinois in 1833 (An Act relative to Criminal Jurisprudence 1833). Not only did the Californian legislature adopt the same structure as in the Illinois criminal code, but it also (with minor exceptions) adopted wholesale the wording of the Illinois legislation. The Illinois legislation was, in turn, influenced strongly by the movement to reform and codify the common law of crime.

It was not just the American colonies that felt the intellectual influence of the European reformers. From the 1760s, reformers in England called for the repeal of the 'Bloody Code', which was the name given to the large number of capital offences that littered English criminal law (Farmer 2000: 406). Law reform in the 1820s and 1830s reduced the number of capital offences, but the law remained complex and unconsolidated (Finn 2005: 224). In the same year that the criminal code was enacted into law in Illinois, a Royal Commission on the Criminal Law was appointed in Britain by Henry Brougham, the Lord Chancellor. The Commission's brief was to consider English criminal law as a whole and 'produce a digest that would replace the existing common and statute law' (Farmer 2000: 407). Various codes were drafted, but opposition to codification on the ground that it threatened the deeply rooted traditions of the English common law meant that the work of the Commission did not result in comprehensive legal reform in England. However, in a small consolation, it did lead to the consolidation of the statutory law of crimes in England in 1861. This was described by James Stephen as 'a sort of imperfect Penal Code in respect of all the common offences' (Leader-Elliot 2006: 392). Demonstrating the scope of the transnational reform movement, these draft codes were adopted by other nations, particularly in Central America.

The influence of the transnational reform and codification movement was felt indirectly in the Australian colonies as a result of the adoption of various English reforms, and also more directly in that early Australian law reformers consciously applied the teachings of Bentham and the nineteenth-century English law reformers (Currey 1937: 227). Although this perhaps overstates the position, it is nevertheless clear that the consolidation of statute law was a concern of colonial lawyers (Castles 1982: 445). This was certainly the case in Queensland, which on separation from New South Wales in 1859 inherited a complex mixture of English and New South Wales law. The first attempt to define the laws in force in Queensland was by Ratcliffe Pring, who published an alphabetical digest of Queensland statutes in 1862. A more comprehensive consolidation and revision of the criminal law was undertaken by Chief Justice James Cockle, Justice Alfred Lutwyche and the

Attorney-General Charles Lilley, in 1866 (Bennett 1970: 219–20). This revision was based on the English criminal law, which itself had been consolidated in 1861. The English influence is unmistakable and offences entirely unsuited for Queensland such as 'stealing deer in an unenclosed part of the forest', being 'found in possession of venison', and 'killing hares or rabbits in a warren in the night time' remained on the statute books (Act to consolidate and amend the Statute Law of Queensland relating to Larceny and other similar offences 1865 (Qld)).

The task of codification in Queensland, in the sense understood by David Dudley Field, did not occur there until the 1890s, when Sir Samuel Griffith drafted a criminal code for Queensland. Griffith drew on a number of existing European codes, as well as draft English codes. Griffith was influenced, in particular, by the Italian Penal Code, and the New York Penal Code, drafted by David Dudley Field (who Griffith had met in 1887) (Gibbs 2003: 235).

The Californian and Queensland experiences illustrate the convergence of legal norms in various jurisdictions around the globe, the influence of the international criminal reform movement in the eighteenth and nineteenth centuries, and the corresponding emergence of a transnational system of criminal governance. In both regions, there existed a comprehensive body of criminal law that covered the field of both violent and property offences. The substance of these laws was so similar because the law had the same origins and was transformed by the same influences. This system of transnational criminal governance affected not only Australia and the United States, but was felt around the world. For example, as a direct result of the transnational exchange and adoption of the idea that probation might be an alternative to punishment, the concept became 'part of the penal systems of countries with such different political and social histories and diverse cultural traditions as Chile, Japan, the Philippines, France, and Russia' (Vanstone 2008: 735). Sir Samuel Griffith's draft code of 1897 (which was largely adopted unchanged as the Queensland Criminal Code in 1901) was itself exported. The Griffith Code was adopted (substantially unmodified) in Western Australia, Tasmania and the Northern Territory. Further afield, nations as diverse as Cyprus, Israel, many African nations, and other British dependencies all adopted versions of Griffith's Code (Leader-Elliot 2006: 394; Gibbs 2003: 237–8).

It was not just the content of the criminal law in various jurisdictions that was influenced by transnational reform movements, but also its enforcement. Police reform in the nineteenth century, which began in Britain (particularly using the model of the Irish constabulary) and influenced reformers in Australia and the United States, sought to create a professional police force. Accordingly, when the colony of Queensland was established, a professional police force was constituted along these modern lines and deployed to the populated districts. This force was controlled by the colonial government, and supervised by a police commissioner who was appointed by the governor. The police commissioner appointed inspectors (who were responsible for the management of the police force within their districts), sergeants and constables. A report on the prevention and repression of crime in Queensland, tabled before the Queensland legislature in 1872, noted that the professional police force in Queensland took much of the 'character of the Irish constabulary, allowing for differences occasioned by sparseness of population, and the great area of country over which it is scattered' (Journals of the Legislative Council 1872: 889). The police had many functions in Queensland's colonial bureaucracy, but their primary purpose was to act as peace officers. Police were required to be 'ever on alert for the prevention of crime and the protection of person and property' and 'any circumstances which may, in the most remote degree, appear to affect the public peace' (ibid. 1869: 292).

In the United States, the creation of a 'modern' professional police force was linked to the development of urban bureaucracies. Unlike Australia where the police force was controlled by a central colonial government, in the United States, the police were controlled at a city level and not at a state or national level. Nevertheless, many cities in the United States adopted the same type of reforms as the Australian colonies. The metropolitan police of London, established in 1829, provided the model that was adopted in part in Boston in 1838, and in New York in 1845. This model was then adopted in other major cities throughout the first half of the nineteenth century (Friedman 2005: 213). In New York, as in Brisbane, police were professional, divided into ranks, wore uniforms and badges, and were tasked with maintaining the peace (ibid.: 438).

As in relation to the transnational spread of the criminal law, the movement to modernise policing was felt further afield than the United States and Australia. In colonial Africa, nineteenth-century police forces had European senior officers, and many of the colonial forces were based on the model of the Royal Irish Constabulary (Killingray 1986: 425). The similarities in the reform of the criminal law and the enforcement of that law in the Anglo-American world (and further afield) meant that the criminal law formed part of an emerging transnational system of governance.

Exchange of National Laws and the Development of a Transnational Commercial Law

It is not just in relation to the criminal law that national or regional laws were part of a wider transnational lawmaking enterprise in the nineteenth century. In the field of commerce, similar methods of exchange and forms of governance were adopted around the common law world, laying the basis for a transnational system of commercial law and corporate governance. This was in part born out of commercial necessity. California and the Australian colonies, for example, were both frontier outposts of a global network of credit. In December 1852, it was reported via San Francisco that the first express company between New York and the gold regions of Australia was to be established by the house of Berford & Co. of New York for the purpose of forwarding gold dust, parcels and freight (The *Courier*, 11 December 1852). In 1853, the Melbourne *Argus* praised the number of trans-oceanic steamships in Australian ports and noted a 'real commercial brotherhood among nations' (The *Argus*, 20 January 1852).

It would not have been possible for commercial exchange to develop in the nineteenth century if the commercial law in each region did not share important features. A key development was the negotiability of promissory notes. A promissory note is a primitive form of credit, and negotiability is a principle whereby the rights attached to a promissory note were transferred by delivery of the document. This principle allowed international commercial networks to prosper because it provided an efficient and convenient method of payment for imported goods.

The negotiability of promissory notes was recognised in English law in 1704 with the Statute of 3 & 4 Anne (1704). The English legislation of 1704 did not immediately apply in the American colonies, but three colonial legislatures did directly adopt the English statute. By 1800, two more states had adopted the principle of negotiability, including the state of New York, which was growing in importance as a financial centre (Horwitz 1977: 215). This was a critical development because it both demonstrates the law evolving to accommodate transnational economic processes, and in turn, by virtue of New York's emerging status as a commercial centre, added momentum to the transnational movement to adopt similar commercial legal norms. During the nineteenth century, promissory notes became increasingly important in the economy of the United States. For this reason, as settlement moved west, 'the law of negotiable instruments went with it' (Friedman 2005: 196). This was certainly the case in California. On 16 April 1850, the Californian legislature passed An Act Relating to Bills of Exchange and Promissory Notes 1850 that was almost a complete reproduction of the equivalent New York statute. In this way, the English law of negotiability found its way into California by way of New York.

The law of negotiability arrived in Queensland through a similar (but more formalised) process of adoption of English law. As has been previously discussed, Queensland adopted the laws of New South Wales, which in turn received the laws of England in 1828. In 1867, the laws in relation to promissory notes were consolidated in Queensland in the Bills of Exchange Act 1867. Thus, in both California and Queensland, promissory notes had the characteristic of negotiability, which allowed notes to be transferred and therefore allowed the regions to participate in global economic exchange, and facilitated the development of a transnational credit system. This was a result of the shared legal history of the Australian colonies and the United States, the continuing influence of English legal developments, and the global economic forces that operated in the nineteenth century.

Even more than the transnational nature of the law of credit, the story of corporate governance on either side of the Pacific was remarkably similar and driven by the same transnational forces. The story of corporate law in each region began with the English law of partnership. The law of partnership is arguably the oldest form of business organisation and is a creature of the common law. English partnership law provided that a partnership could be formed by businesspeople through a simple agreement to act as partners and to share the profits of the business. Contracts entered into with third parties were legally binding on all partners, each partner was liable for all debts incurred during the course of the partnership, and no share of the partnership could be transferred without the consent of the other partners. From the beginning, the English law of partnership was part of the law of both the Australian and American colonies.

While the law of partnership was a creature of the common law, other corporate forms were a result of legislative invention. The origin of the modern corporate form can be traced back to the fourteenth century in Genoa, when shares were sold in large state-backed companies formed for the purpose of mining, importing of materials, and even the conquest of two Mediterranean islands. From the sixteenth century, English joint stock companies, operating under a government charter that provided them with certain corporate privileges, were able to amalgamate large pools of private capital and 'led the nation's charge overseas for conquest and profit during the Age of Exploration' (Hansmann et al 2006: 1376; Banner 1998: 23–4).

Each of these early joint stock companies had to be approved individually by the government. However, notwithstanding the popularity of the chartered joint stock company, the English Parliament was circumspect in its issuing of charters (Hansmann et al 2006: 1378). This reluctance led to the emergence of the unincorporated (unchartered) joint stock company in the late seventeenth century. The unincorporated joint stock company combined the law of partnership and the law of trusts to allow stockholders to transfer shares without the consent of all other shareholders (which was the feature of the chartered joint stock company that was most attractive to investors) (ibid.: 1383–4). These unincorporated joint stock companies were not registered or regulated by the government and speculation in them was rampant. As a result of this speculation in unincorporated companies, the English Parliament passed the Bubble Act 1720. Among other things, this legislation prohibited unincorporated companies from selling shares. The Bubble Act remained on the statute books until 1825, but as a practical matter was rarely enforced (Banner 1998: 78).

American corporate law owes much to its English origins. Although the partnership form was the most common way of organising business enterprises in the United States until well into the nineteenth century (Blair 2003: 414), the first American settlers would certainly have been familiar with the chartered joint stock company. Several of these companies, including the Hudson's Bay Company, operated in colonial America (Hurst 1970: 7–15). In the late eighteenth and early nineteenth centuries, the state legislatures of the United States granted charters to companies, primarily for the same types of businesses that the English Parliament had allowed to incorporate, such as those concerned with the construction and operation of canals, bridges and turnpikes. Unincorporated joint stock associations were also popular and, just as in England, businesses in America looked to achieve corporate status without seeking a charter from one of the state legislatures (Blair 2003: 416). In the early development of the corporate form, therefore, developments in the United States mirrored those in England.

Early corporate law in Australia also reflected English legal developments and those across the Pacific. Although the partnership form was the most popular form of association, the Australian colonists were also familiar, like their American counterparts, with the concept of the chartered joint stock company. In 1817, Governor Macquarie purported to confer a charter on the Bank of New South Wales (although the charter was not approved by London) (Salsbury and Sweeney 1988: 8). Several unincorporated joint stock companies were formed in Australia, including the Australian Agricultural Company in 1824, and the Australian Gas Light Company in 1836. By the middle of the 1830s there was 'a sort of mania for the formation of companies' (Lipton 2007: 808–9).

By the first decade of the nineteenth century, American corporate law began to develop independently of English law (albeit moving in a parallel direction and, importantly, in response to the same economic forces). By the late eighteenth century, the first incorporation statutes had been passed in a number of states. This legislation allowed companies to be incorporated for specific purposes, usually religious. In 1809, the Massachusetts legislature passed a general incorporation statute for manufacturing, and in 1811 a more general incorporation statute was passed in New York (Blair 2003: 426). In 1836 and 1837 respectively, Pennsylvania and Connecticut passed general incorporation laws. The passage of these laws opened the legislative floodgates and by the end of the 1850s, 24 states had enacted similar statutes. A general incorporation law was passed in California on 22 April 1850, and this law was based on the precedents provided by the eastern states (Hamill 1999: 102–3).

In respect of general incorporation law, English law lagged behind the United States. It was not until 1844 that the English Parliament finally relented to pressure and passed the Joint Stock Companies Act 1844. This legislation required all unincorporated companies with more than 25 shareholders, or with transferable shares, to register as public companies (Dodd 1954, p. 1351). In 1855, the principle of limited liability was granted to registered companies (Limited Liability Act 1855 (UK)) and this emerging body of company legislation was consolidated in the Companies Act 1862. The Australian colonies adopted this English corporate legislation almost without modification (McQueen 1991: 24). Within six months of the passage of the Companies Act 1862 in England, a version of the law had been introduced into the Victoria Parliament, and in 1863 similar legislation was passed in Queensland (Lipton 2007: 814).

The historical development of Anglo-American corporate law explains why the legislation on either side of the Pacific was substantially similar. The extent of the similarity is demonstrated by a brief comparison between the legal position in relation to limited liability, calls on shares, and the transfer of shares was almost identical:

- Limited liability: Under the Californian corporations legislation, the liability of shareholders was limited to the unpaid amount on their shares. If the company's debts exceeded this amount, the directors were personally liable. Under the Queensland legislation, shareholders were also only liable for the unpaid amount on their shares. The main difference between the regions was that in California, directors were liable for the debts that exceeded the capital of the company. This was not a significant difference, however, because the majority of investors were still protected by the principle of limited liability and directors could avoid the prospect of the company incurring debt by issuing additional shares.
- Transfer of shares: Under both the Queensland and Californian corporations legislation, shares were freely transferable. This meant that investors were able to dispose of their shares at any time if they wished to realise the value of their investment.
- Calls: Under both the Queensland and Californian corporations legislation, the directors could call upon shareholders to pay amounts to the company up to the value of their subscription. Failure to pay meant that the share was liable to be forfeited. This stimulated investment by allowing miners to invest in a company with a small initial outlay. The only noticeable difference between the legal regimes in each region was the development in the Australian colonies of the 'no liability' mining company. This form of company emerged in Queensland with the passage of the Mining Companies Act 1875 (Qld). Under this legislation, the acceptance by a shareholder of a share did not oblige that shareholder to contribute to the debts or liabilities of the company. However, if a company did make a call upon the shares, and that call was not paid, then the shareholder was not entitled to a dividend upon that share and the share could be forfeited and sold at public auction. While important, this difference did not change the operation of the law in a significant way. This is because it did not alter the principle that a shareholder could invest a certain amount in a company without having to pay that entire amount immediately.

Again, as in relation to the reform of the criminal law, it was not only in Australia and the United States that company law developed along such similar lines. Chartered companies operated throughout the world and traded across national borders, facilitating the need for a simple method of exchange. International banking houses, such as the House of Baring and Rothschilds, issued letters of credit that allowed importers to buy goods from all over the world. The Baltimore agency of Brown, Shipley & Co., for example, issued letters of credit to importers of coffee, sugar, hides, copper ore and guano (South America), iron (England) and assorted dry goods (Europe) (Perkins 1971: 429). In this way, the nineteenth century saw the origins of transnational corporate governance, born out of the emerging international network of commerce, and the continuing exchange of commercial legal principles.

Conclusion

Although the story of law and legal governance in the nineteenth century has often been told within the prism of the nation-state, it cannot be separated from its historical, social, economic, geographic and political context. This context often had an international dimension. Laws across jurisdictions were influenced by the same factors that crossed regional and national boundaries. This network of laws created informal systems of transnational governance in the nineteenth century.

It is clear that much work still needs to be done to assess the extent of transnational governance in the nineteenth century. Scholars who search for a paradigm to explain the development of national laws continue, in large part, to tell a story that implicitly entrenches the distinctive nature of each national regime. Morton Horwitz in his seminal work, *The Transformation of American Law*, argues that judges in the United States framed 'general doctrines based on a self-conscious consideration of social and economic policies' (Horwitz 1977: 2). By confining his discussion to the impact on American legal institutions of the nation's social and economic policies, Horwitz implicitly confirms the distinctive nature of American law. Even William J. Novak, who notes the dangers of exceptionalism and credits transatlantic customs and traditions for important aspects of American society and government, nevertheless begins his excellent exposition on nineteenth-century government regulation with the observation that 'A distinctive and powerful government tradition devoted in theory and practice to the vision of a well-regulated society dominated United States social and economic policymaking from 1787 to 1877' (Novak 1996: 1). It is unquestionable that the work done by legal scholars to unravel and explain the development of national laws is invaluable, but these national or regional legal histories tend to obscure the connections, transfers and exchanges of law between nations, and the similarities in the development of law in different geographic settings. Bruce Kercher, in calling for a more international legal history, suggests that 'it is time to look at cross-Pacific influences' and 'the circulation of legal ideas' including the 'multi-directional influences on official and popular thought' (Kercher 1995: 204–5).

This chapter has considered the transnational character of laws that operated in the United States and the Australian colonies, specifically California and Queensland, and suggests that the same transnational forces gave particular systems of governance in each region a substantially similar shape. While there were certainly differences between each region, these differences should not obscure the substantial similarities, and the fact that an analysis of the similarities can illuminate the emergence of transnational systems of governance. In this way, a history of transnational governance in the nineteenth century can be written by considering each legal regime as a system of 'inputs' and 'outputs'. The 'output' is the actual content of the law (including both the text of the law and its practical operation). The 'inputs' of the law are those forces (many of which were international) that determine the 'outputs'. By investigating the nature of the 'inputs' and the extent to which they transcend national boundaries, it is possible to construct a picture of the various systems of transnational governance that operated in the nineteenth century. This chapter, for example, identified two main 'inputs': the influence of a shared English legal heritage; and the exchange of laws between nations, which gave rise to particular systems of transnational governance. There are, of course, many more transnational 'inputs' that shaped nineteenth-century systems of governance, including the influence of shared social norms on the development of law, and the influence of shared geographical and geological settings. Put another way, it is suggested that legal regimes in the nineteenth century were shaped by shifting patterns of tensions, many of which had a transnational character. By defining that pattern of tensions, and connecting that pattern across national borders, it is possible to identify a history of transnational governance that had its origins well before the twentieth century.

References

Asante, Samuel B. 1987. 'Over a Hundred Years of a National Legal System in Ghana: A Review and Critique', *Journal of African Law* 31 (Spring): 70.

Banner, Stuart 2007. *Possessing the Pacific: Land, Settlers, and Indigenous People from Australia to Alaska*. Cambridge, MA: Harvard University Press.

—— 2002. *The Death Penalty: An American History*. Cambridge, MA: Harvard University Press.

—— 1998. *Anglo-American Securities Regulation: Cultural and Political Roots, 1690–1860*. Cambridge: Cambridge University Press.

Beckman, Gail M. 1966. 'Three Penal Codes compared', *The American Journal of Legal History* 10 (April): 148.

Benton, Lauren 2002. *Law and Colonial Cultures: Legal Regimes in World History, 1400–1900*. New York: Cambridge University Press.

Bennett, J. 1970. 'Historical Trends in Australian Law Reform', *University of Western Australia Law Review* 9: 211.

Blair, Margaret M. 2003. 'Locking in Capital: What corporate law achieved for business organizers in the nineteenth century', *UCLA Law Review* 51 (December): 387.

Boorstin, Daniel 1996. *The Mysterious Science of the Law: An Essay on Blackstone's Commentaries*, 1st edn 1941. Chicago, IL: University of Chicago Press.

Castles, Alex C. 1982. *An Australian Legal History*. Sydney, NSW: Law Book Co.

Chapin, Bradley 1989. 'Law Reform in the Early Republic', *The Pennsylvania Magazine of History and Biography* 113 (April): 163.

Currey, C.H. 1937. 'The influence of the English Law Reformers of the Early 19th Century on the Law of New South Wales', *Royal Australian Historical Society* 23: 227.

Djelic, Marie-Laure and Sahlin-Andersson, Kerstin 2006. 'A world of governance: The rise of transnational regulation', in Djelic and Sahlin-Andersson (eds),

Transnational Governance: Institutional Dynamics of Regulation, Cambridge: Cambridge University Press, pp. 1–28.

Dodd, E. Merrick 1954. *American Business Corporations until 1860*. Cambridge, MA: Harvard University Press.

Farmer, Lindsay 2000. 'Reconstructing the English Codification Debate: The Criminal Law Commissioners, 1833–45', *Law and History Review* 18(2) (Summer): 397–425.

Finn, Jeremy 2005. 'Codification of the criminal law: the Australian parliamentary experience', in Barry S. Godfrey and Graeme Dunstall, *Crime and Empire, 1840–1940: Criminal Justice in local and global context*. Cullompton: Willan.

Friedman, Lawrence 2005. *A History of American Law*, 3rd edn. New York: Simon & Schuster.

Gibbs, Harry 2003. 'Queensland Criminal Code: From Italy to Zanzibar', *Australian Law Journal* 77: 232.

Hall, Ford W. 1950–51. 'The Common Law: An Account of its Reception in the United States', *Vanderbilt Law Review* 4: 791.

Hamill, Susan Pace 1999. 'From Special Privilege to General Utility: A Continuation of Willard Hurst's Study of Corporations', *American University Law Review* 49: 81–180.

Handlin, Oscar, and Mary Handlin 1969. *Commonwealth: A Study of the Role of Government in the American Economy: Massachusetts, 1774–1861*, 1st edn 1947. Cambridge, MA: Harvard University Press.

Hansmann, Henry, Reiner Kraakman and Richard Squire 2006. 'Law and the Rise of the Firm', *Harvard Law Review* 119 (March): 1333.

Herman, Shael 1996. 'The Fate and the Future of Codification in America', *American Journal of Legal History* 40(4) (October): 407–37.

Horwitz, Morton 1992. *Transformation of American Law, 1870–1960*. New York: Oxford University Press.

—— 1977. *The Transformation of American Law, 1780–1860*. Cambridge, MA: Harvard University Press.

Hurst, James Willard 1970. *The Legitimacy of the Business Corporation in the Law of the United States, 1780–1970*. Charlottesville: University of Virginia Press.

Kercher, Bruce 1995. *An Unruly Child*. Sydney, NSW: Allen & Unwin.

Killingray, David 1986. 'The Maintenance of Law and Order in British Colonial Africa', *African Affairs* 85 (July): 411.

Kimball, Bruce A. 2007. 'Langdell on Contracts and Legal Reasoning: Correcting the Holmesian Caricature', *Law and History Review* 25(2) (Summer): 353.

Kleps, Ralph N. 1954. 'The Revision and Codification of California Statutes, 1849–1953', *California Law Review* 42: 766–802.

Leader-Elliot, Ian 2006. 'Benthamite reflections on codification of the general principles of criminal liability: towards the panopticon', *Buffalo Criminal Law Review* 9: 391.

Levi-Faur, David and Jacinta Jordana 2004. *The Politics of Regulation: Institutions and Regulatory Reforms for the Age of Governance*. Cheltenham: Edward Elgar.

Lipton, Phillip 2007. 'A History of Company Law in Colonial Australia: Legal Evolution and Economic Development' (August). Monash University Department of Business Law & Taxation Research Paper No. 11. Available at SSRN: <http://ssrn.com/abstract=1030196>.

McPherson, B.H. 1989. *The Supreme Court of Queensland, 1859–1960: History, Jurisdiction, Procedure.* Sydney, NSW: Butterworths.

McQueen, Rob 1991. 'Limited Liability Company Legislation – The Australian Experience', *Australian Corporate Law Journal* 1(1): 22.

Novak, William J. 1996. *The People's Welfare: Law and Regulation in Nineteenth-Century America*. Chapel Hill, NC: University of North Carolina Press.

Perkins, Edwin J. 1971. 'Antebellum Importers: The Role of Brown Bros & Co in Baltimore', *Business History Review* 45(4) (Winter): 421–51.

Salsbury, Stephen and Kay Sweeney 1988. *The Bull, the Bear and the Kangaroo: The History of the Sydney Stock Exchange*. Sydney: Allen & Unwin, 1988.

Saunier, Pierre-Yves 2008. 'Learning by Doing: Notes about the Making of the Palgrave Dictionary of Transnational History', *Journal of Modern European History* 6(2): 159–80.

Schidhauser, John R. 1992. 'Legal Imperialism: Its Enduring Impact on Colonial and Post-Colonial Judicial Systems', *International Political Science Review* 13 (July): 321.

Subrin, Stephen N. 1988. 'David Dudley Field and the Field Code: A Historical Analysis of an Earlier Procedural Vision', *Law and History Review* 6(2) (Fall): 311–73.

Thelen, David 1999. 'The Nation and Beyond: Transnational Perspectives on United States History', *Journal of American History* 86(3): 965–75.

Tyrrell, Ian 1991. 'American Exceptionalism in an Age of International History', *American Historical Review* 96(4): 1031–55.

Vanstone, Maurice 2008. 'The international origins and initial development of probation', *British Journal of Criminology* 48 (November): 735.

Weaver, John C. 2003. *The Great Land Rush and the Making of the Modern World, 1650–1900*. Montreal and Kingston: McGill-Queen's University Press.

Chapter 2
Challenging Neoliberal Ideology in a Global Financial Crisis

Scott Mann

Introduction

This chapter traces the global financial crisis (GFC) back to the major structural changes from social liberal to neoliberal ideology and policy in the early 1980s. Following major defeats for the organised working class in the West from the mid-1970s, these changes marked the end of the welfare state consensus across major political parties and the end of government committed to moderating and stabilising the effects of market forces in the interests of full employment, redistribution and global development.

The ideas guiding and legitimating this transition were drawn, amongst other sources, from the social contract ethics and ethical egoism of Thomas Hobbes, the classical economic theories of Smith and Ricardo, the neoclassical microeconomics of Jevons, Marshall and others, and the monetarist macroeconomics of Milton Friedman and the Chicago School. Such ideas, put together in universities, research centres and private think tanks, have functioned as effective tools of class struggle, wielded by business leaders and business-friendly governments to guide and legitimise the winding-back of the gains of workers and peasants in the post-war boom period.

Where previously interest rate cuts had been used to support full employment, interest rate rises were now used to weaken, demoralise and discipline working people through re-instituting chronic unemployment and underemployment. With workers appropriately weakened and cowed, interest rate reductions were instituted to protect investors when share prices fell as a result of instability produced by financial deregulation.

Where previously fiscal intervention – and deficits – had supported full employment and expansion of welfare provision, now the ideology called for balanced state budgets, along with tax cuts for the rich to increase productivity. Supposedly, all were going to benefit from the high growth produced by neoliberal deregulation.

But real growth stalled while inequality increased at an accelerated rate. Powerful nations now felt free to impose unrestricted free trade, free investment and balanced budgets upon weaker nations, while reserving the right to protect their own territories through tariff and non-tariff barriers and general regulation of foreign investment. At the same time, more and more of their taxpayers' money went into no strings hand-outs, subsidies and bailouts for big business.

The Argument

Political and legal responses to the GFC have generally been grounded in an analysis which attributes the crisis to a failure of the US Federal Reserve to effectively control the money supply, particularly following the dotcom crash in 2000, and a failure of financial regulatory authorities to effectively monitor and control risk taking in the production, proliferation and dissemination of financial derivatives.

Avoiding a repeat of the crisis is seen to involve central banks – particularly the Federal Reserve – keeping a tighter rein on the money supply in the future, keeping supply in line with the expansion of production, and restricting the growth of private debt. There is dispute about the nature and extent of governance and regulatory reform needed in relation to financial institutions and operations. The most radical response is to call for a return to effective separation of retail and investment banking, to protect the savings of households and businesses, and to protect taxpayers and citizens from future bailouts of wealthy gamblers. But relevant authorities seem to favour the resumption of business as usual as soon as possible, with government borrowing to fund the bailouts rapidly repaid, nationalised financial institutions returned to private ownership, megabanks left intact and a minimum of new regulatory reforms, to encourage more 'efficient risk management'.

It is clearly true that loose money contributed to massive asset inflation, particularly in the US housing market, built upon increasingly risky – subprime – mortgages. This boom, in turn, became the basis for the proliferation of mortgage-based securities (CDOs) and derivative-based insurance (CDSs) of such securities, with limited regulation justified by the alleged benefits of greater dissemination of risk.

Billions and ultimately trillions of dollars worth of such securities and insurance commitments became increasingly widely distributed throughout the financial world, with banks, insurance companies and investment funds treating them as valuable investments.

When rising – inflation-targeted – interest rates led to accelerating subprime mortgage defaults, institutions which had accumulated large amounts of such assets, or provided insurance for them, found themselves in serious difficulties, leading to failure of lending (to other banks, to businesses and to the public), insolvency and collapse. This led to a first round of government intervention – shoring up key financial institutions through handouts and takeovers.

With reduced lending, deleveraging of households, banks and firms, and falling confidence and consumption, the financial crisis rapidly impacted upon the real economy, leading to deepening recession and a second round of government intervention in the form of major stimulus programmes of deficit spending. With recession easing, the orthodox approach calls for major welfare cut-backs and loss of government jobs to allow for rapid repayment of huge government debts.

But the orthodox analysis fails to consider any broader structural, global, ideological and historical contributions to the crisis. In particular, thirty years of neoliberal policies of deregulation, of restriction of jobs and wages and conditions of the working population around the world, major global trade imbalances, with permanent current account surplus in China and deficit in the US, and structural adjustment of poor developing-world countries, are seen as largely or essentially irrelevant.

This chapter contests an orthodox explanation which looks no further than recent US monetary policy and an orthodox response of forcing working people to carry the costs of the bailout through loss of jobs and services, while maintaining current structures of wealth and power, and in particular, the globalised 'free market', essentially unchanged. It argues that the case for much more radical governance and policy reforms, not just to avoid another, deeper financial crisis in the near future, but also to address issues of increasing inequality, poverty, pollution and climate change driven by neoliberal policies and priorities.

Neoliberal policies have limited the share of wealth going to working people in the West through the abandonment of full employment fiscal policies, through the destruction of trade union power and of effective collective bargaining, and through encouraging transfer of manufacture to low-wage regions of the developing world. They have stunted the growth of the developing world – apart from China and India – through massive wealth transfer to the developed world, through enforced repayments of odious debt, repatriated profits and unrequited resource appropriation, dumping, and all of the problems of IMF and World Bank-imposed structural adjustment. The rapid growth of the Chinese economy has been bought at a terrible price in terms of pollution, ill health, political repression and economic exploitation.

Increasing inequality within and between nations – with a major shift in the share of national income away from wages and into profits – has limited wage-based demand for consumption goods which has undermined the expansion of productive investment in the West. The oligopoly power of big corporations, lack of working-class demand and the ready availability of cheap labour in the developing world have stunted the development of new productive technology to allow for sustainable growth.

At the same time, this shift has increased the excess wealth of elite groups looking for new opportunities for speculative gain. Such increased speculation has destabilised financial markets, encouraging 'loose money' policies to try to protect the real economy. This is the context in which 'loose money' has sustained increasingly debt-based subsistence consumption by the working population in the West and debt-based speculation, leveraged buyouts and paper asset trading by wealthy gamblers and opportunists.

But quite apart from their central role in generating the crisis, neoliberal policies of deregulation, privatisation, monetary inflation control, 'free trade' and 'free investment' have had negative consequences for poorer people and poorer countries, for democratic participation, for the growth and stability of the world economy and for the environment. This chapter examines the true nature and consequences of such policies. And it shows why and how alternative policies are possible and necessary.

The chapter is divided into three main sections. The first deals with corporations, economic policy and democracy, the second with international trade and investment, and the third with banking deregulation, financial markets and the meltdown.

Corporations, Economic Policy and Democracy

History

Prior to the late 1970s, post-Second World War policies in the developed economies were based upon Keynesian and social democratic ideas of the need for government intervention, nationally and internationally, to maintain full employment and economic stability. In the developed world, fiscal demand management, progressive taxation, strong trade unions and capital controls (with fixed but adjustable currency exchange rates) contributed to maintaining close to full employment while also allowing the construction of substantial welfare systems. In the developing world, high tariffs protected agriculture and import-substituting industrialisation contributed to social progress.

From the late 1960s, neoliberal critics identified simultaneous increases in inflation and unemployment as a result of excessive government – deficit – spending and regulatory 'distortion' of the operation of free markets. Margaret Thatcher came to power in Britain in 1979 and Ronald Reagan in the US in 1980 promising to address these problems through government budget balancing, deregulation of markets, winding back of taxes and of trade union power, with accelerated tariff reductions and free currency trading replacing capital controls. They were committed to fighting inflation through big interest rate rises and privatising state operations in the name of increased efficiency.

Free Markets

Neoliberals followed classical economic theory in maintaining that with free markets, rational consumers, through their purchasing decisions, and rational firms, through their investment decisions, ensure that productive resources are efficiently transferred from areas of declining to those of increasing demand, without the need for central control. The prices of goods (to such consumers) are continually falling and overall social wealth growing as productivity increases through competition driven capital accumulation.

This system is powered by rational self-interest – with consumers trading off the costs and benefits of particular purchases to maximise their 'utility', and producers balancing productive inputs and outputs to maximise their profits.

Neoliberals appealed to the neoclassical theories of Marshall and Walras to argue that free markets, driven by such rational self-interest, 'naturally' gravitate towards an 'equilibrium' condition in which productive resources are fully and efficiently employed. External 'shocks' such as the sudden oil price rises of 1973–74 can disturb such an equilibrium, but, left to its own devices, the free market automatically readjusts to a new and still optimally efficient equilibrium position. The fundamental role of government is to facilitate the free operation of such natural market forces with a minimum of intervention.

Corporations

Neoliberals have generally treated the public business corporation, with ownership of corporate assets vested in private shareholders, as the ideal vehicle of such competition and capital accumulation, and the ideal model of efficient governance, to be applied or emulated as widely as possible. In particular, they have favoured the Anglo-American model of corporate governance, with no direct input for workers, unions, governments, or the wider public into senior management decision-making.

The professional and hierarchical structure of the modern corporation allows general policy to be translated into specific directives by experts. The hierarchy allows for ongoing monitoring of policy and action with information from the base centralised for policy review. The work of professional experts (scientists, accountants, lawyers, and so on) can be effectively integrated and directed on a large scale, by a central authority, in pursuit of high levels of productivity and efficiency.

Large size allows for economies of scale and concentration of resources for large-scale projects, which sustain further scale economies. It allows for substantial research budgets, for increased division of labour, specialisation and automation of production, along with bulk purchase, storage and application of inputs to bring down costs.

Neoliberals justify very substantial remuneration of senior managers of big corporations by reference to the high levels of stress and responsibility of their positions, and intense international competition to gain the services of the limited numbers of top talents. Greater power and remuneration up the hierarchy provides a powerful incentive to upward mobility through optimum productive and creative input into corporate profit-making. Higher profits are both the consequence of effective management and the means to ensure the rewards which drive such effective management.

Shareholders' limited liability is said to encourage the public to finance ongoing innovation to bring new and cheaper products to market, to fund large-scale productive undertakings, and to facilitate the movement of productive operations around the world, to take advantage of the best available conditions.

Neoliberals claim that representative democracy rules in the corporate world, with each share generally having one vote towards appointment of the board of directors. Where share-ownership is relatively concentrated, it is fair and just that those who have contributed more should have more say in appointing the executives to effectively employ such resources. It is reasonable to expect that successful boards and CEOs will be in the best position to advise shareholders as to who is best suited to replace members who retire or transfer to other positions.

Share-markets offer managers opportunities for raising capital, as and when it is needed, without the need to conform to the strictures and regular interest payments of bank loans. Such share-markets complement freely competitive goods markets to ensure that managers are optimally committed to productivity in the service of shareholder value. They are kept on their toes through the threat of sale of shares, falling values and hostile takeovers.

Privatisation

In contrast to private businesses, state-owned enterprises are frequently run as monopolies, free from competitive pressures to maximise efficiency, and able to rely upon government bailouts if they make losses. In private businesses, owner managers have both the ability and a strong incentive to seek to maximise profit through efficient operation and innovation. Directors of publicly listed corporations can be shareholders and can be motivated to good management with stock options. Even without such direct incentives, they are under continuous pressure of market competition and their performance is monitored by shareholders.

These are the key neoliberal arguments in favour of privatisation of state-owned enterprises. This is why neoliberals see share and bond financing of business operations as – generally – superior to deposit bank financing, because of the greater discipline exerted by the high liquidity of financial markets, as well as the greater flexibility such instruments give to business.

In Britain, the 'reforming' neoliberal Tory governments of the 1980s and 1990s instituted wide-ranging privatisation of previously government-owned instrumentalities. Other governments followed suit, including the Keating Labor government in Australia.

Following the Third World debt crisis of 1982, the IMF and World Bank imposed 'structural adjustment' programmes as conditions for debt renegotiation for developing world debtor nations. Such programmes refashioned the economies in question along neoliberal lines, including privatisation of state-owned enterprises, so as to reduce budget deficits, in so far as government subsidies to such enterprises were seen to contribute to balance-of-payment difficulties, and private ownership was seen as the key to improved efficiency and profitability (Chang 2007: 33–4).

Regulation

Neoliberal supporters of the corporate form acknowledge the possibility of conflict of interest between managers as controllers and shareholders as owners, especially where diversified share ownership allows management to appoint most of the board of directors.

But they maintain that such conflicts are effectively addressed through executive incentives and bonuses in the form of stock options, rewarding managers for increasing capital gains and returns to investors. Influential neoliberal accounting theorists (for example, Watts and Zimmerman 1986) argue that market forces – in particular, the markets for managers and auditors – can ensure effective, conservative and objective voluntary accounting and auditing procedures without external regulation of such practices.

Some neoliberals accept that there is a place for legal regulation of corporate governance including regular and transparent checking and reporting of the company's financial position, and enforcement of anti-monopoly laws to protect businesses as well as consumers from monopoly price fixing. But they are determined to limit the power of enforcement agencies (such as ASIC, the ACCC and APRA in Australia), and encourage the use of persuasive rather than punitive sanctions.

Inflation Control

The principal economic inspiration for the early neoliberal political reformers came from the new classical or Chicago School theories of Milton Friedman, championing a return to free market 'self-regulation' (Skidelsky 2009: 105).

Friedman argued that even relatively low levels of inflation are major obstacles to investment and growth through creating financial instability. Inflation is the product of governments spending beyond their means, running deficits to supplement their tax receipts, and central banks allowing too much money into circulation.

When governments borrow money to finance their investment spending, they 'crowd out' private-sector investment by competing with private businesses for loanable funds, and pushing up interest rates. Such government intervention therefore fails to boost the national economy, and can further weaken it.

Friedman argued that an increase in effective demand through expansionary monetary and fiscal policy attempting to reduce unemployment beyond an equilibrium level (called the 'natural rate') is futile because workers save rather than spend what they see as merely temporary increases in their incomes. When excess funds are spent, they push up inflation. With established inflation, organised workers campaign for ongoing wage increases to keep pace with further anticipated price increases. Employers pass on increased costs in further price increases leading to a positive feedback of increasing inflation.

Friedman agreed with Keynes that in 'normal' times, governments should aim to keep their spending in line with their tax receipts. But Friedman called for permanently low taxes (particularly on higher incomes, assets and profits) to stimulate the growth of the private sector, while Keynes saw the need for progressive taxation to support public welfare and infrastructure spending and repay government debt incurred in such spending. However, Keynes came to see taxation in excess of 25 per cent of national income as problematic (Skidelsky 2010: xviii). Keynes saw deficit-funded fiscal interventions as sometimes necessary to avoid deepening depression, while Friedman argued that any such deficit-funded interventions would create further economic instability. Crises should be self-correcting through falling factor costs and interest rates.

Friedman called for 'independent' Central Banks, mandated to ensure steady growth of the money supply at a rate equal to the long run ('natural') increase in national output to maintain stable growth. Whenever too rapid economic growth or excess workers' pay demands threaten to push up inflation, such banks need to reduce the money supply to push up interest rates. Such restrictive monetary policy reduces 'runaway' investment and growth; by pushing unemployment to the natural equilibrium rate, it cuts back inflation.

In 1979, Margaret Thatcher's Conservative government in the UK and Paul Volker at the US Federal Reserve were guided by Friedman's ideas in instituting big interest rate hikes to protect currency values and squeeze out inflation.

Subversion of Democracy

There are many problems with the theory and practise of neoliberal reform. Neoliberal economics sees 'free market' competition as the norm and the ideal, as long as governments keep out of the picture. But the logic of the market ensures that unregulated competition of private firms leads to increasing concentration of economic power as profits are squeezed in the downswing of the business cycle. Larger operations benefit from economies of scale and grow larger as they take over competitors' resources and markets. Such concentration has proceeded to the point where major industries are now run as national and transnational oligopolies, with a few big firms sharing each market while benefiting from prices fixed to maximise profits.

In many areas of the world economy, half or more of world production of the goods in question is controlled by ten or less major corporations, providing a foundation for oligopoly power over output, prices and employment. The market capitalisation of the world's ten biggest mining companies, for example, 'outmatches those of all other mining companies put together'. (Moody 2007: 13) Most of the newspapers, magazines, television and radio stations in the US are owned by just five big conglomerates: Time Warner, Disney, News Corporation, Bertelsmann and Viacom.

Such concentrated oligopoly power wastes resources through restricting output and innovation. It subverts democratic politics through control of election funding, of the mass media and of job creation (and destruction) by managers and major shareholders of a handful of big corporations. Such subversion extends to control of policies supposedly aimed at restricting and regulating non-price-competitive business practices. So that, in practice, such policies are applied to smaller players or are restricted to achieving 'workable' rather than actual competition.

The fact that some of the biggest of the three hundred transnational corporations (TNCs) that control 70 per cent of FDI and 25 per cent of the world's capital are in the business of selling, burning, or otherwise directly utilising fossil fuels (with seven of the top ten in the oil and gas business – including Exxon, Shell, BP and Sinopec), has particularly disastrous consequences for the future of the human race. Such companies have so far used their economic and political power to block any effective action to check accelerating climate change produced by greenhouse gas emissions. So the world is now on track for massive sea-level rise, and loss of glacial melt-water, threatening future food supplies.

Monopolies per se are far from being a necessarily bad thing. All can benefit from economies of scale and avoidance of wasteful duplication of productive resources. But such general benefit depends upon effective public rather than private control of such production, ensuring that gains are effectively socialised – as more and better jobs, better products and social welfare provision, rather than privatised as wealth and power for a small minority.

Business Ethics

The internal structure of the typical business corporation, as a rigid power hierarchy, with those at the top deciding who will be allowed to join them, and effectively unaccountable to all below them, is incompatible with a democratic, fair, or civilised society. There can be no ethical justification for a situation where, in 2007, chief executives of the largest US companies received well over 500 times the pay of their average employees after tax (with top income tax rate of only 35 per cent in the US), or where, in many of the top companies today, the CEO is paid more in each day than the average worker is in a year.

Senior managers, insulated, assisted and protected by teams of specialists and experts, need exercise little in the way of special skills or effort to carry out their jobs. Rather than any correlation between burgeoning executive salaries and enhanced company performance, there is a strong correlation between the massive inflation of executive compensation in the US and the wave of corporate scandals engulfing the US in 2000, following after the stock market boom. In January 2008, just before the collapse of all major Wall St investment banks, 'bonuses added up to US$32 billion … the losses of those at the bottom of the pyramid [through foreclosures and falling asset values] roughly matched the extraordinary gains of the financiers at the top' (Harvey 2010: 2).

Production is a collective endeavour, with people and technology working together in increasingly complex patterns. It makes no sense to 'blame' workers, with no control over choice of technology, for their low productivity. Orthodox economists anyway acknowledge that there have been substantial increases in working-class productivity throughout the neoliberal period, with no corresponding wage increases. Shareholders, on the other hand, make no contribution to output, beyond original purchase of shares and occasional pressure upon the composition of management boards and upon some aspects of policy. Very few shareholders have actually made any such original purchases, with most rather handing over money to other shareholders.

With corporate finance increasingly based upon investment of profit, bond sales and bank loans, share markets have functioned to drain potential funding away from productive investment and into the pockets of wealthy investors. Profits from productive endeavour, channelled into inflated executive remuneration and dividends (and corporate welfare via taxation) have been increasingly directed into destructive speculation and asset-stripping, which have undermined real growth and job creation, or into the destruction of reasonably paid employment in favour of unprotected and underpaid labour in the developing world.

As Michael Albert points out, the corporation fosters a division 'between those who overwhelmingly monopolize empowering, fulfilling and engaging tasks and those who are overwhelmingly saddled with rote, obedient, [boring or] dangerous tasks'. This leads to a situation where some people – those in the upper reaches – 'have great confidence, decision-making skills, and relevant knowledge obtained through their daily work, while other people are only tired, de-skilled and lacking relevant knowledge' as a result of theirs (Albert 2003: 10).

The epidemiological research of Michael Marmot has shown the radically debilitating consequences of steep occupational hierarchies, in terms of increasing morbidity and mortality down the hierarchy (Marmot 2004: 38–40). With power, enjoyment and financial reward concentrated at the top, stress and responsibility are passed down to the middle and lower ranks, resulting in increasing morbidity and mortality down the hierarchy, with 5, 10 or 15 years difference in average life expectancy from the top to the bottom (ibid.: 26). With increasing export of actually productive tasks to low-wage, low-human rights territories overseas, the difference has further increased in some cases.

Corporations Law

Corporations law has failed to address the issue of management control of board appointments with dispersed share ownership, leading to short-term maximisation of management remuneration at the expense of any other social goal. Stock options have historically encouraged accounting manipulations to maximise reported profits rather than actual profit maximisation. They have encouraged managers to choose high-risk policies that ultimately lead to disaster but maximise short-term gains to the balance sheet.

Where concentration of share ownership delivers power to particular fund managers or particular families, we see how fundamentally undemocratic the system is, not only excluding workers, consumers and those in surrounding communities from any real say in board selection or company policy, but also the majority of shareholders themselves. At the same time, the power of such fund managers has contributed to a 'shareholder value' approach which has channelled an ever greater proportion of the revenue from productive output away from wages and into profits.

There are unfortunate parallels between the pseudo-democracy of the corporation, and liberal representative parliamentary democracy subverted by corporate wealth and power. In both cases, the big wealth holders decide upon the board, and the small fry are left floundering in isolation and ignorance. And like those effected by corporate decisions and actions, plenty of people in the developing world, profoundly effected by political and economic decision making in the developed world, have no say in the process.

In a situation where short-term profit and return to shareholders are typically reduced by socially responsible policies, the legal requirement for corporate officers to maximise dividends for shareholders is a requirement to act without moral responsibility. And even without such a legal requirement, share-markets themselves punish any redirection of resources away from short-term return to shareholders (into long-term sustainability, for instance) with falling share values, takeovers and asset stripping.

Welfare Services

Neoliberals call for, and have instituted, and maintained, privatisation of health care, education and welfare. Faced with continuing public support for surviving state provision, they have none the less extended private systems, supposedly to 'relieve the burden' upon the public systems, and set a standard towards which the public system should aspire.

But private systems have never provided quality services to more than a small minority of wealthy people. The US health care system, with the highest level of privatisation in the developed world, wastes billions in executive salaries, bonuses and benefits, advertising, determining patient eligibility, enforcing complex restrictions on coverage, attempting to collect bad debts, and so on.

The four largest insurance companies – UnitedHealth Group, WellPoint, Aetna and Humana – outside of the control of anti-monopoly laws, now have revenue of US$202 billion, 'almost three quarters of all health insurance' (Monkerud 2010: 1). With increasingly concentrated monopoly power, health insurance costs increased around 100 per cent in many states between 2000 and 2009, with major health insurers increasing their profits over 400 per cent from 2000 to 2008:

> Overall profits rose from $2.4 billion in 2000 to $13 billion in 2007. CEOs … pay reached 468 times the average American worker, with money left over to lobby against reforms … According to the National Institute on Money in State Politics, the health care industry paid almost $400 million to politicians in state governments in the past six years. The Centre of Responsible Politics discovered the industry spent over $1 billion in the past two years to oppose real reform. (Ibid.: 2)

The system costs more than any of the public systems in other developed countries, and has given richer people significant tax breaks, while the number of poorer people without health insurance rose to 46 million, or 15 per cent of the population, prior to President Barack Obama's health reforms.

As long as private systems coexist with public provision in a nation or a region, particularly a region with high levels of economic inequality, they pose an increasing threat to any adequate provision for the majority of the population. With high-quality private systems available, the rich have no incentive to subsidise public provision and they can conspire to reduce their own contribution to the public systems or exploit the resources of such systems to subsidise their own private provision.

State-owned Enterprises

Contrary to neoliberal claims, state-owned enterprises, like Singapore Airlines, the (now privatised) Korean steelmaker POSCO, Brazilian oil company Petrobras and aircraft manufacturer EMBRAER, have competed very successfully with privately owned enterprises in terms of productivity and profitability, both nationally and internationally (Chang 2007: 110–11).

State takeover of private business in times of total war, when rapid innovation and high efficiency are issues of national survival, gives the lie to free market arguments. And all of those developing world countries which have achieved successful modernisation and industrialisation since the end of the nineteenth century have done so on a basis of massive state intervention and control of productive investment.

As noted earlier, business cycle fluctuations contribute to the creation of private monopoly through the destruction of smaller businesses. Where technological conditions make single suppliers much more efficient, multiple private suppliers waste resources and single private suppliers can exploit the public with huge monopoly mark-ups. It is much more efficient to create and run major infrastructural and other larger operations as state monopoles, benefiting from scale economies and avoiding wasteful duplication or destruction of facilities.

State control can allow for implementation of crucial social policies, including provision of universal health care and education, counter-cyclical policies, maintaining employment in a downturn to avoid recession, focused public services and environmental protection. State-controlled banks can support responsible industry policy, through focused lending to sustainable producers.

Fiscal Policy

Government deficit spending can be the only way to maintain employment and prevent a multiplier effect of falling consumption, deepening recession and mass unemployment. Even staunchly neoliberal governments have been forced to acknowledge this, as the financial meltdown generated major downturns in the real economies of the developed world, and bank bailouts were followed by massive fiscal 'stimulus packages' to try to stem the slide into recession.

Government borrowing does not 'crowd out' private investment if there isn't enough private investment to sustain the national economy or if governments borrow in world financial markets, with little consequence for local interest rates (Stillwell 2002: 294).

As Chang and Grabel point out, 'the increase in economic activity that is associated with government spending does not necessarily cause inflation in countries with significant excess capacity.' And 'historically, periods of rapid economic growth in Continental Europe, the USA and Japan were associated with large programmes of public expenditure and … large budget deficits' (Chang and Grabel 2005: 193).

For long periods in the past, high inflation has not precluded sustained and rapid economic growth, with no inevitable progression to runaway inflation. World Bank research showed that for the period from 1950 to 1973, inflation below 40 per cent made no difference to economic growth, but below 20 per cent was positively correlated with such growth (ibid.: 185–6). Minsky showed how high inflation can reduce the severity of debt-driven recession (Keen 2001: 254).

Supposed conservative commitments to state budget balancing have not prevented neoliberal leaders able to get away with it – such as Ronald Reagan and George W. Bush in the US – from running up huge budget deficits to fund tax cuts for the rich, bail out businesses in trouble (as with the savings and loan banks in 1989) and conduct imperialist warfare overseas. Average CPI inflation in the neoliberal era from 1980 to 2008 at 3.2 per cent was little different from the 1950–73 average of 3.9 per cent (Skidelsky 2009: 124).

Neoliberal Government

For those gaining political power in the early 1980s in Britain and the US (as Margaret Thatcher's advisor Alan Budd admitted), the incompatibility of fact and theory was not relevant (Harvey 2010: 15). Neoliberal economic ideas were primarily tools for winding back the gains of ordinary people during the previous thirty years, in terms of secure employment, living wages, improved working conditions, social welfare benefits and empowerment, in the interests of protecting and extending capitalist class wealth and power.

Restricted fiscal policy meant cut-backs in welfare for the poor to fund tax cuts for the rich. High interest rates to control inflation meant recreation of an expanding reserve army of unemployed and underemployed workers through collapse of less profitable or less favoured businesses. Official unemployment rates in the US and UK went up from less than 5 per cent in the late 1970s to over 10 per cent by the mid 1980s. Cheap labour, cheap resources and cheap markets were thus 'freed up' for more effective exploitation.

Weakened union power, along with increasing fear of job loss with the winding-back of social services, left workers vulnerable to being blackmailed into increasing hours of more intensive work, or into inadequately paid casual employment. Instead of working together against their class enemies, they were increasingly turned against one another, competing for limited jobs and services.

Neoliberal regimes in the developed world encouraged racial tensions and conflicts, both indirectly, through reduced provision of jobs and services within their own territories and in the developing world, and directly through targeting 'illegal migrants', 'gangs' and 'terrorists' equated with particular ethnic groups. This further undermined effective collective action by working people.

Privatisation replaced relatively benign public monopolies with malign private ones, pushing up the cost of vital goods and services, reducing quality and safety provisions and shifting profits from public spending into private wealth accumulation. Quiggin estimates that the sale of British Telecom by the Thatcher government in 1985 involved a loss to the British public of more than £15 billion – in government debt servicing (Quiggin 2010: 194). Public bailouts were soon needed to save privatised services, which had been run into the ground by private owners (see, for example, Funnel et al. 2009). And once high interest and budget balancing had destroyed working-class power, neoliberal governments were willing to reduce rates to zero and run up huge deficits in the service of oligopoly capital – including funding of the US$3 trillion Gulf (Oil) War and the (first of many) no-strings-attached US$700 billion bailout of the banking industry by President George Bush in 2008.

GDP and Inequality

Neoliberals have traditionally claimed that a. GDP is a good measure of overall social welfare; with higher GDP meaning increased welfare, and b. neoliberal economic policies are better than any others in maximising such GDP.

GDP measures the economic activity going on within a particular nation-state. It is expressed as the sum of final expenditures on goods and services in the economy (consumer expenditure, government expenditures, gross investment in fixed capital and net exports), as the sum of income generated in order to sustain such expenditures (all wages and dividends including profits and rents), and as the sum of value added by productive enterprise to produce such income (Jackson 2009: 124).

The neoliberals claim that their policies are necessary for effective growth of GDP. But inflation-adjusted or 'real' GDP growth has been slower during the periods of neoliberalism than it was in the previous period of regulation. From a peak of over 5 per cent a year (adjusted for inflation) attained in the 1960–73 period, the average growth rate of the world economy progressively declined from one decade to the next to an average of barely more than 2 per cent a year recorded in the 1990s. And this was despite the very high growth rates achieved during this period by the East Asian so-called 'tiger' economies.

The apparently significant growth achieved in the later neoliberal period has been largely confined to China and India, with global averages distorted by these developments, built upon ruthless exploitation of labour in those countries, and massive extension of destitution in the latter, along with the de-industrialisation of the older industrial nations, particularly the US, Britain and Australia.

There are, anyway, major problems with GDP as any sort of measure of social welfare. It fails to:

> … account properly for changes in the asset base, to incorporate the real welfare losses from having an uneven distribution of income, to adjust for the depletion of material resources and other forms of natural capital; to capture the external costs of pollution and long term environmental damage; to account for the costs of crime, car accidents, industrial accidents, family breakdown and other social costs; to correct for defensive expenditures and positional consumption or to account for non–market services such as domestic labour and voluntary care. (Jackson 2009: 179)

Above about US$5,000–6,000 GDP per capita (on purchasing power parity), and throughout the developed world, GDP levels and increases bear no relation to real measures of social welfare. But levels of inequality are strongly correlated with a range of key measures of social welfare. The higher the inequality – as measured by how much greater the income (after tax and benefit) of the richest 20 per cent (of families) is than that of the poorest 20 per cent (Wilkinson and Pickett 2009: 17) – the higher the levels of social mistrust, mental illness, homicide, infant mortality, imprisonment and obesity, and the lower the levels of life expectancy, social mobility, and children's educational performance (ibid.: 19).

The gap between the richest and poorest 10 per cent in the developed English-speaking world has increased by 40 per cent since 1975 to reach a level 'unprecedented since records began' (ibid.: 234). In the US, the richest 20 per cent have increased their income to the point where it is more than 8 times greater than that of the poorest 20 per cent. In the UK and Australia, the income of the richest 20 per cent is around 7 times greater.

As Wilkinson and Pickett point out, those countries which have gone furthest down the neoliberal path, including reduced taxation of high incomes and private wealth, reduced welfare payments and employment protections, are precisely those with the highest levels of inequality and resulting social tensions and problems.

Such inequality has played a central role in precipitating the current crisis. Restricted income for working people has encouraged increasing accumulation of debt to finance consumption. Restricted monetarily effective demand for consumer goods by working people has discouraged investment in real material production. The increased wealth of those at the top has flowed into destructive speculation driving massive inflation of the prices of paper assets. Without real economic growth, there has been no way to pay for burgeoning debts and maintain the value of such assets.

SOEs and Workers' Cooperatives

Nationalisation of major corporate operations, of big oligopolies and services vital for the functioning of the rest of the economy and a civilised social system – including comprehensive health, education, information and welfare provision, provides an obvious foundation for beginning to address some of these problems. In particular, this could reverse private corporate subversion of the political process. Rather than allowing such operations to undermine representative democratic government, they could be made answerable to it, in fulfilling major public policy goals. And steep income gradients could be radically reduced.

This need not preclude the internal democratisation of such state-owned operations, with boards elected by, and answerable to, the whole workforce. Such managers are bound by government policy and answerable to executive authority to maintain agreed levels of service to the public. But this leaves considerable scope for workers' self-management and sharing of rewarding and empowering – and less rewarding – labour processes within the organisations.

Beyond such state-controlled monopolies, the success of the Mondragon system in the Basque region of Spain shows the possibility for smaller businesses to be very effectively run as worker-controlled cooperatives, supported and financed by state- or worker-controlled savings banks.

In the Mondragon system, a cooperative bank played a key role in funding and organising an expanding system of cooperatives. Individual cooperative enterprises are directly owned by the worker-members. At this level, workers' democracy most often takes the form of democratic elections to various councils and boards, rather than direct democracy of regular workers assemblies (Wright 2010: 242). But there are also periodic General Assemblies of worker-members which are formally the sovereign bodies of the cooperatives. They are responsible for 'appointing the managing director and, in principle, have the power to determine the broad strategies of the cooperative' (ibid.).

Inevitably, there have been problems with such a system developing within a hostile capitalist world, without 'supportive social and economic infrastructure for cooperative activity' (ibid.: 239). It has, to some extent, become a victim of its own success, with the takeover of other, overseas firms creating major problems for a system based upon 'solidarity and trust' (ibid.: 245). But the survival of the core system and expansion of the Mondragon Cooperative Corporation overseeing redistribution to aid cooperatives in difficulties, provides the beginning of a viable model for a post-corporate world.

Fiscal and Monetary Policies

As Chang and Grabel argue, rather than 'independent' central banks concentrating on inflation, 'politically embedded and accountable central banks should be charged with pursuit of monetary policy that promotes sustainable growth, employment and social welfare objectives', including increasing political and economic equality.

'The prevention of high rates of inflation should be pursued only as far as it is consistent with these broader goals' (Chang and Grabel 2005: 187).

Fiscal policy should be based upon genuinely redistributive taxation, with higher and unearned incomes (from property, shares, and so on) taxed at much higher rates (than lower and earned ones), as long as radical income disparities and asset-based incomes continue to exist. Income-bearing assets should themselves be taxed, in the interests of reduction of inequality, and comprehensive death duties would begin to tackle the radical inequality of opportunity created by inheritance. Issues of small to medium-sized businesses being destroyed by such a tax could be easily addressed through partial government ownership and/or extended payment periods.

In an unequal society, it makes sense to institute progressive goods and services taxes, with luxuries taxed at high rate, and necessities exempted. And as long as financial speculation is allowed to continue, this too should be taxed, both to discourage its prevalence and transfer funds to more constructive activities. This issue is addressed in Chapter 4, which discusses the Tobin Tax.

In the case of mineral deposits, the costs of private development of the least productive and accessible sources need to be covered and a standard rate of profit added in order to motivate production and establish the price of the mineral in question. The excess profits of those whose production costs are lower, their differential mineral rent, should clearly also be taxed at a very high rate, not least in order to sustain development of effective recycling and alternatives to non-renewable resources (Harvey 2010: 81).

A carbon tax – which puts a substantial and gradually rising price on all carbon, levied as a flat fee per tonne at the mine, well, or port of entry into the country with the proceeds handed back to the public (with no exemptions or special cases or opportunities for large scale speculation) and used to support sustainable technologies ,– could also have a part to play in addressing climate change. With such a tax, the goods people and companies buy increase in price in proportion to their fossil fuel costs, motivating them to change their consumption patterns. Incomes subsidised by the tax would help to offset high costs of such a transition.

Such taxation policies can reduce inequality – and all of the social ills associated with it – through redirection of excess wealth into job creation and welfare, while also promoting sustainable growth through appropriate public investment: 'There is no empirical basis for the neoliberal claim that private investment is superior to public investment' (Chang and Grabel 2005: 195); '… cross-country and historical experience shows that strategic, well-designed and well-managed programmes of public expenditure are critical to the promotion of economic growth investment and the alleviation of important social ills' (ibid.: 197).

Protecting Democracy

Beginning to address radical inequality through genuine progressive taxation, through a shift from private to public investment and workers' cooperatives, restricted executive remuneration and wages boosted in line with workers productivity, would also begin to put some restriction upon the subversion of parliamentary democracy by moneyed interests. But such economic reforms need to be supported by corresponding political reforms, outlawing contributions to parties' funds other than flat-rate subscriptions from members and state funding in proportion to actual membership (Shutt 2001: 157). Similarly, parties in power need to be prevented from using public funds for campaigning purposes.

The power of 'individuals and sectional interests' to exercise 'effective editorial control over significant parts of the media' is quite incompatible with any meaningful democracy (ibid.). Ways must be found to ensure meaningful and ongoing access for all shades of political opinion to be communicated to voters. Genuine voter participation needs to be extended, through public consultation in the development of election manifestos, increased used of referenda and opportunities for 'fringe parties and campaigning groups' to submit legislative proposals to a popular vote. Political parties themselves could be effectively democratised, with the power of senior political appointments shifted from party leaders to the legislature as a whole. And absolute freedom of public access to 'all information and documents relating to government activities' is vital to ensure genuine accountability of all public officials (ibid.: 159).

Strengthening the democracy of individual nation-states is a fundamental step towards democratic reform of existing global institutions, including the United Nations, the Bretton Woods institutions, the WTO and the international courts. Or better, towards the creation of new international institutional arrangements, better adapted to drive the various reforms considered here.

Free International Trade and Investment

Adam Smith argued that free trade between nations allows all to benefit from an international division of labour, with each nation concentrating its resources in those industries where it has an absolute cost advantage. The later theory of comparative advantage said that countries could benefit from free trade even where their trading partners have an absolute cost advantage in all areas. Where one nation specialises in that industry for which it has the greatest production cost advantage, while the nation's trading partner specialises in the industry that has the smallest cost disadvantage, a greater overall output of goods can be obtained than if the same productive resources had gone into self-sufficiency for both countries. This extra output can be shared between the trading partners to their mutual benefit through appropriate prices and quantities of goods exchanged.

Supposedly, big corporations will only shift technology and skills offshore in direct foreign investment if such resources will increase productivity more offshore than if utilised in the home country. So complete freedom of international trade and investment benefits all parties through increasing productive efficiency and output.

Floating currencies – instituted from 1971 through 1973 – were supposed to ensure that such trade was balanced, so that no one had to 'drop out' because of increasing deficit, which would threaten to propagate deflation around the world. If a country's currency value is determined by the level of demand in free world currency markets, with central banks supplying whatever amounts of currency are demanded at the going price, then low demand for a currency, due to low demand for goods from, or investment in, that country, will lead to such currency's value dropping. This will encourage the development of local industry, as consumers turn away from expensive imports. It will bring down the price of deficit-country goods, and of investment in the country. This will increase demand for its exports and help it get out of its trade imbalance problems.

Debt Crisis and Structural Adjustment

The reality, once again, is a bit different. Powerful neoliberals have acted as though they have seen removal of all barriers to international trade and investment as a policy to be inflicted upon the weak and the gullible, rather than adopted by themselves. This interpretation is supported by reference to the US position in multilateral and bilateral trade negotiations. Others must immediately dismantle all tariff and non-tariff barriers to entry of US products into their territories, while the US keeps many such barriers in place – particularly special government purchasing arrangements (Weiss et al. 2004).

For poorer countries, tariffs have been a major component of government tax income, available to fund health, education, agricultural subsidies and other infrastructure. They have thus provided some protection for the development of local industry. Yet international pressure from the US-dominated World Bank, IMF and WTO has led to their abolition in the name of free trade.

From the 1970s onward, the World Bank and western investment banks loaned increasing amounts of Gulf State petrodollars to developing countries. The monetarist interest rate rises of the early 1980s led to increasing crisis in these countries, no longer able to service such inflated debts. IMF structural adjustment programmes as conditions of debt renegotiation served both to protect western bankers from default and to create economic conditions increasingly supportive to developed-world economic operations, including the removal of import tariffs and barriers to foreign investment and acquisitions of valuable assets in the developing world.

Such programmes meant cheaper raw materials as inputs to western production and consumption systems, as governments of the global South competed in boosting output of export crops and minerals to try to acquire foreign currency to service their debts. This, in turn, created increasing pools of surplus labour displaced from subsistence agriculture by such expanded plantations and mining operations, along with unrestricted entry for developed -world business operations to low-regulation, low-wage, low-tax, high-subsidy conditions.

The increasing transfer of land from subsistence farming to more 'efficient' large-scale capitalist agricultural exporters, miners and electricity producers, mass tourism and the destruction of imports substituting for local industries and smaller farming operations, produced by the removal of agricultural and industrial protection in the name of free trade, has created a huge pool of desperate, destitute unemployed people, which, along with repressive government control (or use of unregulated Export Processing Zones), has kept wages down to an absolute minimum.

By demanding cut-backs in state taxation, spending and subsidies, along with such dispossession, in particular through the dismantling of effective post-colonial resources taxes on foreign mining multinationals, and the undermining of import substituting industrialisation, such IMF and World Bank packages have created desperate poverty, starvation, ill health and misery on a huge scale. Hundreds of millions of people have been driven into destitution, with tens of millions more joining them each year.

In India, with 6% per cent annual growth in GDP from 1995 to 2005, 5 million peasants were displaced from the land each year (Shiva 2005), the majority reduced to destitution, living in slums, without clean water, health care, or education, where 'life expectancy is short and infant mortality shockingly high' (Harvey 2010: 152). More than 800 million people in the developing world now suffer chronic malnutrition, 1.2 billion are in extreme poverty, 2.8 billion earn less than US$2 per day.

The International Division of Labour

What is called world 'trade', is now mostly (60+ per cent) planned exchange within transnational corporate structures, with 'prices' determined as much by tax minimisation as by any real cost considerations. Transfer pricing enables TNCs to claim that profits are generated in low tax areas, including offshore tax havens. They also pressure weaker governments to provide fiscal concessions in the form of tax breaks and subsidies.

In a world where big corporations easily and cheaply transfer technology and output across national boundaries, where some countries have outlawed sweatshop production while others have not, corporate leaders striving to maximise profits increasingly transfer production to the latter locations, where real unit labour costs are significantly lower. Then they just have to (temporarily) charge a bit less than the going rate in higher tax but low tariff areas for the same good in order to displace established local industries (that actually pay taxes and living wages) and reap huge profits.

Such job transfer is justified on the grounds of its driving the emergence of new 'higher-value' jobs in the developed world, sustained by cheaper imports. In fact, it has left the western neoliberal heartlands reduced to industries that produce goods and services that are not tradable across national boundaries. These jobs are weakly unionised with workers in a poor position to fight for better conditions. Intensified competition for such 'service industry' jobs amongst those displaced from the manufacturing sector by 'free trade' and capital export has further helped to force wages down (Davidson 2009a: 136).

Meanwhile, workers in China, the most 'successful' developing world economy, struggle in often appalling conditions for hopelessly inadequate wages; in many cases below US$2.50 per hour at purchasing power parity. Things are bad enough for skilled workers in the formal sector, of large and medium-sized state-owned, partly foreign-owned and private enterprises, with only Communist Party-controlled unions, and no meaningful wage negotiations or even wage contracts. For unskilled workers in the formal sector and all workers in the informal sector – of smaller private companies – things are worse. Many industrial workers are under 16 years old; workers are sacked for refusing massive overtime (with many working 60 hours per week or more), or attempting to organise strikes; many have only one day off in a month, and work with hazardous chemicals without protection, sleeping in dirty, fire-prone dormitories.

Exchange Rates

The neoliberal floating currency regime – supposedly introduced to help balance world trade – opened up huge new speculative possibilities, through betting on, or forcing, short-term changes in relative currency values. Such speculative transactions massively outpaced currency sales to finance foreign purchases, or provide 'insurance' against fluctuating prices, with daily forex trading volume increasing from US$18 billion per day in 1977 to US$1500 billion in 1998.

Wealthy foreign speculators can sell a nation's currency in anticipation of a fall in its value, thereby leading to a fall, leading to more selling. This can lead to major financial crises for the countries concerned, with interrupted debt service and further foreign takeover of vital resources.

Many poorer trade deficit countries whose exchange rates have been forced down by market forces, currency speculators, or structural adjustment requirements, have actually found themselves much worse off, with a greater deficit in the export–import balance because of limited price elasticity of demand for both their exports and their imports. Even with an increased volume of exports, the increase was frequently not sufficient to offset the loss of earnings through the reduced sale price of such exports.

With inelastic demand for key imports, again, a country can find itself paying more for less, because it is unable to reduce its import volume sufficiently to compensate for the increased costs. This is a crucial issue in relation to the destruction of local agricultural self-sufficiency by tariff reduction and dumping of subsidised US and European agricultural produce. Devaluation or speculation-driven commodity price rises can have disastrous consequences for poorer countries increasingly dependent upon food imports, leaving ever more people in hunger.

Reduced demand is passed on to exporter nations, increasing unemployment and lack of demand in the world market. With 'free trade and investment', poorer countries' devalued currencies have allowed all of their valuable assets to be pillaged by foreigners at bargain basement prices.

The major capital and currency devaluation in, and capital flight from, Asia in 1997–98, facilitated by free currency markets, encouraged leading Asian economies to accumulate vast reserves of US dollars to avoid the disastrous consequences of similar rapid devaluation of their own currencies, including highly destructive conditions associated with IMF rescue packages. The Chinese government was also motivated to accumulate US dollars to keep the value of the dollar high compared with the value of the yuan, thereby keeping cheap exports to the US growing rapidly to drive employment and growth in the Chinese manufacturing industry (Skidelsky 2009: 182).

The huge loss of aggregate demand produced by taking hundreds of billions of US dollars worth of purchasing power out of the global economy each year, locked up in reserves has exacerbated trade imbalances, with such funds unavailable for purchase of goods of deficit nations. Keynesians see failure of consumption demand, including the huge potential consumption demand of 1 billion Chinese workers, leading to failure of investment and employment as the underlying cause of the current crisis.

Reforms

There is an urgent need to move beyond neoliberal 'free trade', as championed and imposed by the WTO, the IMF and the World Bank, which is mainly just unrestricted looting and pillaging by big corporations, and return to an appropriately 'regulated' system, built upon high levels of national or regional self-sufficiency and effective self-governance. State takeover of big TNCs should go along with the handing-back of resources and compensation to those they have robbed in past decades. Pursuit of economic growth through trade and current account surplus should be recognised and treated as socially irresponsible.

With national governments or regional blocs genuinely committed to full employment, redistribution and social welfare policies, international trade could be reorganised along the lines proposed by Keynes in 1941, to avoid radical imbalances and associated inequalities and crises, and facilitate such self-sufficiency and local control of employment. In particular, Keynes's system was designed to preclude the accumulation of big trade surpluses based upon undervalued currencies, creating huge problems for debtors, leading to reduced consumption, reduced investment and deflation.

Keynes's system centred upon the idea of a new currency through which all international trade would be directed. Each nation's central bank would hold its reserves of this currency, bancors or International Money Clearing Units, in an account in a 'clearing house'. International trade would involve a buyer in country A providing local currency to the agreed IMCU value to their central bank, which would transfer the corresponding IMCU amount to country B's central bank clearing house account. Country B's central bank would then hand over the relevant amount of local currency to the seller. Initially fixed exchange rates between local currencies and IMC units would be adjusted to take account of inflation within the countries concerned, with greater amounts of (devalued) local currency required to acquire each IMCU (Davidson and Davidson 1996: 204–5).

A trigger mechanism would be in place that encourages any creditor nation to spend what is deemed (in advance) by agreement of the international community to be excessive credit balances at the clearing house (ibid.: 205).

Unless such credits are quickly spent on the exports of other nations or on foreign aid to assist deficit members, they are first taxed, to provide funds for disaster relief, and ultimately confiscated to be distributed to deficit nations.

Instead of promoting deflation through keeping reserves out of circulation and forcing deficit nations to tighten their belts, thereby further reducing trade, this system provides opportunities and assistance for debtor nations to work their way out of trouble (ibid.: 206).

Both developing world industry and developing world agriculture can be run upon a cooperative basis, using resources transferred from transnational and corporate capitalist control. In many areas, the most pressing need is for significant land- reform, restoring to local communities the subsistence base taken from them to sustain export agribusiness.

Via Campesina, the international peasant movement, is taking a lead here. In particular, they call for radical land reform throughout the developing world, reversing the 'consolidation of land by landlords and transnational firms' to ensure that agricultural production is 'carried out mainly by small farmers or cooperative or state enterprises', with 'the distribution and consumption of food … governed by fair pricing schemes' taking account the rights and welfare of both farmers and consumers' (Bello 2009: 137). This involves returning to protection of national food production, with the 'rebuilding of nationals grain reserves, public sector budgets, floor prices, credit and other forms of state support' (ibid.).

Via Campesina aims for food self-sufficiency – with a country's own farmers producing most of the food consumed domestically. They reject the industrial agriculture of the Green Revolution, genetic engineering and seed patenting in favour of sustainable organic practices, highlighting the greater productivity (in terms of actual output of useable products per acre of land, rather than labour time) – as well as sustainability and health benefits – of small integrated farming systems, allowing for the elimination of hunger and food insecurity around the world. Maximum self-sufficiency can be complemented by extension of current fair-trading practices to allow for sharing of the benefits of increased productivity.

As well as organising rural communities to pursue such goals, so do they campaign internationally to neutralise the operations of the WTO, seen as 'the lynchpin of the neoliberal order'. And they have been successful in derailing the agriculture negotiations of the Doha Round (ibid.: 134–5).

Banking Deregulation

A central part of the neoliberal programme has been deregulation of financial markets, including relaxation of the rules that had previously restricted the size and scope of activities of banks, separation of the activities of investment and deposit-taking banks, with the latter precluded from using depositors' money for speculative operations.

The Glass-Steagall Act of 1933 made it illegal for a bank that holds people's savings to engage in speculative activity. But in 1987, the Federal Reserve changed the rules to allow commercial banks to use 5 per cent of their turnover for speculative activities. By 1996, this had reached 25 per cent and in 1999, the Act was finally abolished (Mason 2009: 62).

State-controlled deposit banks were privatised. Private banks were allowed to operate freely across borders, supposedly increasing competition and thereby reducing bank charges to customers. This allowed for the creation of huge diversified global banks (including Citigroup, JP Morgan Chase, Bank of America, UBS, Credit Suisse, HSBC, BNP, Deutsche, Fortis, ING) doing everything from high-street banking and home loans to investment banking and insurance.

Efficient Markets Hypothesis

These deregulatory policies were justified by the 'efficient [stock] markets hypothesis', which says that there is a natural equilibrium value for shares in listed companies which reflects the real profit potential of the productive operations underlying such shares – around which actual market values oscillate in response to the random flow of relevant information to buyers and sellers.

In so far as governments ensure appropriate reporting and transparency – but otherwise keep out of the picture (and assuming market participants are rational, and can and do respond immediately to all available relevant information, without extra costs), then prices of such instruments represent the best possible estimates of prospects and risks, with investors able to trade off risk (understood as average deviation from average returns) against greater expected rates of return.

Neoliberals argued that governments should allow investment banks a free hand to create and market new financial instruments, allowing investors to protect their investments through new and 'flexible' forms of insurance. In these largely unregulated markets, free competition supposedly ensures the survival and proliferation of the fittest, new, more efficient investment vehicles – again to the benefit of the system as a whole. The sophisticated financial institutions principally involved in trading these new instruments (over the counter) were eminently capable of defending themselves through application of appropriate mathematical tools to accurately gauge the true value of such assets without the need for any 'external' oversight or regulation.

Derivatives

The earliest derivatives – futures – were obligations to buy or sell material goods. Then came options, as rights to buy or sell something at a specified future date for a specified price. With put options, the seller pays for falling prices of the asset; with call options, the seller pays for rising prices. After derivatives with prices based upon the underlying value of a material asset, came financial derivatives based on the value of an underlying share, bond, currency, or other financial asset.

Later, bankers at JPMorgan invented a third type of derivative: swaps. The principle was that of swapping debts, so that different organisations would get the income streams and take on the risk of default of bonds owned by each other. Companies could, for example, gain payment in different currencies as interest payments on each other's bonds. The system then spread to other sorts of debts.

Later still came Credit Default Swaps (CDSs), invented in Europe in the early 1990s, which involved a swap-selling, protection-buying bank agreeing to pay an annual fee for a set period of years to a swap-buying, protection-selling bank, with respect to a specific portfolio of loans. The seller would commit to making good the buyer's losses on portfolio defaults during the life of the swap. Such contracts grew to a value of a trillion dollars by 2000. The idea of insuring against loan defaults appealed to bankers. Given the requirements of the reserve – set at 8 per cent by the Basel Accords (meaning that banks can lend the other 92 per cent of funds deposited with them) – it could also benefit banks to pay others to take on their loan risks even if they thought such risks were small, to remove debt from their books and open the way for more profitable loans.

Securitisation involved the bundling of loans into packages – called Collateralised Debt Obligations (CDOs) – to provide security to purchasers without time-consuming negotiation and investigation (if some defaulted others wouldn't). 'Tranching' was the division of such packages into more and less risky debt bundles, 'tailored' to buyers 'needs'. Banks got fees for such securities and insurance against their loans, investors got streams of revenue – as debt repayments – and established levels of risk.

Whereas relevant historical data on risks and returns in the goods markets formed the basis for valuing non-financial derivatives, there were initial problems for both buyers and sellers of how to value financial derivatives. Supposedly, these were solved in 1973 by Fisher Black and Myron Scholes, who produced a formula for valuing (call or put) options. With cycles of resales of an increasing variety of different types of derivatives, world trading reached hundreds of trillions of dollars or 10 times real economic output world-wide.

Banks Creating Money

Once again, the reality is a bit different from the theory. Deposit banks have huge liabilities in the form of customer deposits while their assets are mainly other people's debts. They must have high levels of assets to cover high levels of deposits.

This means that they are inherently vulnerable to insolvency and therefore unable to continue to operate legally when debtors default and assets lose value, or when all depositors lose faith and try to withdraw their funds simultaneously. But the bigger their loan-to-deposit ratios, the more profitable they can be.

How vulnerable banks are depends upon how big they are, and how big their liabilities are compared to their equity. Neoliberal deregulation, by encouraging increases in both size and leverage, through mergers in pursuit of increased oligopoly power (along with falling reserve ratios) – enhanced the vulnerability of the banking sector. The merging of deposit and investment banking in increasingly bigger operations represented further huge increases in risk, with the savings of workers and businesses now exposed to increasingly unregulated speculative transactions in global markets.

Most of the functional money supply is created by private commercial banks when they accept deposits and make loans – with more purchasing power in checking and other account balances than in actual circulating currency. In so far as the money commercial banks loan comes back to them as deposits, they can expand such loans and spending (and therefore also their profits as interest and dividends), while retaining enough to cover the internationally agreed 'cash ratio' of funds immediately available to pay back to depositors. Investment banks are paid for the services of financial asset creation and asset trading. And such assets can be resold to create new 'values'.

But private bankers undertake this money and asset creating role purely for their own profit, rather than any higher public purpose. And in so far as new money is created as debt, ever more new wealth must somehow be created in order to service and repay such debt and avoid default. Unregulated economic growth is driving accelerating resource depletion and pollution. There are good reasons for believing that such growth must be stopped in order to avoid catastrophic climate change. On the other hand, an end to growth means an immediate debt crisis, and 'growth' simply built on more debt merely increases the size of the ultimate financial collapse.

Investment

The 'efficient markets' model assumes that there is no feedback from share market valuations to investor perceptions. But investors always pay attention to the actions of other investors, via changing share prices – and need to do so if they are going to cash in on rapid price appreciations or avoid becoming victims of rapid depreciations.

Risk is assumed to be measurable as standard deviation by reference to a normal distribution of relevant past returns. But historical records of yield volatility can be of limited value as a guide to future outcomes, which depend upon future economic circumstances, leaving the future yield of an investment fundamentally uncertain.

In recent decades, directors' 'disclosures' to shareholders and regulators have increasingly become accounting constructs, generally designed to present a picture of appropriately steady growth, in line with securities analysts' profit projections (rather than accurate pictures of companies' situations). And what counts as profit and dividends to shareholders, as opposed to executive salaries, depends upon the – changing – balance of power within corporations.

There is a substantial body of empirically supported 'behavioural theory' demonstrating that individuals never behave in a fully 'economically rational' manner, as required by the EMH (Keen 2001: 250). Amongst other things, they tend to over-react to what are seen as changes to the prevailing status quo, and then over-adjust when the over-reaction is recognised. And markets react to their own volatility, building price movements upon price movements (Skidelsky 2009: 168–9).

A rising market, driven at first by some real phenomenon (like a new technology) will tend to encourage investors to believe that the market will continue rising. Even if they don't believe this, there will still be pressures to buy to cash in on such rising prices. 'Such a market can find itself a long way from (anything that could be called) equilibrium' as 'self-reinforcing waves of sentiment sweep through investors'. And of course, eventually, inevitably, such waves break, when it becomes clear that 'valuations have gone far beyond what is sustainable by corporate earnings' (Keen 2001: 239).

In so far as regulators strive to maintain confidence and promise to bail out failing banks (and investment funds), they encourage excessive risk taking and contribute towards such uncontrolled expansion and subsequent collapse.

Hyman Minsky found that when an economy grows at a time of risk aversion and low borrowing because of a previous crisis, firms that do borrow heavily can prosper (ibid.: 251). This drives a decline in risk aversion on the part of investors and banks. Increasing bank lending and money supply drive the accelerated growth of asset prices. And even with increasing interest rates, continued demand-driven asset price inflation motivates further borrowing in anticipation of further increases. This allows for the appearance of Ponzi financiers who continue to borrow and buy when their debt servicing exceeds the cash flow from the assets because they anticipate that capital appreciation will still exceed the interest bill. But such accelerated borrowing pushes up the interest rate which ultimately leads to falling asset prices. Banks increase interest rates still further to try to compensate for increasing defaults. With the boom collapsing, high inflation can allow for debt repayments. But without it, further asset sales drive a deflationary spiral into depression (ibid.: 253).

Along with Ponzi schemes, whereby business operations borrow to meet their interest payments so that their debt burden continuously increases, such debt-driven speculative booms also encourage leveraged buyouts. Here, big borrowing fuels buyouts of healthy companies, whose assets are then sold (and staff sacked) to get back the initial collateral for the loans. As the buyout-fuelled stock prices keep rising, the depleted company is sold on again for a substantial profit. Wealth destruction replaces wealth creation as source of profit (Morris 2009: 61).

Recent History

In the neoliberal period, disempowered labour, with productivity increasing while wages remained stagnant or fell, meant increasingly inflated profits, dividends, executive salaries and bonuses. With reduced and ineffective taxation of profit and high income, and little or no taxation of wealth and inheritance, this meant that the gap between rich and poor grew wider. As the rich became ever richer, the increasing income 'gap' contributed to increasing disintegration of social cohesion and trust, increasing frustration and desperation of those at the bottom, and increasing arrogance of those at the top. Such desperation at the bottom has been effectively channelled into debt-driven consumption of ever more electronic gadgets, fast foods, clothes and drugs.

Governments failed to effectively combat the tax avoidance packages developed by clever lawyers and accountants for companies and wealthy individuals. In Australia, the dividend imputation credit system massively increased the proportion of income going to the wealthy minority of major shareholders.

The huge excess of capital generated by intensified exploitation of the workforce, and unable to be profitably invested in production because of inadequate monetarily effective demand due to workers' low wages and living standards, along with oligopoly price-fixing by big corporations, was a major contributor to low long-term interest rates in the later neoliberal period.

Surplus capital, low interest, low inflation and oligopoly encouraged an increasing shift away from investment in expanding production of new goods and services and into purchase of existing assets of various kinds, particularly stocks and shares and property, into speculation and into mergers and acquisitions, including leveraged buyouts and asset stripping. Low interest rates encouraged risky speculation both because of the relatively low returns from less risky ventures and because of the ready availability of very cheap money available for 'leveraging'.

Speculators would borrow money to buy shares along with options to sell them for just a bit less. If the share price increased, they could make big gains essentially from nothing – no money or productive activity of their own. If it fell, their losses were limited – they could probably still pay back the debt. If values plummeted, the option seller, forced to buy back the assets, was in trouble. But for a while it could seem that everyone was winning. Futures, as obligations to buy or sell, were more risky to the buyer but as a result were generally cheaper than options, and capable of delivering big profits if underlying values changed significantly (Lanchester 2010: 38–9). This process was encouraged by neoliberal taxation policy, which reduced or eliminated taxation of the income from rich people's assets, and the gains from reselling them.

The great majority of share transactions in recent decades have simply involved resales of already issued shares. With limited shares available, the more surplus wealth flowed into share markets, the more inflated share values became. This led to ever more self-expanding bubbles, as big purchases in expectation of price increases produced the expected increases, to drive further purchases and so on. New markets – around the developing world – offered huge new possibilities for speculative bubbles, and free movement of finance allowed for contagion to spread quickly from one market and one country to another.

Financial crises therefore became ever more frequent and deeper throughout the neoliberal period, compared to the earlier post-war boom period. The Federal Reserve in the US responded to each developing crisis (as new threat to the value of the assets of the rich) with interest-rate reductions to encourage recovery and renewed growth of the system (and prevent the spread of crisis from specific financial markets into the wider economy). But so did each interest rate fall after a crisis pave the way for the next crisis, by making ever more cheap money available for further speculation.

Greater surplus wealth from increased exploitation of the working population drove the creation of new financial instruments, with the ultra-rich putting their vast excess wealth into hedge funds and investment banks, to gamble on short- or medium-term changes in the values of commodities, currencies, shares, and so on.

With exotic instruments ever further removed from the real-world operations upon which they were supposed to be based, asset-creators and investors came increasingly to rely upon complex mathematical operations (understood by few) to price such instruments. Black and Scholes' model was followed by a succession of new derivative pricing models, including, most significantly, David Li's 'copula function'. All these models revolved around risk understood as volatility (measured by standard deviation) on historical measures of underlying returns (Lanchester 2010: 136), as in the models of share valuation underlying the EMH. But now the chosen data became increasingly far removed from underlying realities – particularly in the case of the booming market in securitised mortgages. There was no historical data on subprime mortgages.

Houses

Low interest rates due to the glut of capital and the Fed's efforts to protect the financial assets of the rich, contributed to maintaining the profitability of the productive economy by making loans ever more readily available to poor working people to maintain relatively high levels of consumption, despite stagnant, inadequate and declining real wages.

Under demand pressure, US home prices rose by 124 per cent from 1997 to 2006, from 3 to 4.6 times the average wage, with an increasing rush to build more houses (Skidelsky 2009,: 5). By early 2005, half of the US's GDP growth was based on the housing boom, including refinancing of mortgages. The megabanks set up special trusts as 'investment vehicles' to take on, and sell off, their mortgage risks as securities, to pension and other investment funds. Long-term repayments and possible default were replaced by immediate short-term gain, and with the debts off their balance sheets, this paved the way for more loans, to create more securitised debt to sell, and finance the purchase of more financial derivatives.

In the early 2000s, other asset classes were not doing well or looked dangerously inflated in value. Bankers were able to persuade investors that credit risk in the form of CDOs gave higher returns than government bonds, ignoring the fact that, unlike government bonds, CDOs could also produce losses rather than gains. Investors like super funds 'insured' their purchases of CDOs through CDSs offered by other investment banks, hedge funds and insurers (like AIG). These institutions further resold the risks of the CDOs. Non-owners of mortgage bonds were able to purchase CDS insurance in anticipation of massive default. By 2006, the CDO market was worth US$4.7 trillion and by the end of 2007, the CDS market was worth US$62 trillion.

Neoliberals had successfully resisted any effective oversight or regulation of the new markets, so no one had responsibility to ensure that the insurers could actually make good on the 'policies' they had sold, in the event of large-scale default.

The story is well-known. With increasing demand for such securities from investors ('hungry for yield'), home loans were increasingly sourced by brokers offering initial below-market rates to people with ever lower credit ratings, ultimately to buyers without jobs, income, or assets. Such loans were then sold to investment banks that produced the CDOs to sell to institutional investors and so on (Soros 2008: xvii).

Commercial banks, which had become investment banks, borrowed increasing amounts of money in short-term inter-bank money markets to supplement that provided by their depositors for speculation in the new securities markets.

This great Ponzi scheme, with global banks, investment banks and credit hedge funds borrowing more and more to pay for the selling of financial derivatives back and forth amongst themselves, recording profits at every stage (Harvey 2010: 30), driving the value of such securities to more than 10 times global GDP, eventually fell apart as inflation-fighting interest rate increases (from 1 per cent to 5.25 per cent between 2004 and 2006) by the Federal Reserve drove increasing mortgage defaults and rapidly falling property values in 2007 (Skidelsky 2009: 6). By the end of 2007, nearly 2 million people in the US had lost their homes with 4 million more close to foreclosure. Many were on the streets with credit rating that denied them access to rented accommodation.

Uncertain of their own exposure, or that of others, banks stopped lending to each other. Banks that had borrowed heavily in short-term money markets to provide funds for speculation and long-term loans found that they could not repay their debts or borrow any more to sustain their operations. Banks and insurance companies that had counted big stores of mortgage-backed securities or insurance of such securities as assets found themselves insolvent.

The fusion of investment and deposit banking meant that the megabanks were not just gambling with rich people's surplus capital, but their losses encompassed the savings of companies and households. So bank executives felt free to demand that governments bail them out. With depositors rushing to withdraw money, the collapse of the banking system threatened the collapse of the capitalist economic system.

Bank bailouts took the form of government share purchases, public ownership with debt guarantees, enforced takeovers, and multibillion dollar asset buy-ups. They were followed by big fiscal stimulus packages to support stock markets and real economies, undermined by loss of credit and loss of confidence as a result of the banking collapse.

But governments have to pay back such rescue funds by increasing their taxes – on those who actually pay taxes – and cutting back on crucial services – for those who rely upon government services. And these are not generally the wealthy gamblers who created the crisis – but rather ordinary people, many of whom have already been its principal victims – through loss of their houses and their jobs and their credit ratings. Meanwhile, the big banks that remain, with still greater oligopoly power, continue to accumulate funds for huge executive bonuses (Harvey 2010: 12).

As weaker governments have sought to sell more government bonds – to overseas banks, governments, corporations, funds, in order to finance bailouts, increasing fear of default has allowed buyers to demand ever greater interest rates, and undermined confidence in share markets around the world. With government debt-servicing absorbing ever more of declining GDP, so have the pressures increased for greater and greater cut backs in social welfare spending, to restore 'balanced' state budgets. In some cases the IMF and EU have stepped in to supervise such welfare cutbacks. But accelerated spending cuts are undermining economic growth, cutting into tax receipts for future debt reductions, threatening a long term deflationary spiral of deepening recession and misery.

Reforms

Neoliberals and others call for greater 'transparency' and 'improved corporate governance' as ways to avoid similar financial crises in the future, without any change to basic financial structures or processes. Better external monitoring of banks' capital adequacy, better accounting procedures (to anticipate problems ahead), extra reserves and bonus systems for managers would discourage, rather than encourage too much risk taking. Some even go so far as to call for a return to Glass-Steagall, with a new separation of 'utility' from 'investment banking' (Skidelsky 2009: 176).

Paul Davidson, a leading Keynesian critic of neoliberalism, calls for both an SEC-enforced prohibition against securitisation 'that attempts to create a public market for assets that originated in private markets' (for example, mortgages, commercial bank loans, and so on) and a return to Glass-Steagall, forcing financial institutions 'to be either ordinary bank lenders creating loans for individual customers in a private financial market or underwriter brokers who can deal only with instruments created and resold in a public financial market'. Since deposits at the former institutions would be 'insured by a government agency' so would they be 'subject to government regulation, oversight and strict auditing procedures'. The latter, meanwhile, might need no regulation beyond 'margin requirements' to maintain the 'orderliness of the financial markets in which they engage' (Davidson 2009b: 99–100).

Along the same lines, other social liberal reformers call for accountable central banks to be empowered to intervene to prevent asset bubbles through means other than interest rate rises, for an end to the unregulated 'shadow' banking system, for careful vetting of any new financial instruments and a requirement for them to be traded in organised exchanges.

But the reforms really necessary to address these problems and avoid bigger ones in the future have already been outlined. Share markets, derivatives and private banks have not only outlived their usefulness but have become major threats to the future well-being of the species and the world. Transnational corporations run by little cliques of rich people should no longer be allowed to control the resources of the world and dictate government policy. A genuine nationalisation of banks, with responsible governments effectively taking control of use of credit in the public interest, allows for principled lending of workers savings to workers' cooperatives, without any of the 'financial intermediation', rampant speculation and fictitious wealth creation of the current system.

Along with employment, education and medical care, so should quality housing be recognised as a basic human right, with government responsibility to ensure its provision to all. Adoption of Keynes's international clearing house for international trade, as updated by Davidson and others, along with appropriate recompense for past looting of the developing world by the developed; redistribution of the developing world land currently held by transnational corporations (for export crops) to local farmers' cooperatives on long-term government leases, could allow for increasingly stable and fair, rather than free and unfair trade.

Conclusion

The universities have been complicit in the creation of the economic and social problems considered here, to the extent that they have taught and endorsed and continue to teach and endorse neoliberal ideas as the core of the economics syllabus.

Skidelsky suggests that future 'undergraduate degrees in economics' and finance need to be 'broadly based', taking account of 'Keynes's dictum that 'economics is a moral and not a natural science' (Skidelsky 2009: 189). But in order to apply moral judgements to contemporary ideas and policies, it is crucial to develop theories which actually do cast light upon real economic phenomena, that have a solid foundation in social reality. Keynes and latter-day Keynesians have made valuable contributions in this area.

References

Albert, M. 2003. *Parecon: Life After Capitalism*. London: Verso.
Bello,W. 2009. *The Food Wars*. London: Verso.
Chang, H. 2007. *Bad Samaritans*. London: Business Books.
—— and Grabel, I. 2005. *Reclaiming Development*. London: Zed Books.
Davidson, G. and P. Davidson. 1996. *Economics for a Civilized Society*. Houndsmills: Macmillan.
Davidson, P. 2009a. *John Maynard Keynes*. Houndsmills: Palgrave-Macmillan.
—— 2009b. *The Keynes Solution*. Houndsmills: Palgrave-Macmillan.
Eliot, L., D. Teacher and J. Treanor 2010. 'Capitalism is still the only game in town', *The Guardian Weekly*, 13–19 August, pp. 1–2.
Funnell, W., R. Jupe and J. Andrew 2009. *In Government We Trust*. Sydney; UNSW Press.
Harvey, D. 2010. *The Enigma of Capital*. London: Profile Books.
Jackson, T. 2009. *Prosperity Without Growth*. London: Earthscan.
Keen, S. 2001. *Debunking Economics*. Sydney: Pluto Press.
Lanchester, J. 2010. *Whoops!*. London: Allen Lane.
Marmot, M. 2004. *Status Syndrome*. London: Bloomsbury.
Mason, P. 2009. *Meltdown; The End of the Age of Greed*. London: Verso.
Monkerud, D. 2010. 'A Predatory System; The Health Insurance Monopoly', *Counterpunch*, 14 January <http://www.counterpunch.org/monkerud01142010>.
Moody, R. 2007. *Rocks and Hard Places*. London: Zed Books.
Morris, C. 2009. *The Two Trillion Dollar Meltdown*. Melbourne: Black Inc.
Quiggin, J. 2010. *Zombie Economics; How Dead Ideas Still Walk Among Us*. Princeton, NJ: Princeton University Press.
Shiva, V. 2005. *Earth Democracy*. Cambridge, MA: South End Press.
Shutt, H. 2001. *A New Democracy*. London: Zed Books.
Skidelsky, R. 2009. *Keynes; The Return of the Master*. London: Allen Lane.
Skidelsky, R. 2010. *Keynes; The Return of the Master*. London: Penguin Books.
Soros, G. 2008. *The New Paradigm for Financial Markets*. New York: Public Affairs.
Stillwell, F. 2002. *Political Economy*. Melbourne: Oxford University Press.
Watts, R. and J. Zimmerman 1986. *Positive Accounting Theory*. Edgewood Cliffs, NJ: Prentice Hall.
Weiss, L., E. Thurborn and J. Matthews 2004. *How to Kill a Country*. Sydney: Allen and Unwin.
Wilkinson, R. and K. Pickett 2009. *The Spirit Level*. London: Allen Lane.
Wright, E. 2010. *Envisioning Real Utopias*. London: Verso.

Chapter 3

Trade Governance: Legal Institutionalism as a Magnet for Non-trade Issues. A study of the mixed benefits of WTO dispute settlement for enforcing international obligations

Simon Kozlina

Introduction

Legal institutionalism is a form of international governance characterised by a heavy reliance on legal rules, action and processes to exercise authority, especially as seen through formal regimes, lawyers and courts. A modern example of legal institutionalism is the World Trade Organization (WTO), in particular its compulsory dispute settlement system. Its apparent success, as seen in a perceived high level of compliance by member states with their international trade obligations, generates a 'magnet effect' that pulls or attracts other 'non-trade' issues such as human, labour and environmental rights into its regulatory reach. The challenge is to understand whether this attraction to legal institutionalism is beneficial for the enforcement of non-trade issues.

This chapter examines the concept of legal institutionalism as embodied in the WTO to assess the concept's significance for the international enforcement of trade and non-trade obligations. The chapter considers the experience of developing and developed member states in the WTO's dispute settlement system over 15 years (from 1995 to 2010) to determine the extent to which a heavily legalised dispute settlement system provides an equality of opportunity for strong and weak states to enforce heavily legalised obligations. The chapter concludes with a discussion of the mixed blessings of legal institutionalism for transnational governance.

A Question of Governance

There are two perspectives on 'governance' implicit in this chapter. The first is a focus on the form of governance – legal institutionalism, as embodied in the WTO. The second is a focus on an area of governance – international trade law and the framework of international and domestic economic law in which it exists. This chapter focuses on the first issue more than the second, and examines the area of governance (international trade) in order to evaluate the form of governance (legal institutionalism) and assess its benefits and problems for the enforcement of international obligations.

Legal Institutionalism

Governance by legal institutionalism is the exercise of shared authority through the creation and operation of heavily legalised regimes or organisations, in which obligation, rights, process and authority is based on 'law' rather than diplomacy or power. While 'institutionalism' can refer to any regime for coordinating action among states, legal institutionalism is a narrower concept and is limited to describing institutions that display an overt sense of 'legalisation' through their processes, language and values. This notion of legalisation is embodied in court-like dispute settlement procedures, increasingly precise treaty obligations and the reliance on authoritative interpretation of text as the basis of that obligation (Goldstein et al. 2000; Abbott et al. 2000). In other words, in this framework, state cooperation is facilitated through overt legal channels and institutions.

Establishing the focus as 'institutionalism' means this chapter places importance on the reality of how humans act in relation to law in the real world. To identify the 'institution' as the basis for study is to recognise the operation of law beyond a strict 'black-letter' approach to interpretation, legal analysis and governance. 'Institutionalism' reflects the importance of regimes, the actions of actors within those regimes and the effects produced by the existence of the institution's rules, practices and expectations.

The notion of legal institutionalism is at the crossroads of several perspectives in law and international relations (on the growing interdisciplinary work in this field see Beck, Arend and Lugt 1996, and Simmons and Steinberg 2006). Legal positivists like MacCormick and Weinberger (1986) argued that it was critical to identify the norms and practices that exist around a set of black-letter rules to gain a better understanding and evaluation of law. Institutionalist thinkers in international relations (for example, Krasner 1983) recognised the limitations of the realist approach to understanding the role of regimes in shaping the interaction of states in the global system. In this vein, constructivist approaches provided insights into the social understandings through which institutions take shape (Ford 2003). The cross-disciplinary work undertaken by international liberal institutionalist writers like Slaughter (2005) have clarified and developed the nature of law and institutions that operate in these forms of international governance through the rubric of 'legalization' (see Abbott et al. 2000). The criticisms of Reus-Smit (2001), that these approaches fail to explain change, and Finnemore and Toope (2001), that it adopts an overly narrow understanding of law, do not diminish the benefits provided by operationalising notions of law in international governance.

In other words, it is the existence and operation of the institution, not just the text of treaties establishing the institution, that explains the nature of this form of governance and, in the context of this chapter, makes legalised institutions appear attractive to epistemic communities concerned with non-trade issues.

The significance of this conception of governance is how it helps states to translate power from one area of influence to another (Braithwaite and Drahos 2000: 482). Power is often exercised by leveraging military, economic, or cultural strength in one setting into another situation. The effect of legal institutionalism on power and governance is that it both disables and re-imagines the methods of exercising traditional state-based authority while remaining within a strict framework created and reinforced by other forms of power. The combination of enervation and empowerment forms the basis for the so-called 'magnet effect' of the WTO and legal institutionalism to enforce other non-trade issues.

Law is only the power of words – it does not manifest itself as physical authority to compel compliance or obliterate resistance. Mostly, international law provides legitimacy for physical action such that those actions are more acceptable or effective when labelled 'legal', to the extent such actions and laws remains consistent with key international rules such as *pacta sunt servanda* and sovereign equality (see Franck 1990; 2006). The challenge is to better appreciate the mechanisms for enforcing international law, whether it be through force, self-interest, or even adherence to a belief in the rule of law, and to understand how legal institutionalism fits within this framework.

The normative claim of legal institutionalism is that it is good to remove authority or legitimacy from other sources of power (such as relative economic power or military might) and to replace them with power that is only justified or accepted when exercised within a specific 'legalised' framework that reifies logic, argument and consistency. The naive acceptance of this 'surface' understanding of a heavily legalised institution leads to a belief in the need to subjugate raw or unequal power to the fairer or more equal application of power according to law.

Establishing this form of institution requires a belief in the normative values that underpin law, including that logic, rationality and the objective interpretation of fact are possible; that shared understandings can be achieved through dialogue; that outcomes of a legal process demonstrate objectivity, certainty and finality, and perhaps most crucially, that law is equally accessible to all (Abbott et al. 2000).

Essentially, it is the failure of these assumptions and values to be true in the real world that points to the potential weaknesses of heavily legalised institutions. The rational language of law tends to hide rather than illuminate the values of decision makers behind a façade of objectivity. Law does not represent the collective good if strong states use relative power imbalances to close down negotiation of a treaty. Access to law is limited by barriers like prejudice, culture, language and a lack of resources (see also Koskenniemi 2000; Rajagopal 2003).

These flaws do not mean that international law or legal institutionalism are failed concepts. Rather, the purpose of this chapter is to highlight the strengths and limitations with this form of governance in order to better appreciate when it can be used effectively as a valuable alternative to military or economic power.

Legal Institutionalism as a Form of Governance

The challenging feature of considering the concept of legal institutionalism is that it appears 'old' or 'traditional' in form and style. An international regime consisting overwhelmingly of nation-states, international treaties and an autonomous international organisation is a 'classic' form of formal and explicit international coordination and requires little consideration of the more diffuse notions of regimes, governance and informal rule making examined in more contemporary research (Krasner 1983). In this context, 'legal institutionalism' seems a throwback to a time before the emergence of 'governance theory' and the appreciation of state and non-state actors working in networks of networks to achieve regulatory outcomes. At that level, legal institutionalism focuses on the traditional forms of international relations: states, treaties and international organisations.

However, this study assumes two points: first, the world still operates through the creation and operation of large-scale, state-based international organisations – we are not so decentralised and post-state in nature that states or international organisations are irrelevant for the resolution of international or transnational disputes. Secondly, the renewed interest in the nature and quality of 'legality' in international relations provides an opportunity for a reappraisal of the operation of these 'traditional' structures and the ideas that underpinned them.

The significance of legal institutionalism is that it still conveys a notion of an 'ideal type' – a form of reified governance rarely achieved in international regulation. The WTO in this sense is the most recent, and in some respects only, working model of this ideal type and allows a close examination at the reality of aspect of the governance spectrum. (By comparison, see Toope (2000) on the benefits of adopting an enlarged notion of 'governance' to appreciate less formal methods of rule making in international relations.) In that sense, this chapter examines with caution the 'drive toward harder and more coercive forms of enforcement' (Hurrell 1999: 67, in Toope 2000) as embodied in a heavily legalised international institution.

A Question of Compliance?

Any discussion about international law and governance necessary touches upon the question of 'compliance', especially if compliance is used as a measure of effectiveness. Bull was correct when he wrote:

> … the basic factors making for compliance with international law – acceptance by the parties of the ends or values underlying the agreement, coercion by a superior power, and reciprocal interest – exist independently of legal commitments, and without their operation legal commitments are ineffective. But the framework of

> international law serves to mobilise and channel these factors in the direction of compliance with agreements. (2002: 136)

In other words, compliance is not driven by international law but by other factors along with law, such that compliance is not a valid measure of effectiveness. Scott (1994, 1998) argues against compliance as a factor in determining the relationship between law and international action, instead focusing on the changing relationship between law and action as seen in rhetoric, norms and modifications to behaviour over time. To be clear, this chapter examines state action, especially as it changes over time and compliance (such as with WTO law) is an inherent aspect to that measurement. However, 'compliance' is not held up as the most valid lens through which to analyse legal institutionalism. In some ways, the level of compliance in the WTO is a secondary concern to the broader consequences of exercising international governance through this form of institution.

The WTO as a Legalised Institution Governing Trade

The WTO's dispute settlement system is a meeting point of legal institutionalism and trade governance. The Dispute Settlement Understanding ('DSU') demonstrates all the characteristics of a heavily legalised or juridical process. It adopts the language of lawyers, not diplomats. It employs the processes of law as seen in trials, appeals and sanctions. It utilises the techniques of legal argument to provide definitive resolutions to disputes. In this sense, the WTO is a heavily legalised dispute settlement system (McCall Smith 2000). The perception may be that these characteristics give the WTO a strength or power to enforce its obligations more effectively than international obligations enforced through other regimes or institutions, such as the International Court of Justice (see, generally, Krueger 1998).

It is important to clarify that not all of the WTO is heavily legalised like the dispute settlement system. The description by Chayes and Chayes of the role and effect of international bureaucracies applies in equal measure to the WTO, but in that sense those aspects of the WTO mirror and replicate the political and social realities of other international organisations, such as the United Nations or the World Health Organization (Chayes and Chayes 1995: 271–85). Also, this chapter does not adopt the 'bureaucratic' lens of Barnett and Finnemore (2004) to examine the non-dispute settlement aspects of the WTO (such as the Trade Review Mechanism and Committee structures), although their work does highlight very well the organic role of a secretariat in the development and effectiveness of international organisations.

To avoid ambiguity, the WTO as examined in this chapter is an international institution, exercising powers and authority as an independent international organisation established by nation-states but separate from them. In this sense, the WTO is an institution within the broader international economic governance regime, in which a more diffuse set of actors, norms and institutions exercise governance. The focus of this work is on the governance exercised by a specific, formal arrangement characterised by its highly legalised nature and operation (see Krasner 1983 and Keohane 1988 on regime theory and institutions).

The Shift to Legalism in International Relations

'Legal institutionalism' is a label applied to both a perspective on governance and an institution that heavily relies on law in its method of governance. International Relations theorists in recent years developed the notion of 'legalisation' as a way to explain the turn to law in some aspects of international governance in order to better understand this particular form of control and authority (Abbott et al. 2000).

Law has long been used to resolve international disputes through the operation of legal obligations established in treaties, enforced by institutions and understood by lawyers. In that sense, the label 'international' merely emphasised that the participants were 'international' actors like states rather than municipal actors like individuals and companies. However, the 'turn to law' highlights a shift to establishing and resolving more and more transnational issues through the lens of law rather than diplomacy. The turn to law incorporates the values, language and processes of law into the field of diplomacy and relative might (see Weiler 2001). The supposition is that a heavily legalised system will be more precise, less biased, have higher levels of compliance than regimes based on diplomatic governance and, most of all, be less susceptible to interference by the economically or politically powerful over the weak (McCall Smith 2000).

The shift to legalism represents a normative belief that labelling something as 'law' grants legitimacy to the regime, values, or obligations (Franck 2006). The shift also conveys a belief in the 'effectiveness' of law to change behaviour and to force compliance. The shift suggests a lack of belief in the ability of diplomatic, consensual, or voluntary regimes to achieve effective participation and compliance.

The focus of this chapter is on the WTO's dispute settlement system rather than the entire institution. The court-like appearance and operation of the dispute settlement regime is the clearest indication of the WTO's legal institutionalism and the element that most defines the 'magnet effect', although the agreements, committees and ongoing Doha Round negotiations provide an important context to the dispute settlement regime. In fact, given the drawn-out nature of the Doha negotiations, the dispute settlement system represents one of the main ways in which WTO obligations can be clarified and developed and is therefore a key aspect of the regime.

The Reasons for the Shift in Trade Law

In trade law, the gradual development over time of the obligations encapsulated in the General Agreement on Tariffs and Trade (GATT) witnessed a shift from a largely 'diplomatic' arrangement in the years following the Second World War to an increasingly legalised regime by the late 1980s. The reason for the necessarily diplomatic structure of GATT was partly the United States Senate failing to adopt the Havana Convention 1948 that would have established the 'International Trade Organization' to administer the GATT and other international trade obligations; in the absence of this institution, the GATT developed along a largely consensus-driven diplomatic path for forty years. The negotiation and completion of the Uruguay Round in 1994 and the creation of the World Trade Organization in 1995 represented the further development of that legalising trend with the establishment of a heavily legalised governance regime for international trade and, in particular, a form of juridical dispute settlement that strongly resembled the powers of municipal courts – clear legal rules, the possibility of appeals and penalties for non-compliance; a process that was described as finally 'having teeth'. (See, generally, Charnovitz 2001; cf. for an alternate description of GATT history that emphasises the factors driving 'judicialization', see Stone Sweet 2002).

The desire for change was due to a perception that under the earlier GATT dispute settlement procedures, member states could avoid 'compliance' because the GATT's dispute settlement system was not compulsory, could not always give a 'verdict' and could not authorise sanctions against a party in breach (Hudec 1999). While some of these problems were resolved through the adoption of the 'negative consensus' model before the establishment of the WTO, the creation of a 'sanctions' power represented an important break from the earlier model of WTO dispute settlement.

Outline of the WTO Dispute Settlement System

Before engaging in a close analysis of WTO law and practice, it would be useful to outline the structure of the WTO's dispute settlement body and its relationship with the WTO's other constituents. WTO dispute settlement consists of three stages – notification, panel hearings and the Appellate Body (DSU: Articles 4, 6, and 17) – plus oversight by member states through the Dispute Settlement Body ('DSB'). Notification requires the parties to consult with each other to determine if a resolution can be negotiated without third-party intervention. If negotiation is unsuccessful, the complaining party has the right to establish an ad hoc panel composed of experts in international trade, which will hold hearings then deliver a (binding) report on the facts and outcome of the dispute. Once a panel report has been circulated, an appeal may be sought with the permanent standing Appellate Body. Formally, panels and the Appellate Body issue 'recommendations' to the DSB, and the DSB chooses to adopt or not adopt the 'recommendations' (DSU: Articles 16 and 17). However, as the DSB uses a 'negative consensus' decision-making rule, all panel and Appellate Body recommendations are adopted unless all member states agree not to adopt it, including the 'winning' complainant, an event that has never happened since the WTO was established. The dispute settlement system also includes a further panel enquiry to determine if member states successfully implement recommendations

(DSU: Article 21.5) and arbitration procedures for determining the level of authorised sanctions, if allowed (DSU: Article 22).

The 'Other' Issues – Human Rights, the Environment, Public Health and Labour Rights

Since the creation of the WTO, there have been arguments about the scope of its authority – in particular, whether member states should extend their obligations to include specific 'non-trade' promises (see Guzman 2004; DiMatteo et al. 2003, although consider McGinnis and Movsesian 2004 for a contrary view). Putting to one side the inherent arbitrary and political division in identifying matters as 'trade' and 'non-trade', the debate tends to assume the matters covered by existing obligations are 'trade' issues and other potential matters are 'non-trade'. In that sense, a common call is for human rights, environmental rights, public health rights and labour rights, amongst other issues, to receive a more explicit consideration and protection under WTO law. In a sense, all of these rights are recognised in the WTO-covered agreements and are protected through the establishment of specialist committees (such as the WTO Committee on Trade and Environment) and close cooperation with other international organisations (such as joint publications with the United Nations Environment Program (WTO-UNEP 2001, 2009) and the International Labor Organization (2007, 2009)). However, this is not what supporters of these rights are seeking. As argued by Guzman (2004), it is the ability to enforce these obligations through the dispute settlement system that provides the real incentive for including them in the WTO's sphere of influence. The 'magnetic attraction' is the power to bring complaints to independent third-party arbiters, to have binding decisions made and be able to support those decisions with sanctions.

The argument is often one of 'linkages', in which the WTO is linked to other issues. Alvarez (2002) argues that the GATT/WTO is a 'linkage machine' in its ability to expand over fifty years to encompass a range of issues such as subsidies, government procurement and intellectual property, albeit slowly and with much struggle.

Three compelling areas of international concern ripe for effective international enforcement mechanisms are international environmental law, international labour law and international human rights law. All three areas have extensive international law regimes with complementary, overlapping and sometimes contradictory frameworks for creating and enforcing rights.

There are several reasons why the epistemic communities related to human rights, labour and the environment are attracted to the form of legal institutionalism displayed in the WTO dispute settlement system. First, the process of enforcement becomes simplified. Secondly, the nature of the sanctions are clear. Third, the very broad nature of WTO membership makes the enforcement regime virtually global.

Fourth, the institutional framework within which the obligations are enforced makes compliance more likely.

Current Involvement of the WTO in Non-trade Issues

The explicit incorporation of important human, environmental and labour rights into the WTO-covered agreements has been problematic since the completion of the Uruguay Round. The tension is between a strict focus on keeping the WTO agreements related to one issue – 'trade' – and a recognition of the broader effect of liberalised trade on societies, in particular on human rights, the environment and labour. A more explicit recognition by the WTO of human rights has long been argued for (Petersmann 2000; Marceau 2002). For more than a decade, there have been calls for labour and environmental rights to be integrated more effectively into the interpretation and application of WTO obligations (Anderson 1998). Although WTO member states make positive noises in the Doha Declaration and other statements on areas such as human rights and public health, no substantive movement exists in any particular area, except perhaps for sustainable fishing in the context of WTO fishery negotiations. (On the environment, see WTO-UNEP 2009; on public health, see WTO 2003, 2005). Underlying the broader 'linkage' push is a simplistic belief that the expected and perceived effectiveness of the WTO in enforcing international obligations can be harnessed to achieve good outcomes for these other important international rights, despite the reality that human rights compliance by states and citizens is more often a product of acculturation or changes in state conceptions of itself and its interests (Goodman and Jinks 2004–5).

The Characteristics of the WTO Dispute Settlement System

The story of WTO dispute settlement is that it largely remains the battleground of strong states battling other strong states (Busch and Reinhardt 2002). It has also become a place for weak states to attempt to address disputes with strong states, but without the same likelihood of success (Busch and Reinhardt 2003). Iida (2004) argues that the system is moderately effective in settling disputes but with limited success for encouraging developing member states, or for levelling the 'playing field' between strong and weak states.

These broad descriptions of the system, however, need to be examined in the context of specific stages in the dispute settlement process to assess how legal institutionalism, as a form of governance, can be relevant for non-trade issues.

Notification and Panels

State practice has changed markedly over time, with the number of dispute notifications rising quickly in the WTO's first few years with a peak over forty new disputes in 1997, followed by a gradual reduction ever since. Dispute notifications by developed member states peaked in 1998, well before notifications by developing member states in 2002. Importantly, a significant majority of all disputes are between or involve developed member states, with virtually no involvement by Least Developed Country ('LDC') member states, except as third parties. Similarly, the proportion of notifications that resulted in disputes sent to panels increased over time, despite the falling overall number of notifications.

These two points suggest that the reality of WTO dispute settlement is one of low-level on-going participation, largely involving strong states battling other strong states or weak states challenging strong states. In other words, by its nature, the heavily legalised dispute settlement system attracts disputes to it that involve one of the parties seeking an alternative to power to resolve the dispute.

In other words, this ability to attract disputes against 'strong' states is a measure of the 'magnet effect'; the system exerts a positive effect to bring disputes into the process, and the 'attraction' rises as the size or power of at least one of the parties is strong. This means that legal institutionalism could provide a benefit to the examination of non-trade issues by independent international third parties.

WTO litigation is largely used to overcome a strong power – either by another strong state or a weak state. The 'missing' interaction in WTO litigation is weak states against other weak states and, after several years of 'experimentation', strong states against weak states (see Bown and Hoekman 2005).

So, the benefit for most states of a heavily legalised dispute settlement system is that, at one level, it provides an opportunity to challenge the position of a strong state. In that sense, it mirrors the function of municipal courts that allow all parties, whether strong or weak, to seek justice through law. The unusual feature is to see this practice demonstrated in an international tribunal in which sovereign, equal states engage with the process in very different ways.

When considered from the perspective of governance, the nature and degree of engagement by member states in the DSU highlights that this form of governance is not based on broad participation – an apparently inherent characteristic of legal institutionalism in practice. Legal institutionalism does not ensure equal access to the system of governance. However, it does provide an important opportunity for equality of access and thus a chance to achieve some degree of fairness through the rule of law. The changes in state engagement with the DSU over time highlight the unrealistically high expectations of early participants.

The other important aspect of the changes to how states engage with the system is the extent to which the notification stage has lost some relative importance, as seen in the increasing proportion over time of disputes that escalate from notification to a panel hearing. The significant gap between the number of notifications and the number of panel hearings (allowing for the time delay between one stage and the next) in the early years of the WTO and the relative narrowing in recent years suggests that more disputes rush through to the panel stage rather than be resolved at the notification stage. In other words, the mediation and two-party aspect of the system is becoming relatively less important than the third-party arbitration available at the panel stage. This suggests the independent, unbiased third party is the most attractive feature of the institution for participants.

Appellate Body Action

Member states regularly continue action through to the Appellate Body stage, with developed member states displaying a greater propensity for appeals than developing member states. This remains the case even if cross-appeals by developing member states are taken into account. While the number of appeals has generally been quite low throughout the WTO's existence, it has remained at a persistent level.

The significant use of the Appellate Body, for disputes that proceed beyond notification, indicates the need the system has for authoritative interpretation of international obligations. The Appellate Body provides a strong sense of certainty through its legal and formal method of decision making, as well as its protection from being easily overruled by disagreeing member states. Even in circumstances where many member states strongly disagreed with the Appellate Body (for example, allowing *amicus curiae* briefs to be submitted by non-government organisations in the line of cases from United States – Shrimp (DS58) to United States – Lead and Bismuth II (DS138)), the Dispute Settlement Body did not reject an Appellate Body report (see Charnovitz 2002).

The implication of such a central role for the Appellate Body is that legal interpretation, 'precedent' and the implicit removal of authority from member states accentuates the pressures of legal institutionalism. An appellate role in any international forum is a very radical concept. Only the ad hoc tribunals prosecuting war crimes and the International Criminal Court have an appellate function – see ICC Appeals Division; although the European Court of Human Rights does have a 'Grand Chamber' to deal with 'exceptional' cases (Convention for the Protection of Human Rights and Fundamental Freedoms: Article 27).

An appeal process that focuses on matters of law represents one of the strongest mechanisms for establishing and maintaining a heavily legalised institution. Its effect is to encourage and reinforce legal reasoning and the language and logic of law throughout the institution. In the context of this form of institutional governance, a defensible decision on appeal is one that can be legally justified. A decision that reflects the relative power imbalances of the parties, or the non-legal pressures imposed on the third-party decision maker, will be hard to justify on purely legal grounds on appeal.

Standard of Review

The key challenge of heavily legalised dispute settlement is the challenge it presents for defending sovereign decision making according to strict legal criteria and the strictures of a rational, probative, court-based approach to decision making. The nature and standard of review conducted by panels and the Appellate Body can make it very difficult for member states to defend measures. The kind of review can extend from the very broad (did the local authority have the power to make the decision?) to the very specific (what was the best decision in the circumstances?). In the WTO context, the legal answer has been that a 'middling' level of review is conducted, in which the power of the local authority and the merits of the decision are considered but due respect must be shown for the determinations of the local authority on questions of fact (see DS141 EC — Bed Linen (Article 21.5 India)). The effect of this form of heavily legalised dispute settlement is that international bodies have rejected the 'merits' or 'factual' conclusions of domestic authorities. The result is that the opportunity for states to pursue different policies or social values as an exercise of sovereignty is curtailed by the extent to which those policies or values can be defended in a heavily legalised context.

Thus, the third-party international review process is not a mechanical or direct comparison of an action and a standard (compared to determining in a domestic criminal matter whether an item was stolen or not). These particular decisions involve judgment and the application of opinion or values through the prism of 'necessity' or 'reasonableness'. They represent a significant challenge to the independence and autonomy of nation-states operating at both the domestic and international level. This form of decision making is endemic to legal institutionalism as it conveys both the legal nature of the process and the independent authority of the institution.

The Role of States and Legal Institutionalism

The distinguishing feature of WTO trade law governance is that it is still a state-to-state method of control and interaction. Unlike some other areas of international economic law, individuals have a very limited formal role to play in WTO dispute settlement (for example, individuals cannot notify disputes at the WTO, although *amicus curiae* briefs can be submitted to WTO panels and the Appellate Body by individuals or non-government organisations – see United States – Shrimp, United States – Lead and Bismuth II). By contrast, international investors via bilateral investment treaties receive rights to bring claims against State Parties to an independent arbitral tribunal (for example, the Agreement between Australia and Uruguay on the Promotion and Protection of Investment, signed 3 September 2001, [2003] ATS 10, entered into force 12 December 2002). Of course, WTO disputes still reflect the interests of the individual or industry actors who lobby member states to bring or defend an action. However, the 'real world' complainants and defendants do not directly participate in the proceedings as the final decision to litigate or defend is taken by the state, although some disputes make that distinction appear wafer-thin (see DS285). This means that the state in its competing, coordinating and non-unitary way intervenes and regulates, not just in the decision to litigate but in the implementation of any underlying trade measures.

The Nature and Use of Sanctions

The relationship between legal institutionalism and a power to sanction is problematic but also predictable. There are heavily legalised institutions that have no direct sanction power, such as the International Court of Justice, which lacks the ability to enforce its decisions – other than the 'compliance-pull' power of legal decisions (see Franck 1990).

Sanctions were seen as the 'crowning glory' of the new WTO because they finally 'gave teeth' to international enforcement in ways the earlier GATT and other international organizations fail to possess (Mora 1993). The key features are that sanctions are decentralised in application, are only a 'suspension of obligations' and not compensation, and are intended to compel a respondent into compliance (Jackson 1997, 2004).

Charnovitz (2001) explains the circuitous history by which a 'sanctions' power appeared in international trade governance in which WTO member states took a radical step to extend sanctions beyond merely 'rebalancing' trade barriers between parties in dispute, yet the word 'sanction' makes no appearance in the WTO Covered Agreements ('suspension', 'countermeasure', 'compensation' are the closest terms used to describe these actions). The intention was to compel parties to comply, although Charnovitz argues that this was achieved implicitly rather than explicitly in the drafting of the DSU.

However, the WTO exercises a 'decentralised' method of enforcement, in that the WTO itself does not apply, levy, or extract penalties or fines from the wrongdoer. The 'sanctions' or countermeasures authorised by the WTO through the DSB are in the form of the suspension of obligations by other member states. As the 'obligations' in WTO law include promises not to impose tariffs about a promised 'bound' rate (for example, 20 per cent of the value of the imported good), the suspension of the obligation means 'successful' complainants can impose higher tariffs on imports from the member state in breach. It might also include the 'suspension' of intellectual property rights, which means the production of another country's protected intellectual property without penalty during the 'suspension'. In that sense, the enforcement of WTO sanctions is by other member states acting with the authority of the WTO, rather than the WTO institution itself imposing them.

In examining the possible effect this form of governance may have when applied to other issues, it is important to remember that 'sanctions' in the WTO context are not payments or penalties in the sense of compensation being paid for past wrongs, but rather a right to 'suspend concessions' and thus impose higher tariffs in most circumstances.

The unusual feature of state practice on sanctions is how few times member states sought authorisation to impose sanctions on other member states. Actually imposing sanctions is even rarer. In 15 years and over 400 notified disputes, authorisation for sanctions has only been obtained 15 times – and in reality, they constitute only eleven distinct disputes, around 3–4 per cent of all WTO disputes.[1]

WTO obligations have only ever actually been suspended in three disputes: EC – Bananas (WT/DS27), EC – Hormones (WT/DS26 and WT/DS48) and US – Offset Act (Byrd Amendment) (WT/DS217). Suspensions were authorised but never implemented in three disputes as a result of negotiations between the parties (DS222, DS234, DS267), of which DS267 represents the most interesting example in which the United States agreed to a 'Framework' for the resolution of the dispute outside of the dispute settlement system and in return Brazil 'suspended' its intention to implement sanctions. In the remaining disputes, the authorisation for sanctions has never been utilised.

In other words, sanctions are a rare aspect of WTO dispute settlement. While the possibility of sanctions can colour all aspects of the dispute, the reality is a power that is seldom wielded. As argued by Charnovitz (2002), the use of sanctions by complainants has resulted in very mixed success for enforcing compliance. It does not represent a improved method of guaranteeing compliance. Busch and Reinhardt (2002) argue that the best outcomes are achieved for complainants when disputes are resolved as early as possible in the process.

The implication for governance is that incorporating a sanctions power into a heavily legalised institution does not guarantee better enforcement. While the possibility of sanctions may be useful, the reality is a much more limited mechanism for achieving compliance.

The Role of Procedural Arguments

Procedural arguments, in which the parties debate the method for determining a dispute, generally involve attempts to restrict the scope of a panel's decision making. The battle over establishing the 'correct' procedure is a characteristic element of heavily legalised dispute settlement systems. Respondents may raise them to avoid consideration of the substantive merits of the case.

A common form of procedural argument is over the jurisdiction or ability of the panel to address specific issues or measures. In many disputes concerning jurisdiction, the respondent seeks to restrict the panel's ability to consider aspects

---

1 The disputes in which the suspension of concessions has been authorised are: EC – Bananas (US), WT/DS27/49, 19/4/1999; EC – Bananas (Ecuador), WT/DS27/54, 18/5/2000; EC – Hormones (US), WT/DS26/21, 26/7/1999, EC – Hormones (Canada), WT/DS48/19, 26/7/1999, Brazil – Aircraft (Canada), WT/DS46/25, 12/12/2000; Canada – Aircraft (Brazil), WT/DS222/10, 18/3/2003; US – Foreign Sales Corporations (EC), WT/DS108/26, 7/5/2003); US – Offset Act (Byrd Amendment) (multiple complainants), WT/DS217/31-42, 26/11/2004; WT/DS234; US – Copyright Act (EC), WT/DS160; US – Tubular Goods Sunset Review (Argentina) WT/DS268; US – Gambling (Antigua and Barbuda), WT/DS285; EC – Biotech Products (multiple complainants) WT/DS291, US – Zeroing (Japan) WT/DS322; US – Upland Cotton (Brazil), WT/DS267.

of the complainant's case due to flaws, limits, or vagueness in the notification provided by the complainant when initiating the dispute. Another common procedural argument is over notions of procedural fairness, in particular whether there are implicit natural justice requirements in the DSU. In one example from an early WTO dispute (Turkey – Restrictions on Import of Textiles and Clothing Products, DS34), the respondent argued a series of procedural fairness grounds, for example, that the panel's terms of reference were too narrow to give the respondent notice of the issues, a third party (the EC) should be joined as a relevant party, the complainant had not followed correct procedures to initiate the dispute and consultations were inadequate. All were dismissed by the Panel (WT/DS34/R, 31 May 1999). In another example, this time from the long-running US – Tax Treatment of Foreign Sales Corporation dispute (DS108), the United States argued that incomplete evidence had been attached to request for consultations making the subsequent process unfair and, at the second Art 21.5 panel hearing, that new measures adopted by the US to resolve the dispute should not be part of the panel's terms of reference. Again, the procedural arguments were rejected by the panels (WT/DS108/R, 8 October 1999; WT/DS108/RW2, 30 September 2005).

Process arguments have routinely been ineffective in the WTO. Panels and the Appellate Body have regularly dismissed or minimised the significance of procedural flaws or inadequacies (except in anti-dumping cases) with the effect of keeping dispute complainants on foot and viable. The ineffectiveness of procedural arguments reflects a choice in this institution to privilege one aspect of legalism over another. It de-emphasises the manner or form of the complaint and necessarily emphasises the importance of the substantive legal issues in the dispute. In choosing to adopt a more flexible legal standard on procedural obligations, while maintaining a rigorous legal standard for substantive legal obligations, the institution expands the scope of its authority but reduces the inherent protections for participants. Remembering that generally respondents raise procedural arguments, the significance for governance through legal institutionalism is that access to the institutions' enforcement powers is enhanced but the protections for defending state interests are reduced.

Conclusions

The Problem of Legitimacy – Technical Interpretation vs Policy Decision Making

The implicit power of a juridical regime is its ability to declare certainty in its interpretation of law and finding of fact. The WTO-covered agreements purport to establish a comprehensive and consensus framework, structure and regime for the implementation of trade law obligations. The legalised structures, language and form of decision making reinforce the legitimacy of the institution's outcomes and prescriptions.

The challenge presented by autonomous decision making by panels and the Appellate Body is whether its decision making crosses into distinctly political realms. While this chapter does not examine that issue directly (see Roessler 2000 for a discussion of this view), the direct consideration of non-trade issues is likely to present similar 'political' issues. The challenge is not whether such decisions are 'lawful' or juridically determinable. The real concern is whether these decisions undermine the authority or legitimacy of the institution making the decision.

The Role of Negotiation in a System of Governance

A key feature of legalised institutionalism is that it is not bureaucratic in nature. It is not about empty procedure and the completion of 'process' for the sake of process. The reality of WTO dispute settlement has been that 'litigation' is brought and continued in order to achieve a better position for negotiating a beneficial outcome. A challenging feature of state practice in the WTO is that the vast majority of disputes are resolved by negotiation and consent. For many years, the majority of disputes were settled before the panel or trial stage. In long-running disputes, the successful outcomes are negotiated settlements rather than 'fait accompli' judgments, such as the interrelated Brazil – Aircraft (DS46) and Canada – Aircraft (DS70). If the lodgement of a dispute is enough to shift the power balance between two parties and achieve settlement, then settlement will be achieved early. When the third-party determination of an independent panel increases the pressure on one party relative to another, then that may lead to a negotiated outcome. Even if the matter proceeds to sanctions (rare as that is), the deployment of sanctions has almost never been the factor leading to eventual compliance – it is the threat of sanctions or more precisely the authorisation of sanctions by the WTO that then shifts the relative position of the disputants and allows a settlement to occur.

However, this practice creates a very different image of authority from the quasi-court edifice suggested by a heavily legalised institution. Authority is seen as a weapon or resource taken up by member states and deployed against other member states. It is a rhetorical weapon as much as anything else. The dispute, the process, the findings, even the sanctions, are themselves all instruments of state action. Yet, the legalised institution has its own structures, motivations and interests, but the reason for state interaction with the institution is to co-opt this inchoate power to further state interests.

Final Thoughts

The effect of adopting a legal institutionalist regime for the enforcement of WTO obligations has been to privilege strong states over weak states, although with some benefit for weak states through access to a process that provides at least an opportunity for disputes to be resolved equitably.

The implications are that legal institutionalism, at least as seen in the WTO dispute settlement system, does not present a neutral and unbiased process for the resolution of trade disputes. Legal institutionalism privileges particular types of interests – ones that benefit from the precision, fixed interpretation and legal reasoning inherent in the process. The adoption of heavily legalised dispute settlement methods of governance in trade is not necessarily as effective as expected and will still present problems for state and non-state actors wishing to enforce these rights.

The traditional methods of governance, especially by states in very formalised international institutions, are still limited means to achieve justice. A 'more perfect' form of legalised dispute settlement (in the sense of a more heavily legalised regime of obligations) does not improve the chances of compliance or enforcement. Heavily legalised dispute settlement is a product of a specific set of forces and its continued relevance is also a product of that same political and economic context. However, the establishment of this form of governance regime is meaningful in that it requires, encourages, or impedes particular types of interests and supports a specific conception of power, which may be accessible by both strong and weak state and non-state actors.

The WTO represents the limits of this method of 'strong enforcement' for global governance. The inherent challenge of combining a strict international legalism with the anarchic freedoms of national sovereignty is in stark relief in the WTO dispute settlement system. The regime addresses this complexity by maintaining a narrow area of responsibility and attempting to frame decisions in terms of technical interpretation and application. The potential expansion of the WTO's ambit undermines this balance and reinforces the tension between strict enforcement of international obligations and the defence of legitimate state interests.

If the exercise of power is the transfer of influence from one area to another, then the power harnessed in legal institutionalism is by its nature open to all but is usually only effectively exercised by those already powerful in other ways.

The turn to law in trade governance is not without its risks and problems. These problems are likely to be exacerbated if the 'other issues' were included in the trade governance regime. A proper understanding of the regime's strengths and weaknesses makes it appear less attractive to some issues because of the removal of national discretion, the 'front-loading' of obligation to the negotiation of the agreement, the belief that the 'deal' that establishes the international law obligation and the institution is the best that can be achieved and that future flexibility is over-rated. The nature of the system emphasises precision and certainty. It undervalues sovereignty and flexibility. Such a system may be appropriate when the subject matter is the determination of tariff rates (or the procedural strictures of anti-dumping investigations), but it becomes more problematic in areas with less clarity in application – such as national treatment (see Verhoosel 2002). This tension is then heightened when brought into other non-trade areas such as labour rights and the environment. In other words, the 'magnet' should be resisted, not because these issues are inappropriate to be examined at the WTO, but that governance by legal institutionalism will not be effective. In a manner, this is consistent with McCall Smith's argument (2000) that heavy legalisation usually requires a high degree of integration between nation-states, which is not the case with WTO member states

The risk with legal institutionalism is that a strict court system, by itself, lacks the flexibility to deal with change. The WTO remains hamstrung on the negotiations of the Doha Round; reform is at best piecemeal because all parties want outcomes to be traded as part of a grand bargain. It may be that the European Court of Justice provides sufficient flexibility through the operation of municipal parliaments and the European Commission to rectify the law in these areas.

The reality of legal institutionalism, at least as expressed in the WTO, is a system that still privileges relative power over truth, due to differing member-state capacity to marshal the necessary resources to effectively use the institution. However, the heavily legalised form of governance provides some opportunities for weak states to defend their interests and in that sense justifies its use in international affairs.

Heavily legalised international institutions embody a particular model of global governance which privileges precision, certainty and a lack of flexibility in the interpretation, implementation and enforcement of international obligations. These characteristics support regimes in which detailed, specific and measurable promises can be made and enforced, but may not be suitable for other issues, such as international human and environmental rights.

References

Abbott, Kenneth W. et al. 2000. 'The Concept of Legalization', *International Organization* 54(3): 401–19.

Alvarez, J.E. 2002. 'The WTO as Linkage Machine', *American Journal of International Law* 96(1): 146–58.

Anderson, Kym 1998. 'Environmental and Labor Standards: what role for the WTO?' in A.O. Krueger (ed.), *The WTO as an International Organization.* Chicago, IL: University of Chicago Press, pp 231–55.

Barnett, Michael and Martha Finnemore 2004. *Rules for the World: international organizations in global politics*. Ithaca, NY: Cornell University Press.

Beck, Robert J., Anthony A. Arend and Robert D.V. Lugt 1996. *International Rules: approaches from international law and international relations*. Oxford: Oxford University Press.

Bown, C .P. and B. Hoekman B, 2005. 'WTO Dispute Settlement and the Missing Developing Country Cases: engaging the private sector', *Journal of International Economic Law* 8(4): 861–90.

Braithwaite, John and Peter Drahos 2000. *Global Business Regulation.* Cambridge: Cambridge University Press.

Bull, Hedley 2002. *The Anarchical Society*, 3rd edn. New York: Columbia University Press.

Busch M.L. and Eric E. Reinhardt 2003. 'Developing Countries and General Agreement on Tariffs and Trade/World Trade Organization Dispute Settlement', *Journal of World Trade* 37(4): 719–35.

—— 2002. 'Testing International Trade Law', in D.L.M. Kennedy and J.D. Southwick (eds), *The Political Economy of International Trade Law: essays in honor of Robert E. Hudec*. Cambridge: Cambridge University Press, pp 457–81.

Charnovitz, Steve 2002. 'Judicial Independence in the World Trade Organization', in Laurence Boisson de Chazournes, Cesare Romano, and Ruth MacKenzie (eds) 2002. *International Organizations and International Dispute Settlement: trends and prospects*. New York: Transnational Publishers.

—— 2001. 'Rethinking WTO Trade Sanctions', *American Journal of International Law* (95): 792–832.

Chayes, Abram and Antonia Handler Chayes 1995. *The New Sovereignty: compliance with international regulatory agreements*. Boston, MA: Harvard University Press.

DiMatteo, Larry A. et al. 2003. 'The Doha Declaration and Beyond: Giving a Voice to Non-Trade Concerns within the WTO Trade Regime' *Vanderbilt Journal of Transnational Law* (36): 95–160.

Finnemore, Martha and Stephen J. Toope 2001. 'Alternatives to "Legalization": richer views of law and politics', *International Organization*, 55(3): 743–58.

Ford, Jane 2003. *A Social Theory of the WTO: trading cultures*. London: Palgrave Macmillan.

Franck, Thomas M. 2006. 'The Power of Legitimacy and the Legitimacy of Power: International Law in an Age of Power Disequilibrium', *American Journal of International Law* 100(1): 88–106.

—— 1990. *The Power of Legitimacy among Nations*. Oxford: Oxford University Press.

Goldstein, Judith et al. 2000. 'Introduction: Legalization and World Politics', *International Organization* 54(3): 1-15.

Goodman, Ryan and Derek Jinks 2004–05. 'How to Influence States: socialization and international human rights law', *Duke Law Journal* (54): 621–704.

Guzman, Andrew T. 2004. 'Global Governance and the WTO', *Harvard International Law Journal* 45(2): 303–52.

Hudec, Robert 1999. 'The New WTO Dispute Settlement Procedure: An overview of the first three years', *Minnesota Journal of Global Trade* 8 (Winter): 1–53.

Hurrell, Andrew 1999. 'Socieddae Internacional e Governanca Global', *Lua Nova. Revista de Cultura e Politica*, 55–75.

Iida, Keisula 2004. 'Is WTO Dispute Settlement Effective?', *Global Governance* 10: 207–25.

ILO-WTO 2009. *Globalization and Informal Jobs in Developing Countries*. Geneva:WTO.

—— 2007. *Trade and Employment: challenges for policy research*. Geneva: WTO.

Jackson, J.H. 2004. 'International Law Status of WTO Dispute Settlement Reports: Obligation to Comply or Option to Buy Out Editorial Comment', *American Journal of International Law* 98: 109–25.

—— 2000. 'The Role and Effectiveness of the WTO Dispute Settlement Mechanism', *Brookings Trade Forum*, 179–236.

—— 1997 'The WTO Dispute Settlement Understanding – Misunderstandings in the Nature of Legal Obligation', *American Journal of International Law* 91: 60–84.

Keohane, Robert O. 1988. 'International Institutions: two approaches', *International Studies Quarterly* 32: 379–96.

Koremenos, Barbara, Charles Lipson and Duncan Snidal 2001. 'Rational Design: looking back to move forward', *International Organization* 55(4): 1051–82.

Koskenniemi, Martti 2000. 'Carl Schmitt, Hans Morgenthau and the Image of Law in International Relations', in Michael Byers (ed.), *The Role of Law in International Politics*. Oxford: Oxford. pp. 16–34.

Krasner, Stephen (ed.) 1983. *International Regimes*. Ithaca, NY: Cornell University Press.

Krueger, A.O. (ed.) 1998. *The WTO as an International Organization*. Chicago, IL: University of Chicago Press.

MacCormick, Neil and Ota Weinberger 1986. *An Institutional Theory of Law: New Approaches to Legal Positivism*. London: Kluwer.

Marceau, Gabrielle 2002. 'WTO Dispute Settlement and Human Rights', *European Journal of International Law* 13(4): 753–814.

McCall Smith, James 2000. 'The Politics of Dispute Settlement Design: explaining legalism in regional trade pacts', *International Organization* 54: 137–80.

McGinnis, J.O. and M.L. Movsesian 2004. 'Against Global Governance in the WTO', *Harvard International Law Journal* 45(2): 353–66.

Mora, Montana I. 1993. 'A GATT with Teeth: law wins over politics in the resolution of international trade disputes', *Columbia Journal of Transnational Law* 31(1): 103–80.

Petersman, Ernst Ulrich 2002. 'Time for a United Nations "Global Compact" for Integrating Human Rights into the Law of Worldwide Organizations: Lessons from European Integration', *European Journal of International Law* 13(3): 621–50.

Picciotto, S. 2005. 'The WTO's Appellate Body: Legal Formalism as a Legitimation of Global Governance', *Governance* 18(3): 477–503.

Rajagopal, Balakrishnan 2003. *International Law from Below: development, social movements and third world resistance*. Cambridge: Cambridge University Press.

Reus-Smit, Christian 2001. 'The Strange Death of Liberal International Theory', *European Journal of International Law* 12(3): 573–93.

Roessler, Frieder 2000. 'The Institutional Balance Between the Judicial and Political Organs of the WTO', in Marco Bronckers and Reinhard Quick (eds), *New Directions in International Economic Law*. London: Kluwer Law International.

Sanson, Michelle 2008 *International Law and Global Governance*. London: Cameron and May.

Scott, Shirley V. 1998. 'Beyond Compliance: Reconceiving the International Law-Foreign Policy Dynamic', *Australian Year Book of International Law* 19: 35.

—— 1994. 'International Law as Ideology: theorizing the relationship between international law and international politics', *European Journal of International Law* 5: 313–25.

Simmons, Beth A. and Richard H. Steinberg (eds) 2006. *International Law and International Relations*. Cambridge: Cambridge University Press.

Slaughter, Anne-Marie 2005. *A New World Order*. Princeton, NJ: Princeton University Press.

Stone Sweet, Alec 2002. 'Judicialization and the Construction of Governance', in Martin Shapiro and Alec Stone Sweet, *On Law, Politics and Judicialization*. Oxford: Oxford University Press, pp. 55–89.

Toope, Stephen J. 2000. 'Emerging Patterns of Governance and International Law' in Michael Byers (ed), *The Role of Law in International Politics*. Oxford: Oxford University Press, pp. 91–108.

Verhoosel, Gaetan 2002. *National Treatment and WTO Dispute Settlement: Adjudicating the Boundaries of Regulatory Autonomy*. London: Hart Publishing.

Wendt, Alexander 2001. 'Driving with the Rearview Mirror: on the rational science of institutional design', *International Organization* 55: 1019–49.

Weiler, J.H.H. 2001. 'The rule of lawyers and the ethos of diplomats: reflections on the internal and external legitimacy of WTO dispute settlement', *Journal of World Trade* 35(2): 191–207.

WTO 2003. *Implementation of paragraph 6 of the Doha Declaration on the TRIPS Agreement and public health*, WT/L/540 and Corr.1, 1 September.

—— 2005. Amendment of the TRIPS Agreement, WT/L/641, 8 December. Decision of 6 December 2005

WTO-UNEP 2009. *Trade and Climate Change*. Geneva: WTO.

—— 2001. *Compliance and Dispute Settlement Provisions in the WTO and in Multilateral Environmental Agreements*, WT/CTE/W/191, 6 June.

Young, O.R. 1994. *International Governance: protecting the environment in a stateless society*. Ithaca, NY: Cornell University Press.

Chapter 4
Taxation Governance: Could the Tobin Tax Assist in Democratising Globalisation?

Elfriede Sangkuhl

Introduction

> Transaction taxes are an innocuous way to throw some sand in the wheels of super-efficient financial markets and create room for differences in domestic interest rates, thus enabling national monetary policies to respond to domestic macroeconomic needs (Tobin 1996: 493).

James Tobin made these remarks 24 years after first proposing a currency transactions tax, which has since been called a 'Tobin tax'.

A Tobin tax – a small flat tax to be imposed on the value of all foreign currency transactions – has the objective of reducing the volume of speculative currency trading currently occurring in the largely unregulated world currency markets. Daily trading in world currency markets increased from US$0.2 trillion to over US$1.8 trillion in the twelve years from 1986 to 1998. However, the total trade in goods and services for all countries for an entire year is only US$4.3 trillion (DeFazio and Wellstone 2000). The trade in goods and services in 1998, therefore, only made up less than 1 per cent of the total volume of world currency trades. Or, looked at the other way, 99 per cent of all trading in world currency markets is trading for purposes other than trade in goods and services. This could include spot currency speculation, currency arbitrage, currency hedging, forward exchange contracts and trading in other currency instruments.

The major danger of massive unregulated currency speculation is loss of sovereignty. When countries cannot defend their currency, they effectively lose control of their national monetary policy. The volume and volatility of unregulated currency flows can threaten national currencies with devaluation, higher interest rates and financial crises. This can lead to nations suffering low economic growth, increases in unemployment and inability to implement domestic policy (DeFazio and Wellstone 2000).

The only way to halt currency speculation would be 'permanent currency unification' (Tobin 1996: 493). Introducing a world currency would require convergence of national political and economic interests. This convergence would require an entire reconceptualising and reconfiguring of the notions of national sovereignty. In the alternative, this chapter suggests that if nation-states want to maintain sovereignty over national monetary policy, then a supranational tax, such as the Tobin tax, needs to be implemented.

The proposition of this paper is that:

- If the tax is effective in reducing currency speculation, then the risk of financial instability is reduced, thus returning monetary policy to nation states from the currency speculators.
- If the tax is ineffective to reduce currency speculation, then the tax revenues raised can be used to fund the policy responses required to ameliorate the impact of financial instability caused by the currency speculators.

This chapter will address the following:

- Financial stability a concern of the nation state
- The operation of a Tobin tax
- National and regional currency crises
- The Tobin tax as a 'natural' progression of late sovereignty
- Opposition to the imposition of a Tobin tax.

A Tobin tax is similar in its impact on currency speculators as the goods and services tax (GST) is to individuals. In the year 2000, Australia introduced a GST on the expenditure of individuals in an attempt to combat the erosion of the income tax base in Australia by the use of tax avoidance and tax evasion by individual taxpayers. In this respect, Australia was following the trend of many other jurisdictions where similar taxes (such as VAT) had already been introduced. The Tobin tax is a flat tax based on the value of foreign currency transactions, similar to the GST which is a flat tax based on the final value of all goods and services purchased by an end user of that good or service.

One impact of globalisation is that nation-states have been reduced to being able to 'guard' or maintain their sovereignty almost exclusively by way of border controls over the movement of people, while at the same time the movement of capital across borders is unfettered across most national borders. This unfettered movement of capital makes currency speculation possible. The free movement of capital across borders also prevents national tax authorities from preventing corporations from profit and tax shifting across borders. This makes the reported profitability of transnational corporations a voluntary exercise by corporations of where they wish to declare their profits, if any, and therefore where they wish to pay company tax. In this globalised world of business, corporations are increasingly 'forum shopping' for the most tax-effective jurisdiction to pay income taxes. The Tobin tax could be thought of as a corporate 'consumption tax' of doing business in the global marketplace.

Corporations operate undemocratically in the global market, largely unfettered by currency restrictions with the aim of maximising profits for their shareholders. A portion of corporations' profits are earned by manipulating currency values and from currency speculation. Such entities operate in an unregulated market that is so highly leveraged that they can cause massive currency destabilisation and therefore destabilisation of national or regional economies, including the Australian economy. (Leverage in this context means the ability to trade in large amounts of a currency with a tiny investment. A corporation could buy a currency hedge worth many millions of dollars for a tiny investment, perhaps only thousands of dollars.) This corporate power places the effective control of monetary policy with corporations. The Tobin tax will help nation-states regain some control over their monetary policy.

The recent global financial crisis, which started in the United States and spread across the world in a matter of weeks, has emphasised the reality of the globalised economy and the necessity of a global policy response. John Lipsky, the first deputy managing director of the International Monetary Fund (IMF) in a recent address lauded the fact that the G-20 Leaders Summits resulted in 'a coherent and powerful policy response that helped to halt the global economy's downward spiral, and set the stage for a recovery that is now underway' (Lipsky 2009). The cost of this 'powerful policy response' has been clear in the increase in government indebtedness: 'IMF projections indicate that government debt in advanced economies will reach nearly 120 per cent of GDP by 2014' (ibid.). A Tobin tax may reduce the impact of such a crisis in the future by either minimising the extent of the crisis or providing funds for the appropriate policy response. The issue of financial crises in the future must be addressed by nation-states given the recent frequency of such crises besetting the global economy. Edgar has recently remarked that this global financial crisis, the most significant since the depression of the 1930s 'is only the latest instalment (albeit the most severe) in a series occurring over the past 25 years' (Edgar 2010).

Financial Stability: A Concern of the State

Financial stability is 'a state of affairs which is conducive to the public's welfare' and therefore financial stability is a 'property of a nation state' (Allen and Wood 2006: 154). Allen and Wood in their effort to define financial stability, actually propose a definition of financial instability. They

> … define episodes of financial instability as episodes in which large numbers of parties, whether they are households, companies, or (individual) governments, experience financial crises which are not warranted by their previous behaviour, and where these crises collectively have seriously adverse macro-economic effects. In other words, a distinguishing feature of episodes of financial instability is that innocent bystanders get hurt. (Ibid.: 159–60)

Allen and Wood then go on to assert that because innocent bystanders are hurt by financial instability, as well as those responsible for the problem, 'it is in the interests of public policy to make such episodes unlikely by promoting financial stability' (ibid.: 160). They also hold that nation-states are sometimes required to provide 'emergency official support' (ibid.: 154) to those harmed by financial instability.

The first nation harmed by financial instability caused by the global financial crisis has been identified as Iceland (Danielsson 2008: 9). The reason, given by Danielsson, for the crisis was the fact that high interest rates in Iceland encouraged domestic firms to borrow in foreign currency and trading by foreign-currency speculators leading to high foreign-currency inflows disproportionate to the size of the Icelandic economy (ibid.: 10). As a result:

> Iceland's banking system is ruined. GDP is down 65% in euro terms. Many companies face bankruptcy; others think of moving abroad. A third of the population is considering emigration. The British and Dutch governments demand compensation, amounting to over 100% of Icelandic GDP, for their citizens who held high-interest deposits in local branches of Icelandic banks. (Ibid.: 9)

Iceland did not have the means to deal with the financial instability caused by the global financial crisis and was the 'first developed country to request assistance from the IMF in 30 years' (ibid.).

If nation-states are required to provide support, they require the means. The means, the money, can come from international aid of course, but international aid undermines democracy and sovereignty. The state receiving aid is accountable to the donor. If the means to provide support are generated by taxation, this defends democracy and legitimates the spending: 'Taxes allow governments to have more legitimacy, as citizens can exert pressure for efficient spending and governments can be made accountable' (Kohonen and Mestrum 2009: 39). If taxes are used to finance government expenditure, then the citizens have a say in how the funds are spent and the governments are accountable to their citizens, not to donors.

The ability of nation-states to raise taxes has been seen as:

> … one of the most important expressions of the power of nation states and a defining characteristic of the boundaries of national territories. Fiscal administrations were among the most important components of the 'administrative machinery' through which states asserted control over the nation's territory and population. (Nehring and Shui 2007: 8)

This fiscal control is slipping from the grasp of nation-states because of the 'hollowing out of the state' by the tax avoidance of transnational corporations (TNCs). Tax avoidance has become such a success that 'former IMF tax policy chief Vito Tanzi believes that "fiscal termites" – the growing number of ways the rich evade tax – are hollowing out the state and are an economic threat in the new century' (Castles 2006: 15). If nation-states are unable to effectively impose taxation, it is uncontroversial to assert this as an economic threat: 'Taxes allow governments to provide for public goods, like public services that give equal access to all social services (education, health, environment and so on)' (Kohonen and Mestrum 2009: 39).

However, if nation-states are unable to effectively impose taxation, this also threatens democracy:

> Apart from the old maxim *no taxation without representation* (and vice versa), taxes allow governments to have more legitimacy, as citizens can exert pressure for efficient spending and governments can be made accountable. Taxation can become an important element in the pursuit of good governance and democratisation. (Ibid.: 39–40).

This chapter will demonstrate how the imposition of a Tobin tax will help promote financial stability and provide nation-states the resources to ameliorate the effects of financial instability when it occurs.

The Operation of a Tobin Tax

James Tobin, an American economist, first proposed the introduction of a small tax on foreign currency transactions in 1972 in order to slow what he predicted would be an enormous growth in foreign currency speculation after the collapse of Bretton Woods and the 'freeing-up' of currency trading and floating of currency (Eatwell and Taylor 2000: 1).The Bretton Woods system to manage global finance was determined in 1944 in Bretton Woods, New Hampshire: 'A fundamental aspect of the system was that exchange rates between major currencies were fixed in term of the (US) dollar, and the value of the dollar was tied to gold at a US guaranteed price of thirty-five dollars per ounce.'(ibid)

Tobin was ahead of his time and his fears of the instability that currency gambling would engender have since been realised at the corporate, national and regional level. It becomes urgent to re-examine James Tobin's proposals so that nation-states can regain control over their monetary policy. This control is now in the hands of corporate speculators, who aim to increase their profits via currency speculation, and that comes at the expense of the stability of national currencies. When the gamble doesn't come off, the worst that can happen to the traders in the corporations is that they will be denied a bonus or fired. The consequence for the corporation that employs them is gambling losses that reduce the corporation's profitability. In the aftermath of the global financial crisis, we have seen that even these corporate consequences are not being borne, due to government bailouts of institutions facing liquidation. For example, in the United States, a few months after a government bailout of the firm, the employees of the investment Goldman Sachs had a salary increase of 46 per cent, which put their average earnings up to more than $US500,000 per annum (Patomaki 2009: 4).

The consequences for nation-states can be even more severe. This chapter examines the aftermath of the currency crises in Korea in 1997, Mexico in 1994 and the Asian crisis of 1997.

There are two ways of protecting economies from currency speculators. One is the imposition of currency controls with its attendant disadvantages and the other is controlling the volume of currency speculation. The disadvantages of imposing currency controls are the cost of imposing the controls, the emergence of a black market in the currency being controlled and problems in attracting foreign investment. The Tobin tax is the only well-regarded proposal, gaining international credibility, which would control currency speculation.

Since the deregulation of Australia's currency market in the 1980s, currency speculation here has grown to the point that 49 out of every 50 foreign currency transactions are purely speculative (Stilwell 2000: 226). This is typical of the experience in other countries. This level of gambling with foreign exchange makes the currency, and therefore the underlying 'real' transactions, vulnerable to artificial fluctuations in currency values.

Tobin's suggested imposition of a very small tax of 0.1 per cent on currency transactions would have a negligible effect on commodity trade and long-term foreign investment. The impact on currency speculation of the 0.1 per cent tax would be an effective rate of 24 per cent per annum, if the currency trades were daily trades and therefore obviously speculative. This tax would, to a large extent, eliminate currency speculation by making it unprofitable for corporations. A Tobin tax would result in no revenue or economic loss to nations, like, for example, Australia. This is because currency transactions that are based on a 'real' sale or purchase could not move offshore because the good or service is either being sold from Australia or to Australia. The tax would only impact currency speculators, making such speculation unprofitable.

There is currently no specific tax on the foreign exchange market in Australia or the rest of the world. It could be argued that the relevant entities that facilitate and conduct these transactions, namely banking and broking corporations already pay appropriate tax on their profits. Accordingly, it could be argued that it would be unfair for such corporations to pay tax on their profits and on their foreign-exchange transactions. However, as individuals now pay income tax on their income as well as a goods and services tax on their disposable incomes, there is no equity argument that corporations can raise. All Australian states tax gambling and the '(t)ax arrangements vary greatly across states for the different gambling products' (Productivity Commission 1999: 1) Different gambling activities are taxed in different ways; for example, lotteries and racing are taxed on gross turnover, poker machines and casinos are taxed on player loss or net profit, and licence fees are collected for most gambling activities (ibid.). Taxes on poker machines are around 22 per cent of gross profit in clubs and 30–50 per cent of gross profit in hotels (ibid.: 6). Taxes on casinos range from 8 per cent of player loss in the Northern Territory to 20 per cent in New South Wales, Queensland and the Australia Capital Territory (ibid.). Therefore, the Tobin tax is merely another tax on gambling and a very small one.

Tax Evasion

A Tobin tax has been resisted because of the fear that such a tax would push currency transactions into tax havens (Stilwell 2000: 227). Patomaki believes that using the possibility of tax evasion as an argument against imposing the tax is fallacious because it does not make tax evasion right or imposing the tax immoral (Patomaki 2001: 139). With foreign exchange ('forex') players either inventing financial substitutes for currency transactions and/or locational substitutes for booking forex trades (ibid.: 137), tax evasion could be a serious problem. Tax evasion could make the imposition of the tax ineffective; however, if forex players invent financial substitutes, the tax could be extended to cover the new financial instruments (ibid.: 139). If the tax is not universal when it starts, which it won't be, then members of the Tobin Tax Zone (the Zone) 'can make the banks residing in the tax-free areas pay a higher tax on cross-border credit to non-residents of the Zone. This should prevent banks from transferring funds to the rest of the world for forex purposes' (ibid.: 155) Quiggan suggests that separating the Zone from the rest of the world could be 'an advantage in the context of internationally supported prudential regulation' (Sheil 2003: Ch. 2, p. 8) He suggests countries that choose to operate outside the Zone and their accompanying regulations do so – in the knowledge that they would not have access to the IMF if things went wrong (ibid.).

Financial institutions that chose to operate outside the Zone would be unable to borrow from central banks or the institutions operating within their prudential control (ibid.). Considering the IMF analysis of the causes of, and the detrimental effects of, currency speculation on countries and regions this would probably become IMF policy.

The above consequences would be in control of the nation-states that choose to participate in the Zone. The members of the Zone could also enforce the international consequence of Tobin tax evasion attempts by corporations.

Corporations that object to such a tax would be involved in currency speculation and might be profitable, but are economically unproductive in terms of national and international economics. They do not add to GDP; they are gamblers or speculators, according to Keynes. In November 2003, 47 currency traders in the foreign exchange markets in the US were arrested (The *Australian*: 20 November 2003). The currency traders were charged with 'perjury, money-laundering, extortion, bankruptcy, fraud, narcotics trafficking and even fire-arms offences'. The unregulated foreign exchange market in the US apparently has allowed currency offences to go on for twenty years without detection. The dealers arrested for the above criminal activities include so-called 'boiler-room' dealers as well as dealers with mainstream broking houses, such as JP Morgan Chase, Société

General of France, UBS Warburg Dillon-Reade – an arm of the Swiss-based UBS, Dresdener Kleinwort Benson – a division of Germany's Dresdener Bank AG, and Israel's Discount Bank (ibid.). As casinos, racetracks and other gambling venues attract 'colourful personalities' and people with plenty of cash to launder, it should not be surprising that currency speculation attracts the same type of characters.

Poor law-enforcement practices in place currently are not a good argument for imposing another tax. However, the imposition of a tax would mean that currency speculation would be under more official scrutiny and therefore could assist in improving law enforcement practices. This could be an unintended beneficial consequence of instituting a Tobin tax. While gambling on horses, poker machines and casinos is not illegal in Australia and other countries, it is heavily taxed and regulated. Taxing and regulating the gambling of individuals does not check the gambling of such individuals; however, it regulates the gambling providers and helps check money-laundering activities. Taxing the currency speculation of corporations should check the corporation from attempting to boost profits from currency speculation, by making the speculation less profitable, remembering that corporations are accountable to shareholders.

The Impact of a Tobin Tax on Equity

A Tobin tax is a small, flat tax on currency transactions of, say, 0.1 per cent of the value of a currency transaction. A Tobin tax is, therefore, an indirect tax, that is, a flat rate of taxation on a particular type of transaction. Indirect taxes are regressive taxes and considered bad from a social justice perspective because poorer taxpayers pay a higher proportion of their incomes on the tax. Indirect taxes are also normally considered bad taxes because they lead to a distortion of resources because they are levied on specific types of goods or transactions. A Tobin tax by these criteria would, therefore, be inequitable in that it would be levying a tax on imports and exports; however, because the tax is very small, the impact would be very small. The cost of the Tobin tax would be immaterial to those companies buying currency-hedging contracts as insurance.

In 1996, Tobin wrote:

> Most disappointing and surprising, critics seemed to miss what I regarded as the essential property of the transactions tax – the beauty part – that this simple, one parameter tax would automatically penalise short-horizon round trips, while negligibly affecting the incentives for commodity trade and long-term capital investments. A 0.2% tax on a round trip to another currency costs 48% a year if transacted every business day, 10% if every week, 2.4% if every month. But it is a trivial charge on commodity trade or long-term foreign investments. (Ul Haq, Kaul and Grunberg 1996: xi)

While regressive personal taxes are inequitable and bad from a social justice view, they can be justified if they serve a purpose other than revenue raising as stated earlier. In the case of the Tobin tax the other purpose would be to divert economic resources from currency speculation to protect economies from speculators.

The Zone should be run by the Zone member states. They could use revenues raised by the Tobin tax to administer and collect the tax. The Zone could also determine that taxes, or a portion of the taxes, raised could be kept by the Zone in a form of Zone central bank, or IMF central bank, to protect any currency that faced a 'speculative run'. Such an international currency reserve would be more efficient than currency reserves being held by individual central banks around the world.

The Tobin Tax: Cheap to Administer

The Tobin tax is a flat tax levied on all types of foreign currency transactions whatever they are called. The calculation of the tax would involve no deductions, merely a simple percentage of every foreign exchange transaction. Financial institutions and corporations that engage in foreign currency dealing could simply add the cost of the tax to their transactions and divert the tax on a daily or weekly basis, by an electronic transfer to the relevant taxing authority.

The vast majority of currency trading takes place in a few financial centres, with 82 per cent of trading occurring in only eight countries. The financial centres dominating foreign currency trading are the United Kingdom (32 per cent of all trades), the United States (18 per cent), Japan (8 per cent), Singapore (7 per cent), Germany (5 per cent), Switzerland (4 per cent), Hong Kong (4 per cent) and France (4 per cent) (DeFazio and Wellstone 2000). This concentration of trading in a handful of First World countries by sophisticated players would make the administration of the tax relatively cheap and easy to regulate and collect.

This is a simple tax to calculate; it would have relatively few taxpayers and would therefore be easy to administer and audit by the taxing authorities, and cheap and easy to administer by the taxpayers. In the ever increasing complexity of tax systems around the world, an easy tax to administer and collect would not cause undue additional administrative burdens on those affected taxpayers.

National and Regional Currency Crises

According to Keynes, 'When the capital development of a country becomes a by-product of the activities of a casino, the job is likely to be ill-done' (Patomaki 2001: 120).

A few instances of the effects on a country of a job 'ill-done' are examined below. Economists at the Federal Reserve Bank of St. Louis defined a currency crisis 'as a speculative attack on a country's currency that can result in a forced devaluation and possible debt default' (Chiodo and Owyang 2002: 7). Even the

IMF recognises the fact that currency crises are caused by speculative attacks on currencies caused by 'the unreasoned panic in financial markets'(IMF Staff 1998). Even though the attack on a currency does not stem from any reasoned analysis of the economy under attack, the result of the subsequent panic is real. The damage done by unreasoned panic is permanent damage to a country's economy and its people as the two following examples show.

Korea

The Korean currency crisis in late 1997 resulted in the Korean won depreciating

> ... by 112% against the US dollar while the stock of foreign exchange reserves went down from 22.3 billion to a mere 3.8 billion US dollars bringing the country to the brink of sovereign default. More than 17,000 companies went bankrupt including eight conglomerates in 1997. (Park and Rhee 1998: 2)

The crisis was caused by the flight of speculative capital out of Korea. The flight of capital was caused by panic and not by any underlying problems with the Korean economy, which was growing strongly at the time of the crisis. Park and Rhee, from the Department of Economics at Seoul National University, found that Korea's currency crisis 'had little to do with the mismanagement of monetary and fiscal policy or negative changes in the external environment' (ibid.: 1).

The massive outflow of foreign capital from Korea in October 1997 was as a result of:

- the Korean government agreeing 'to bail out the near-bankrupt Kia Group on October 22; this was the moment when Korea's private banking crisis officially turned into a sovereign one' (ibid.: 15) and
- the crash of the Honk Kong stock exchange on October 23 (ibid.), and
- a weakening of foreign investor confidence because of the 'Asian Crisis that erupted in Thailand in July' (ibid.: 3) of 1997, also impacting on Korea.

Two of the three major reasons cited for the Korean currency crisis had nothing to do with Korean economic fundamentals but more to do with unreasoned panic. For Korea, the unreasoned panic caused the GDP growth rate to fall from 7 per cent before the crisis to a decline in the GDP of –5.8 per cent after the crisis (Lee and Rhee 2002). The GDP growth rate recovered after the crisis but 'the level of GDP remains permanently below its initial trend after the crisis' (ibid.).

Mexico

In 1994, the Mexican economy was enjoying 'economic growth, which averaged 3.1% per year between 1989 and 1994. In 1993 inflation was brought down to single-digit levels for the first time in more than two decades' (Gil-Diaz 1998: 1).

Yet, in December 1994 when the peso was devalued by 15 per cent it precipitated a 'financial crisis' (ibid.). This crisis 'wiped $US75 billion off Mexican securities held by foreigners' and as a result there was a panicked 'exodus of capital' which 'crippled an already fragile economy' (Hunt and Heinrich 1996: 30).

In 1994, the exchange rate of the Mexican peso was operating in a 'moving band system' (Sachs, Tomel and Velasco 1999: 35); that is, the peso was not freely traded. Mexico was operating an 'essentially pegged exchange rate' (ibid.) where the exchange was traded within a band allowed by the government. What Mexico had done was to liberalise their economy so that banking and investment rules were deregulated. This allowed for the operation of private banks and for a large influx of foreign investment in the Mexican economy (ibid.: 24). 'The Mexican currency crisis, unlike many others in Latin America, was not the result of irresponsible fiscal behaviour' (ibid.: 16); it was the result of allowing the economy to become dependent on 'massive ... short-run foreign capital inflows' (ibid.: 21) which became capital outflows in what was called a 'financial panic' (ibid.: 15, 17). These foreign capital inflows were given a boost when the US Congress approved the North American Free Trade Agreement (NAFTA) with Mexico (Gil-Diaz 1998: 4). The financial panic that precipitated a flight of capital out of Mexico was not based on any rational assessment of the future of the Mexican economy. The Mexican government allowing speculative money into the country and then that speculative money fleeing the country in a panic caused the crisis. The panic meant that Mexico had to accept a '$52 billion international support package intended to forestall a default and to bolster confidence in the Mexican economy' (Sachs, Tomel and Velasco 1999: 18), an economy which had been strong and growing before the crisis caused by speculators.

The Australian economy is currently enjoying strong economic growth relative to many developed economies. The Australian economy also shares with Mexico the fact that it has:

- deregulated the banking sector,
- privatised many utilities,
- deregulated its currency trading and capital flows, and
- negotiated a Free Trade Agreement with the United States

The Australian economy is just as vulnerable as the economies of Mexico and Korea to the actions of currency speculators.

The Asian Currency Crisis

An example of regional currency-related speculation was the Asian currency crisis of 1997. This 'lowered the world growth projection for 1998 by one percent and increased worldwide unemployment by 10 million' (DeFazio and Wellstone 2000).

The Asian currency crisis was precipitated by the 'floating of the Thai baht on July 2 [1997] and consequent 35 percent decrease in its international value prompted a generalized currency attack on almost all the Southeast Asian currencies' (Montes 1997: 1). This attack was not precipiated by any careful analysis of fundamentals by astute investors, just speculator panic. Garnaut noted that the countries most seriously affected by the currency crisis were Thailand, Indonesia, Malaysia and Korea and that these countries contain about one-tenth of Asia's population. The serious economic dislocation that had occurred in these four countries in 1998, spread like an infectious disease and transmitted the symptoms of economic contraction, currency depreciation and reduction in imports in other major economies, including the Philippines, Singapore, China and Hong Kong (McLeod and Garnaut 1998: 7).

What caused the currency crisis in Thailand and how did the crisis infect its neighbours with the same crisis?

At the time of the Asian currency crisis, newspaper commentators were blaming 'crony capitalism' – that is, an unhealthy closeness between government leaders and business leaders – for the crisis. A simple Google search linking crony capitalism to the Asian currency crisis resulted in 7,580 'hits'. However, after the dust of the crisis had settled, even the IMF concluded that the Asian currency crisis occurred despite 'several decades of outstanding economic performance *and* even though government budgets were broadly in balance and inflation rates were modest' (IMF Staff 2000: 2). In other words, the crisis happened despite, as economists say, good economic fundamentals. The IMF Staff brief concluded that the crisis occurred because of

> … weaknesses in financial institutions' portfolios; unhedged foreign currency borrowing that exposed domestic entities to significant losses in the event of domestic currency depreciation; excessive reliance on short-term external debt; and risky investments against the backdrop of bubbles in stock and property prices.

All the factors leading to the currency crisis were identified by the IMF to be the result of poor private investment decisions. The IMF Staff brief conceded that in these circumstances, a change in market sentiment could and did lead to a vicious circle of currency depreciation, insolvency, and capital outflows, which was difficult to stop.

Unfortunately these bad private investment decisions and changes in market sentiment lead to widespread misery in the countries affected.

In 1978, Tobin predicted that currency speculation would create the above problems. He stated that:

> National economies and national governments are not capable of adjusting to massive movements of funds across the foreign exchanges, without real hardship and without significant sacrifice of the objectives of national economic policy with respect to employment, output and inflation. Specifically, the mobility of financial capital limits viable differences among national interest rates and thus severely restricts the ability of central banks and governments to pursue

> monetary and fiscal policies appropriate to their internal economies. Likewise speculation on exchange rates, whether its consequences are vast shifts of official assets and debts or large movements of exchange rates themselves, have serious and frequently painful real internal economic consequences. Domestic policies are relatively powerless to escape them or offset them. (Patomaki 2001: 236)

Tobin continued, 'under floating exchange rates monetary policy becomes exchange rate policy' (ibid.). Australia and most other countries have no exchange-rate policy and therefore they have no effective monetary policy.

Three Asian countries not affected by the currency crisis were Vietnam, China and India. These very different economies share the fact that they impose heavy controls on their capital movements (McLeod and Garnaut 1998: 4). Capital controls raise other problems such as:

- the emergence of a black market in the currency being controlled,
- the cost of imposing controls, and
- problems in attracting foreign investment.

An alternative to capital controls is a free market in currencies, but with speculation being 'controlled' by the imposition of a Tobin tax.

The Asian currency crisis infected a region with serious and painful economic consequences that were beyond the reach of power of a single nation-state to control. The proposed Tobin tax will also have to be instituted beyond the sovereign reach and power of a single nation-state. The argument that follows demonstrates that instituting a Tobin tax operating supranationally is a natural progression of late sovereignty.

The Tobin Tax as a 'Natural' Progression of Late Sovereignty

EU scholars have been grappling with the theories of sovereignty in the post-EU world for some time. When considering the imposition of a tax on global currency transactions, it is essential to see where these scholars have taken the notion of sovereignty in the post-Westphalian era and see how it can be applied to a global currency transactions tax. Corporations earn profits world-wide, shift profits by the use of transfer pricing and therefore shift tax payable into favourable tax jurisdictions. Corporations also speculate in currency trading. In order for nations to effectively tax corporations, nations must make a claim to sovereignty as the authority to impose that taxation:

> Sovereignty, in the final analysis is about a plausible and reasonably effective claim to ultimate authority, or in perspective theory a representation of authority made on behalf of a society which is (more or less successfully) constitutive of that society as a political society, or as a polity. Sovereignty claims, when they

> achieve some measure of acceptance, continue to have profound political and social effects, and have to be taken seriously at the explanatory level for that reason. (Walker 2003: 17)

In order to tax currency trading, nations must begin to work beyond their national institutions and national authority in the same way the currency traders operate beyond national boundaries. Different approaches must be found to impose authority outside the normal national taxing authorities.

Walker uses the term 'late sovereignty' to denote the phase we are in now, and calls late sovereignty, that is, the current times, a time, in terms of sovereignty of 'continuity, distinctiveness, irreversibility and transformative potential' (ibid.: 19). Below is an explanation of the terms Walker uses to define our current times.

Continuity

Late sovereignty continuity, in Walker's terms, allow a late sovereign polity such as the EU 'like the state polities of early sovereignty, [to] still make the claim of ultimate authority and, like these state polities, does so through a complex of institutions which, however and wherever derived, comes to claim to be representative of the polity in question' (ibid.: 21).

Distinctiveness

'Sovereignty is always a claim over a particular society … a claim to constitute that society as a polity or political community, as so it always necessarily excludes as well as includes' (ibid.: 21, 22). Late sovereignty distinctiveness recognises that sovereign claims to authority are no longer merely territorial, but also functional. Walker believes that in this post-Westphalian era, even though the 'boundaries between different polities are still deeply contested' (ibid.: 23) assertions of legitimate authority will overlap and intersect and become more systematic.

Irreversibility

Walker holds that late sovereignty is irreversible because

> …the dynamic of globalisation, and of the responses to globalisation through the formation of non-state polities, continues to inexorably unfold. The challenge of multinational capital, of global communications and of free movement of goods, services, persons and capital is beyond the regulatory grasp of the state, and the grant of regulatory authority to non-state polities (as happens in the EU, NATO, ASEAN and other supranational bodies) consolidates and reinforces that process. (Ibid.: 24)

The development of non-state polities cannot be seen as a 'holding measure until states reassert their hegemony, but rather as a process of reallocation of regulatory authority which guarantees that states will never re-establish that hegemony' (ibid.).

Transformative

The transformative potential of late sovereignty poses challenges and offers the capacity 'to consider, balance and co-ordinate the various public goods and private interests' (ibid.: 32) in our globalised environment. The challenge is to maintain the core of sovereignty, which is that 'a sovereign order must assume its own continuing or self-amending sovereignty within its sphere of authority (rules of recognition and change) and must retain interpretive autonomy (rules of adjudication), deciding the boundaries of that sphere of authority' (ibid.: 29). The capacity of late sovereignty is its ability to deal with what Walker calls 'sovereign sites'. Sovereign sites encompass both the territorial and normative reach of sovereignty. Late sovereignty can deal with the

> ... novel, complex and untidy legal arrangements for the development of 'constitutional' relations between sovereign sites we can see the development of a dynamic in which actors with partial and interconnected governance projects in the same policy sectors can begin to imagine and reciprocally enact and co-ordinate polity-transcending comprehensive governance projects. (Ibid.: 30)

The imposition of a Tobin tax appears to be a good example of a 'novel, complex and untidy arrangement' that however, needs to be imposed so that nation-states regain some sovereign control over their currencies and the means to remediate damage caused by currency speculators.

Concern about protecting national economies from speculative attacks on currencies has led to legislation for a Tobin tax being introduced in Canada and is actively being considered in the United Stated and by the European Union.

On 23 March 1999, the Canadian Parliament introduced the Tobin tax in the following terms, 'That, in the opinion of the House, the government should enact a tax on financial transactions in concert with the international community' (Centre for Environmental Economic Development 1999). The Canadian Parliament fixed the rate of tax at 0 per cent for as long as the Tobin tax is not in force in other countries. When other governments enact the Tobin tax, Canada will be ready and prepared to join the Zone and able to protect its economy from currency speculators.

On 11 April 2000, a private members Bill was introduced to the US Congress entitled 'US Congress Concurrent Resolution on Taxing Cross-border Currency Transactions to Deter Excessive Speculation' (DeFazio and Wellstone 2000).

In September 2003, 30 members of the European Parliament and 10 members of national parliaments from 15 countries published an open letter calling for the introduction of a Tobin tax. This was after the issue of a Tobin tax was raised at the European Parliament in June 2000.

Opposition to the Imposition of a Tobin tax

The threat to the viability of the Euro zone in the aftermath of the recent global financial crisis has prompted opposition to suggestions of imposing a Tobin tax. The opposition of the International Monetary Fund (IMF), the World Bank and academics are considered here.

The countries that escaped the Asian financial crisis were Vietnam, China and India. They escaped that crisis because of their exchange-rate controls. In the aftermath of the recent global financial crisis, Lipsky (2009) commented that the economies in Asia were quick to recover because 'Banks built sizeable capital cushions, followed by sound lending practices, and had limited exposure to toxic assets.' What Lipsky failed to acknowledge was that these economies also had in place exchange-rate controls which limited their exposure to the toxic assets that were being readily traded in the advanced economies. Even though exchange controls were a contributing factor in explaining the Asian bounce back from the global financial crisis, the IMF is advocating that Asian economies remove their exchange-rate controls. In the interests of balanced global growth, Lipsky urges that 'all countries must play their part.' These comments are unsubtly directed at China. Lipsky identifies 'underlying policy problems, including outsized fiscal deficits, overly accommodative monetary policies, domestic market distortions, or inappropriate exchange rate policies' as a potential barrier to balanced world growth. Lipsky states that 'the recommended policy response to surging capital inflows *(into Asia)* is a pragmatic question, not a matter for ideology'. The 'pragmatic' answer for China is to become more 'open' and that 'it seems inevitable that increased currency flexibility in many Asian countries, including China, will form part of the rebalancing effort.' Stripping away exchange-rate controls from countries where those controls provided a shield from the Asian currency crisis and the recent global financial crisis without any alternative form of protection from financial stability seems to be an ideologically based, neo-conservative position which will strip the Asian economies of their protection from potential financial crisis.

The World Bank, in a 2010 policy research working paper, concluded that the introduction of a broad-based financial transactions tax would not deliver the 'revenue or efficiency gains hoped-for' by reformers (Honohan and Yoder 2010: 23). This working paper considered the introduction of 'a comprehensive tax on all financial transactions to replace all taxes'. Honohan and Yoder considered the proposals to tax securities transactions as proposed by Keynes, Tobin's currency transactions tax and bank debit taxes (ibid.: 3). Conflating consideration of these different taxes with their different policy objectives and considering them mainly as revenue-raising instruments was disingenuous. Honohan and Yoder concluded that imposing a small transactions tax would lead to 'collapse' in the volume of transactions and undermine the ability to raise tax revenue (ibid.: 23). The aim of a Tobin tax is to reduce the volume of speculative currency transactions and not to raise revenue.

The American academics Aliber, Bhagwan and Yan, have produced a paper presenting a regression analysis to demonstrate that increasing the transaction costs in foreign exchange markets results in a reduction in the volume of trading but also increases the volatility of the exchange rates (Aliber, Bhagwan and Yan 2003: 482). The Tobin tax would increase the transaction costs in foreign exchange markets and so the regression analysis demonstrates that the effect desired, that is, a reduction in volume, would be achieved. Tobin recognised that the Tobin tax could discourage some stabilising transactions such as currency hedging (Tobin 1996: 496). However, Tobin emphasised that 'the purpose of the proposed tax is to expand the autonomy of national monetary policies … and … that does not depend on the success of the tax in reducing volatility' (ibid.).

Conclusion

The currency crises of Korea, Mexico and Asia, described above, have resulted in the people of those countries 'suffering painful and cruel punishments for the crimes of fiscal policy' (Tobin 1996: 498) that they did not commit. The transformative potential of late sovereignty allows for the legitimate imposition of a transnational tax such as the Tobin tax.

The Tobin tax may not be able to address the activities of derivatives-based markets, such as the market in securitised subprime mortgages, which contributed to the recent global financial crisis (Honohan and Yoder 2010). However, the Tobin tax may have contributed to a reduction in the volume of these products being traded in global markets.

Advanced economies which have already embraced the ideology of free global capital markets would do better to consider imposing a global currency tax like the Tobin tax to take the place of the monetary controls they have lost.

Tobin foresaw the problems associated with unfettered currency speculation at the start of the move to currency deregulation. In 1972, Tobin proposed 'an internationally uniform tax on all spot conversions of one currency into another, proportional to the size of the transaction' (Patomaki 2001: 235). He commented in 1978 'the idea fell like a stone in a deep well' (ibid.). The time has arrived to pull the stone out of the well, because currency transactions are presently not taxed in Australia or anywhere else in the world.

References

Aliber, R.Z., B. Chowdhry and S. Yan 2003. 'Some Evidence that a Tobin Tax on Foreign Exchange Transactions May Increase Volatility', *European Finance Review* 7, Kluwer Academic Publishers, Netherlands, pp. 481–510.

Allen, W.A and G. Wood 2006. 'Defining and achieving financial stability', *Journal of Financial Stability* 2: 152–72.

Australian, The 2003. '47 traders face fraud charges', Business section, 20 November <www.news.com.au>.

Castles, Steven 2006. 'Why the poor are paying the price of the rich', *Canberra Times*, 12 January.

Centre for Environmental Economic Development 1999. *Tobin Tax Motion Passes in Canada's Parliament* <www.ceedweb.org/iirp/canadames.htm>.

Chiodo, A.J. and M.T. Owyang 2002. 'A case study of a currency crisis: the Russian default of 1998', *The Federal Reserve Bank of St. Louis*, November/December.

Danielsson, J. 2008. 'The first casualty of the crisis: Iceland', in A. Felton and C.M. Reinhart (eds), *The First Global Financial Crisis of the 21st Century: Part 11 June–December 2008*, VoxEU.org Publication.

DeFazio, Peter and Paul Wellstone 2000. *US Congress Concurrent Resolution on Taxing Cross-border Currency Transactions to Deter Excessive Speculation (H.Con.Res.301)*, introduced on 11 April <www.ceedweb.org/iirp/ushouseres.htm>.

Eatwell, J. and L. Taylor 2000. *Global Finance at Risk: The Case for International Regulation*. London: Polity Press.

Edgar, T. 2011. 'Financial instability, tax policy, and the tax expenditure concept', *Southern Methodist University Law Review* 63(3): 969–1032.

Gil-Diaz, F. 1998. 'The origin of Mexico's financial crisis', *The Cato Journal* 17(3) (Winter) <http://www.cato.org/pubs/journal/cj17n3-14.html>.

Honohan, P. and S. Yoder 2010. 'Financial Transactions Tax: Panacea, Threat or Damp Squib?', Policy Research Working Paper, The World Bank, Development Research Group, Finance and Private Sector Development Team, March.

Hunt, L. and R. Heinrich 1996. *Barings Lost: Nick Leeson and the Collapse of Barings plc*. Sydney: Allen and Unwin.

IMF 2000. *Recovery from the Asian Crisis and the Role of the IMF*, Issues Briefing, June <http://www.imf.org/external/np/exr/ib/2000/062300.htm>.

—— 1998. *Currency Crises the Role of Monetary Policy*, World Bank, March <http://www.worldbank.org/fandd/english/0398/articles/0150398.htm>.

Kohonen, M. and F. Mestrum (eds) 2009. *Tax Justice: Putting global inequality on the agenda*. London: Pluto Press.

Lee, J.-W. and C. Rhee 2002. 'Macroeconomic Impacts of the Korean Crisis: Comparison with the Cross-country Patterns', *The World Economy* 25: 539–62 <http://ssrn.com/abstract=312949>.

Lipsky, J. 2009. 'Building a Post-Crisis Global Economy – an Address to the Japan Society', New York, 10 December.

McLeod, R.H. and R. Garnaut (eds) 1998. *East Asia in Crisis: From being a Miracle to needing one?* London: Routledge.

Montes, M.F. 1997. *The Economic Miracle in a Haze*, Asia Society Publications, December <http://www.asiasociety.org/publications/asean_miracle.html>.

Nehring, H. and F. Shui (eds) 2007. *Global Debates about Taxation*. London: Palgrave Macmillan.

Park, D. and C. Rhee 1998. *Currency Crisis in Korea: How Has It Been Aggravated?*, 31 December <http://plaza.snu.ac.kr/~rhee5/data/kcrisis4.pdf>.

Patomaki, H. 2009. 'The Tobin Tax and global civil society organisations: the aftermath of the 2008–9 financial crisis', *Ritsumeikan Annual Review of International Studies* 8: 1–18.

—— 2001. *Democratising Globalisation: The Leverage of the Tobin Tax*. London and New York: Zed Books.

Productivity Commission 1999. *Australia's Gambling Industries: Public Inquiry*. Commonwealth of Australia, 16 December. Appendix M 'Gambling taxes' <http://www.pc.gov.au/>.

Sachs, J., A. Tornell and A. Velasco 1999. *The Collapse of the Mexican Peso: What Have We Learned?*. National Bureau of Economic Research <http://www.nber.org/crisis/mexico_agenda.html>.

Sheil, C. (ed.) 2003. *Globalisation: Australian Impacts*. Sydney: UNSW Press <http://evatt.labor.net.au/publications/books/12.html>.

Stilwell, Frank 2000. *Changing Track*. Sydney: Pluto Press.

Tobin, James 1996. 'A Currency Transactions Tax, Why and How', *Open Economies Review*, Kluwer Academic Publishers, Netherlands, pp. 493–9 .

Ul Haq, M., I. Kaul and I. Grunberg I (eds) 1996. *The Tobin Tax Coping with Financial Volatility*. New York: Oxford University Press.

Walker, N. 2003. 'Late Sovereignty in the European Union', in Walker (ed.), *Sovereignty in Transition*. Oxford and Portland, OR: Hart Publishing.

Chapter 5
Corruption, International Business Transactions and the OECD

John Juriansz and Marina Nehme

Part 1 Overview of Corruption

1.1 Introduction

In 1997, the Organisation for Economic Co-operation and Development (OECD) adopted the Convention on Combating Bribery of Foreign Public Officials in International Business Transactions (hereinafter 'Convention'), which required each member state to make foreign bribery a crime in their respective jurisdictions by transcribing the Convention into domestic legislation. However, by mid-2011, the collective OECD member states (as well as the countries aspiring to OECD membership) had achieved only moderate success in their progressive goal of eradicating foreign bribery in international business transactions within their economic, legal and political jurisdictions. The lack of significant demonstrable success, whether attributable to a flagging commitment to the ambitious goals of the Convention or to the considerable complexities of corruption, has effectively rendered the collective response of the member states unstable and in jeopardy. Transparency International, a self-proclaimed global civil society organisation established to combat corruption, has warned that 'Unless enforcement is sharply increased, existing support could well erode' (2010b: 8). This chapter considers the scope of the challenge of corruption (in Part 1), traces aspects of the OECD response to the various challenges of corruption (Part 2), highlights the civil cases against bribery (as well as its various defences) (Part 3), and sets out various prospects for reform (Part 4).

1.2 Towards a definition of corruption

Corruption is ubiquitous, complex, multifarious and of seemingly intractable transnational concern. Notwithstanding the abundant international and regional efforts to combat its insidious effects, attempts to achieve a uniform definition and system of measurement have vexed political scientists, as they have progressed very little following Arnold J Heidenheimer's (1970) groundbreaking distinction between definitions centred on public opinion, public office and public interest (Johnston 1996; Dobel 1978: 958; Scott 1972: 3–4; Nye 1967: 419; Rose-

Ackerman 1978: 9; Rose-Ackerman 1999; Shleifer and Vishny 1993; Bayley 1966: 721; Nichols 1997; Friedrich 1966: 74). Accordingly, since the early 1970s, a significant number of distinct corruption and good governance indices have been devised by numerous regional and transnational organisations. Nathaniel Heller (2009) recently examined the most prevalent of these indices, which include:

- Transparency International's National Integrity Systems studies (NIS),
- Transparency International Corruption Perceptions Index (CPI),
- World Bank Institute's Worldwide Governance Indicators (WGI),
- World Bank's Doing Business Indicators,
- Economic Intelligence Unit's Index on Democracy,
- Global Integrity's Integrity Indicators,
- Business Environment and Enterprise Performance Survey (BEEPS),
- Open Budget Index of the International Budget Project,
- Index of African Governance, and
- Freedom House's annual Freedom in the World Survey.

From a review of the literature, it is clear that there are many types of corruption and that it has existed from time immemorial in every jurisdiction the world over. The multiplicity of legal frameworks and standards, of cultural contexts and expectations, and economic practices and imperatives, renders the transnational response to corruption that much more difficult. It has been suggested that such is the inherent complexity and intractable nature of corruption that the Convention is likely to be ineffective (Getz 2006). However, these challenges do not excuse a lack of transnational action. It may well be that 'a single one-dimensional definition that will satisfy all observers will never be found' (von Alemann 2004: 25) as definitions, by their very nature, are prone to the adoption of incomplete descriptions which necessarily draw upon an 'arbitrary selection of attributes chosen to define their character' (Kurer 2005: 223; Wei 2001). Despite such challenges, it is still incumbent upon those concerned with combating corruption to appreciate the scope it has been assigned by the predominant transnational efforts, both internationally and domestically, which have sought to render corruption a nullity in international business transactions. It may be argued that corruption, as Justice Stewart proclaimed when discussing the definition of obscenity, can only be appropriately identified in accordance with the wholly subjective aphorism: 'I know it when I see it' (*Jacobelli* v *Ohio* (1964) 378 US 184, 197). However, such a broad definition lacks the requisite precision necessary for an empirically useful analysis (Gillespie and Okruhlik 1991: 77). Corruption, which is often used interchangeably with the term 'bribery', has commonly been extended to include such offences as the misuse of public office, embezzlement and the misappropriation of State assets (Nicholls et al. 2006: 5). However, despite this common usage, it may be that corruption and bribery are not inseparable terms. For example, Bayley has observed that a 'person bribed is a person corrupt; but a man may be corrupt who does not take bribes' (1966: 700). Notwithstanding these worthy observations, any viable definition of corruption must encompass bribery as well as a host of other behaviours (Rose-Ackerman 1978: 4).

More useful to the task of empirical examination is the recent operational definition proffered by Transparency International which describes corruption as 'the abuse of entrusted power for private advantage' (Transparency International 2010a). They further differentiate this definition by distinguishing between 'according to rule' corruption and 'against the rule' corruption by positing that 'Facilitation payments, where a bribe is paid to receive preferential treatment for something that the bribe receiver is required to do by law, constitute the former. The latter, on the other hand, is a bribe paid to obtain services the bribe receiver is prohibited from providing' (ibid.).

Nichols (1997) applies the term 'petty corruption' to these facilitation payments (or 'grease payments') which may be defined as payments made to minor officials of small amounts of money towards securing a right that is legitimately due (see Nicholls et al. 2006: 3–4). Similarly, the term 'grand corruption' is used to describe cases 'where massive personal wealth is acquired from States by senior public officials using corrupt means' (Society for Advanced Legal Studies Anti-Corruption Working Group 2000; Nicholls et al. 2006: 3–4). In short, this type of corruption involves the making of large payments to people in high positions of official power in order to secure an advantage which would not otherwise be legitimately secured. This chapter adopts the terms 'petty corruption' and 'grand corruption' due to the prevalence of their use in the literature on transnational corruption. While a single authoritative definition has yet to be universally recognised, the OECD has adopted this common approach by simply establishing an offence of bribery of foreign public officials that is broad enough to serve as a useful example for policy development.

Part 2 The OECD Response to the Challenge of Corruption

2.1 Functional Equivalence and the Instruments of the Convention

The Convention, which was adopted by the OECD Negotiating Conference on 21 November 1997 and entered into force on 15 February 1999, has attracted 38 signatory countries made up of the 34 OECD members and four non-members consisting of Argentina, Brazil, Bulgaria and South Africa. On 25 May 2011, the OECD invited Russia to join the Convention. The Preamble to the Convention requires each member to uniformly acknowledge that bribery is a widespread phenomenon in international business which raises moral and political concerns, undermines good governance and economic development, and distorts international competitive conditions. However, despite this uniform vision, the multiplicity of legal, political and cultural paradigms present across each of these 38 independent jurisdictions renders difficult the attainment of a 'functional equivalence' (as opposed to uniformity) in the implementation of the Convention.

The hallmark requirement of the Convention obligates States Parties to criminalise 'active corruption' in their respective jurisdictions (Article 1(1)). For the purposes of the Convention, an act of bribery or corruption is committed where a legal person (either a natural person or a corporate entity) engages in conduct with the intention of influencing a foreign public official in the exercise of their 'official duties' by offering, promising, or giving pecuniary or other advantage. States Parties who have jurisdiction to punish their nationals are required to establish such jurisdiction (Article 4(2)) and to impose proportionate and dissuasive criminal penalties, including imprisonment in the case of natural persons (Article 3(1)).

Article 2 of the Convention requires each member to take measures to establish the liability of legal persons for the bribery of a foreign public official. However, it does not specify whether this liability must consist of criminal or non-criminal (that is, civil and administrative) forms of liability. Accordingly, States Parties have pursued various legislative approaches when implementing this provision. For example, the Working Group's peer-review system has discerned that 25 member countries have established criminal liability for legal persons within their respective domestic legislation, nine member countries have established a non-criminal form of liability. Of the remaining member countries, Argentina has introduced a draft bill which seeks to establish criminal liability of legal persons and Brazil has introduced a bill to its Congress for administrative liability of legal persons (OECD 2010e).

Several provisions within the Convention call upon States Parties to engage in international cooperation and coordination in pursuit of their mutual objectives. For example, Article 4 ('Jurisdiction') of the Convention requires States Parties to consult with a view to determining the most appropriate jurisdiction for prosecution where more than one jurisdiction is in a position to prosecute a case under its domestic law. In particular, Article 4 gives all 38 States Parties to the Convention an extraterritorial jurisdiction to apply the offence of bribing a foreign public official. Similarly, Article 9 ('Mutual Legal Assistance') requires States Parties to provide legal assistance to another States Party concerning offences within the scope of the Convention. However, to fully discern the cooperative scope of the Convention, regard must also be had to each of its ancillary instruments, which are currently comprised of the following:

- Commentaries on the Convention on Combating Bribery of Foreign Public Officials in International Business Transactions ('Commentaries') (adopted by the Negotiation Conference on 21 November 1997) – The Commentaries declare that the Convention, without requiring uniformity, seeks to assure a 'functional equivalence' among the methods employed to combat bribery;
- Recommendation of the Council for Further Combating Bribery of Foreign Public Officials in International Business Transactions ('Further Recommendation') (adopted by the Council on 26 November 2009).

This instrument specifically recognises each of the other ancillary OECD instruments as well as the United Nations Convention Against Corruption (UNCAC) and makes 18 additional recommendations designed to promote conformity with the objects of the Convention. This recommendation, which was awarded the 2010 International Compliance Award by the Society of Corporate Compliance and Ethics (OECD 2010f), also provides two additional good practice initiatives:

1. Good Practice Guidance on Implementing Specific Articles of the *Convention on Combating Bribery of Foreign Public Officials in International Business Transactions* (Annex I) – Pursuant to Article 12 ('Monitoring and Follow Up') of the Convention, this annexure provides interpretive clarifications which seek to ensure that each signatory understands their Convention obligations; and
2. Good Practice Guidance on Internal Controls, Ethics, and Compliance (Annex II) – This annexure sets out methods for companies, business organisations and professional associations to establish internal controls, ethics and compliance programmes for combating the bribery of foreign officials in their international business transactions;

- Recommendation of the Council on Tax Measures for Further Combating Bribery of Foreign Public Officials in International Business Transactions ('Tax Recommendation') (adopted by the Council on 25 May 2009) – The Tax Recommendation encourages member states to enter into bilateral tax treaties to better ensure that each jurisdiction disallows the tax deductibility of expenses that constitutes bribes;
- Recommendation of the Council on Bribery and Officially Supported Export Credits ('Export Credit Recommendation') (adopted by the Council on 14 December 2006) – The Export Credit Recommendation recognises that 'not all export credit products are conducive to a uniform implementation of its recommendation' and encourages each member to 'take appropriate measures to deter bribery in international business transactions benefiting from official export credit support';
- Recommendation of the Development Assistance Committee on Anti-Corruption Protocols for Bilateral Aid Procurement ('DAC Recommendation') (endorsed by the Development Assistance Committee at its High Level Meeting on 6–7 May 1996) – The DAC Recommendation encourages members to introduce and enforce 'anti-corruption provisions governing bilateral aid-funded procurement', and
- Section VI ('Combating Bribery') of the OECD Guidelines for Multinational Enterprises ('Guidelines') – These Guidelines direct enterprises not to offer, promise, give, or demand bribes or to take undue or improper advantage to obtain or retain a business benefit.

The combined effect of each of these ancillary instruments is not one which seeks to impose a strict uniformity of behaviours between each of the States Parties to the Convention. Rather, these instruments seek to attain a 'functional equivalence' between the States Parties to the Convention. As Mark Pieth, Chair of the OECD Working Group on Bribery, has stated:

> … the Convention borrows a principle developed in comparative law. According to the functional approach of comparison, attention is drawn to the overall working of systems, rather than individual institutions. The assumption is that each legal system has its own logic and is not necessarily determined by the legal texts alone. Practices and formal rules are part of this approach as well as other aspects of the legal system taking over ancillary functions. Therefore the focus of comparison would lie on overall effects produced by a country's legal system rather than the individual rules. (Pieth 1999)

In support of this principle, Patrick Moulette opines that the successful adoption of legislation by nearly all of the parties to the Convention 'is a testament to the success of the principle of "functional equivalence" [which enables] Parties to tailor their methods of establishing the liability of legal persons for the foreign bribery offence to the limitations in their legal systems' (Moulette 2010). However, Paragraph 20 of the Commentaries states that 'In the event that, under the legal system of a Party, criminal responsibility is not applicable to legal persons, that Party shall not be required to establish such criminal responsibility.' Accordingly, as each member continues to absorb the requirements of the Convention into its domestic legislation, the litmus test of functional equivalence between the various legal systems – and the impact of the Convention on corruption in general – will be observed in the interaction of the criminal and civil liability schemes resident within the 38 member states. That is, in the exercise of mutual legal assistance (Article 9), Parties will be called upon to treat civil or administrative liabilities as though they were criminal.

2.2 The Impact of the Convention on Corruption

The breadth and scope of corruption makes the accurate determination of the impact of corruption on a given community a near impossible feat. However, in June 2010 and for the first time in the history of the OECD, the Working Group on Bribery Data on Enforcement of the Anti-Bribery Convention ('Working Group'), an assembly which acts as a peer-review mechanism to monitor the implementation of the Convention, published data compiled by the OECD Secretariat and provided by the parties to the Convention which provided 'a realistic picture of the level of enforcement' in the jurisdiction of 37 of the 38 States which are party to the Convention (OECD 2010c). This data was updated in 2011 following the provision of enforcement data by all 38 States which are now party to the Convention (OECD 2011a). In doing so, the Working Group has collected and analysed data regarding the number and outcome of investigations, proceedings, sanctions, settlements and convictions in each participating State. Accordingly, the Working Group (OECD 2011b) reports that:

> … as of March 2011, 199 individuals and 91 entities have been sanctioned under criminal proceedings for foreign bribery in 13 Parties between the time the Convention entered into force in 1999 and the end of 2010. Out of these 13 States, 7 have sanctioned both companies and individuals, one has sanctioned only a company and 5 have sanctioned only individuals. According to the data, at least 54 of the sanctioned individuals were sentenced to prison for foreign bribery. A record amount of EUR 1.24 billion was imposed in combined fines on a single company for foreign bribery. Approximately 260 investigations are ongoing in 15 Parties to the Anti-Bribery Convention. Furthermore, criminal charges have been laid against over 120 individuals and 20 entities in 5 Parties.

Despite the slow take-up by a majority of States Parties to the Convention, data obtained from countries including Germany, the United Kingdom and the United States which represent approximately 30 per cent of the world's export market indicates that some progress is being made in developed countries to investigate and prosecute corrupt practices in international trade. For example:

- Germany: of 117 cases involving allegations of corrupt practices German authorities have concluded 93 which resulted in 30 convictions, with 7 convictions resulting from proceedings concluded in 2009. In addition fines against natural persons and corporate entities were ordered against two former manages of Siemens for allegedly bribing Russian and Nigerian officials.
- United Kingdom: of 10 cases involving allegations of corrupt practices, UK authorities have concluded 7 and have 24 ongoing investigations. In April 2010, a vice-president of DePuy International was convicted and sentenced to one year's imprisonment wholly suspended for payments to Greek health-care officials.
- United States: of 168 cases involving allegations of corrupt practices or bribery and offences under the US Foreign Corrupt Practices Act (1977), US authorities have concluded 138 cases and have 100 ongoing investigations. Concluded cases have resulted in fines and custodial sentences being awarded against corporate entities and natural persons including Halliburton and KBR, Siemens, BAE Systems and Daimler AG. In the Daimler case, it was found that hundreds of illegal payments, approximating to US$ 56 million, had been made to foreign officials between 1998 and 2008 (OECD 2010c).

While these figures may appear encouraging, this record of enforcement is insufficient cause to celebrate the success of the Convention. Nicola Bonucci (the director of the OECD Legal Directorate) and Patrick Moulette point to a general trend towards an increasing number of corruption investigations, prosecutions and convictions for instances of transnational bribery. However, they concede that the 'investigations and prosecutions that have been launched in Europe have seldom resulted in convictions' (Bonucci and Moulette 2008). This observation reinforced the bleak prognosis offered in 2007 by Mark Pieth and Juliette Lelieur who stated that while the introduction of the Convention was a significant event, 'there is still little awareness of the phenomenon of foreign bribery' (2007: 1). Further, they assert that 'the bribery of foreign officials has remained rife in most of the world since 1997', during which time criminal investigations and prosecutions have been rare and convictions rarer still (ibid.: 2).

A more recent assessment of the implementation of the anti-corruption initiatives may be observed in Transparency International's July 2010 Progress Report: Enforcement of the OECD Anti-Bribery Convention ('Progress Report'). Importantly, the Progress Report proclaims that the Convention is 'key to overcoming the damaging effects of foreign bribery on democratic institutions, development programmes and business competition' (Transparency International 2010b: 6). However, the Progress Report records that of the 38 parties to the Convention, only seven are engaged in 'active enforcement' of their obligations, while nine are deemed as moderately engaged in enforcement, leaving an overwhelming majority of 20 States which have engaged in 'little to no enforcement' activities (ibid.: 8, 11–12). This lack of demonstrable improvement in enforcement activity appears to suggest that the majority of the member states continue to struggle with their commitment to the Convention and that the anti-corruption movement has failed to obtain any significant momentum since 1997 – in so far as such success is a measurement of enforcement.

As indicated by the Progress Report, the domestic and international response has been muted by the realisation that a significant number of governments are still not keeping their commitments under the Convention. The seven top performing nations with the best practice were Britain, Denmark, Germany, Italy, Norway, Switzerland and the United States, which represent approximately 30 per cent of world exports (ibid.). The nine nations assessed as providing 'moderate enforcement' of the Convention, which include France, Spain, Japan, Sweden and The Netherlands and represent 21 per cent of the world's exports, are each deemed only to have engaged in inadequate deterrence. The remaining 20 countries, which demonstrated 'little or no enforcement' of their obligations under the Convention, represent 15 per cent of the world's exports, and have been observed to have brought only minor cases, if any (ibid.: 8). Accordingly, those OECD countries which have been deemed to have inadequately engaged in their anti-bribery commitments as set out in the Convention represent 36 per cent of the world's total volume of exports. This represents not only a remarkable lack of political will but also a betrayal of the goodwill, spirit and intendment which welcomed the introduction of the Convention at the end of the twentieth century. The Progress Report remonstrates against this deficient record:

> The most disappointing finding is that there are still 20 countries – including G8 member Canada – with little or no enforcement, representing about 15 per cent of world exports. That number has shown little change in the last five years. This is deeply disturbing because companies in these countries will feel little or no constraint about foreign bribery, and many are not even aware of the OECD Convention. Governments in these countries have failed to meet the Convention's commitment for collective action against foreign bribery. (Ibid.: 8).

Further to this, Bonucci and Moulette assert that there remains a strong impression that European legal institutions and resources are inadequately equipped for combating transnational economic crimes. They suggest that the effectiveness of the Convention hinges upon the implementation by leading emerging countries such as South Africa, which became the first African nation to adhere to the Convention (Bonucci and Moulette 2008). However, in light of the continuing failure of advanced economies to abide by their commitments under the Convention, coupled with the magnitude of their dominant share of the world's export markets, it appears that the reliance upon emerging economies to render the Convention 'effective' is insufficient cause for bullish optimism.

Alarmingly, just one year after the Convention came into force in 1999, the OECD had estimated that wealthy multinational companies were paying bribes amounting to well over US$80 billion a year – a figure which, in the estimation of the United Nations, was sufficient to eradicate global poverty (Hawley 2000). More recently, the World Bank has estimated that more than US$1 trillion is spent annually on the payment of bribes to public officials in exchange for commercial advantages (OECD 2010b).

The Australian Wheat Board (AWB) Oil-for-Wheat Scandal provides a ready example of a wealthy commercial enterprise (empowered by the Federal Government with the grant of a monopoly over the Australian wheat trade) engaging in corrupt behaviour in dereliction of domestic Australian law, United Nations sanctions and Convention obligations. In short, a Royal Commission found that the AWB had paid, through middlemen, over AUS$290 million in bribes to officials within the regime of Saddam Hussein in exchange for lucrative wheat contracts so as to obtain approximately 90 per cent of the Iraqi wheat market by 2005 (Overington 2007). The 28 November 2010 WikiLeaks publication of many of the 251,287 leaked US Embassy cables revealed aspects of the diplomatic reaction to the economic and political impact of these bribes. In particular, then Federal Opposition Leader, the Honourable Kim Beazley MP, is said to have complained to the US Ambassador to Australia, Robert McCallum, that the Australian government had both sanctioned and facilitated significant corruption in the wheat export industry:

> Beazley maintained the Howard government had had full knowledge of the Australian Wheat Board's appalling bribes that undermined the sanctions regime against Saddam. It had repeatedly turned a blind eye to numerous indications

> of wrong doing, and had lied about what it had known and when. Not only had it sanctioned blatant wrongdoing, but the government had facilitated the destruction of the one mechanism that might have forced Saddam to satisfy international demands to prove he was not pursuing weapons programs. The US had every reason to be outraged with Howard, and Beazley urged that Washington express disapproval. (WikiLeaks 2010)

This anecdote of corruption is important for several reasons. It provides an example of how bribery can undermine both domestic and international objectives for peace and stability. Further, it is an important example how corruption can continue to be practiced in wealthy OECD nations irrespective of whether the nation is a signatory to the Convention. Corruption in OECD nations will continue to flourish where the ruling class both condones and participates in the nefarious pursuits of the corrupt. That the AWB Oil-for-Wheat Scandal occurred at all should not come as a surprise considering the assessment of Transparency International that only seven of the 38 parties to the Convention have been adjudged to be actively enforcing their Convention obligations (Denmark, Germany, Italy, Norway, Switzerland, the United Kingdom and the United States) (OECD 2011a). It is overwhelmingly evident that the Convention has yet to effectively curb foreign bribery in international business transactions. To achieve the goals of the Convention, the collective commitment of all the parties will need to be further harnessed. Otherwise, corruption will continue as an impediment to economic growth and will continue to restrict the flow of the economic benefits of globalisation – especially to developing countries ill equipped to deal with systemic corruption within their borders. Corruption will continue to generate a high risk of macroeconomic instability in developing countries, will continue to threaten economic development, and will further undermine the international financial system.

2.3 The Domestic and International Response

That corruption within the public and private sectors presents a real and serious problem for the international community cannot be doubted. Despite this grim prognosis, the register of achievement in the anti-bribery campaign has not been all doom and gloom. Beyond the OECD, the number of international agreements dedicated solely to the eradication of corrupt practices throughout the world, and the ancillary agreements which buttress the obligations under those agreements, attests to this view. In addition to the Convention there have been numerous international initiatives:

- United Nations Convention Against Corruption (and related United Nations initiatives) – International;
- Inter-American Convention Against Corruption – the Americas;
- Southern African Development Protocol Against Corruption – Africa;

- The Economic Community of West African States Protocol on the Fight Against Corruption – Africa;
- African Union Convention on Preventing and Combating Corruption – Africa;
- Criminal Law Convention on Corruption – Council of Europe;
- Civil Law Convention on Corruption – Council of Europe;
- Model Code of Conduct for Public Officials – Council of Europe;
- European Union Convention on the Protection of Financial Interests and Protocols – European Union;
- Convention on the Fight Against Corruption involving Officials of the European Communities – European Union;
- The joint Asian Development Bank (ADB)/OECD Anti-Corruption Action Plan for Asia and the Pacific – the Asia-Pacific region;
- The various initiatives of the International Chamber of Commerce, the World Bank and the International Monetary Fund (IMF) – International.

These agreements seek to eradicate corrupt practices by increasing cooperation between countries in policing, investigating and prosecuting individuals and corporate entities who engage in corrupt practices and by ensuring, as far as possible, uniformity in domestic anti-corruption laws.

The two most significant of these international agreements are the United Nations Convention Against Corruption (UNCAC) and the Convention with a majority of countries, including developing countries and those with the highest percentage of exports, being parties to either one or both. Of those countries that have ratified the Convention, only Korea and Iceland are not signatories to UNCAC. UNCAC, adopted by the United Nations General Assembly on 31 October 2003, is an exceptionally ambitious and all-encompassing anti-corruption document which also deals with the bribery of foreign officials. However, unlike the Convention, it prohibits both 'supply side' bribery and 'demand side' bribery – the latter of which is not covered by the Convention. Interestingly, while the Convention deals with the bribery of foreign officials in transnational business transactions, it only criminalises the act of the bribe offerer (the 'supply side'). The demand side encompasses the recipient/offeree of the bribe. In addition to criminalisation and law enforcement (Articles 15–44), UNCAC also focuses on other aspects of corruption, including asset recovery (Articles 51–9), international assistance (Articles 43–9) and corruption prevention (Articles 5–14). While there has been criticism of the Convention for not addressing the demand side (Kaikati et al. 2000), the unitary focus upon foreign bribery and its impact on the economic interests of the States Parties which makes the Convention more effective than UNCAC in combating the bribery of foreign officials in international business transactions. Comparatively, UNCAC's broad scope is overly ambitious and relatively toothless. When introduced, it was quickly ratified by 140 States (United Nations 2003), including those nations notorious for their entrenched corruption. Ratification, however, does not constitute political will. Accordingly, UNCAC has often been used as a fig leaf whereby countries uncommitted to an anti-corruption reform agenda can deflect criticism from donors or political adversaries. While UNCAC provides an international legal basis for cooperation, it is not a blueprint for anti-corruption reform. In addition to these international instruments, there are two predominant domestic legislative instruments with extraterritorial application: the US Foreign Corrupt Practices Act of 1977 ('FCPA') and the Bribery Act 2010 (UK) ('Bribery Act').

The FCPA, like the Convention, employs the dual approach to combating the offering of bribes by providing anti-corruption provisions which are enhanced by specific accounting measures. However, unlike the FCPA, the Convention is better situated to enforce its anti-bribery provisions due to being a multilateral instrument – so long as the pursuit of its enforcement objectives are vigorously and faithfully pursued (Weiss 2009). As the FCPA is a unilateral law that is mainly applicable to US corporations, it had been argued that prior to the advent of the Convention, the FCPA posed a competitive disadvantage to US corporations (Darrough 2010: 257). Regardless of these differences, scepticism has been expressed about the effectiveness of the self-regulatory mechanisms such as the Convention and the FCPA (Cragg and Woof 2002; Weismann 2009).

The Bribery Act 2010 (UK), which has came into force on 1 July 2011, reforms the United Kingdom's archaic patchwork of anti-bribery legislation enacted in the late nineteenth and early twentieth centuries and implements much of the Convention. Moreover, while it prohibits a person from requesting, agreeing to accept, or accepting a bribe, the legislation primarily focuses upon the briber or facilitator of the bribe. Significantly, the Bribery Act 2010 (UK) offers numerous regulatory and prosecutorial enhancements, including:

- The extension of the jurisdiction of authorities within the United Kingdom to prosecute claims against natural persons and corporate entities;
- The broadening of the scope of application of the legislation to corporate entities or partnerships which are not only incorporated or formed in the United Kingdom but also to corporate entities or partnerships which carry on business in any part of the United Kingdom. The effect of this is that multinational corporations which are established outside of the United Kingdom but operate a business inside its jurisdiction will be deemed to have committed an offence where a person associated with the corporate entity commits an act of bribery involving a foreign public official.
- Impliedly removes the defence of 'Act of State Doctrine' providing that an offence of bribery will not have been committed if the payment of the bribe is one which is sanctioned under the written law of the country in which the payment is made.

Importantly, s7 of the Bribery Act 2010 (UK) creates a new criminal offence which can be committed by a commercial organisation where it fails to establish and enforce adequate procedures to prevent persons associated with them from committing bribery on their behalf. Section 7(2) contains a complete defence for the relevant commercial organisation where it can prove that it had in place adequate procedures designed to prevent persons associated with it from undertaking the corrupt conduct. Section 9 of the Bribery Act 2010 (UK) is also integral to this new anti-bribery regime. This section requires the Secretary of State to publish guidance about procedures that relevant commercial organisations can put in place to prevent persons associated with them from bribing. This guidance seeks to explain the anti-bribery policy behind s7 so as to assist commercial organisations to comprehend the manner, scope and content of procedures it may set in place to prevent s7 bribery and to ensure that the determination of adequacy is not established following a determination by a court. The Secretary of State, Kenneth Clarke, has stated that commercial organisations wishing to prevent the commission of bribery on their behalf should be guided by six (non-prescriptive) principles (Ministry of Justice 2010) when establishing their procedures:

1. Proportionate procedures – A commercial organisation should ensure its procedures are proportionate to the bribery risks it faces and to the nature of its activities.
2. Top-level commitment – This principle seeks to engage the senior management of the commercial organisation (such as the board of directors or the business owners) through the establishment and fostering of a business culture which shuns bribery.
3. Risk Assessment – Commercial organisations should undertake periodic assessment of the types of risk and exposure it may potentially possess (both internally and externally) to situations which may lead to occurrences of bribery by its employees and by persons associated with the organisation.
4. Due diligence – Taking a proportionate and risk-based approach, commercial organisations are expected to conduct due diligence on those who perform or will perform services on its behalf so as to mitigate identified bribery risks.
5. Communication (including training) – Commercial organisations must ensure that its policies are clearly communicated both internally and externally to its employees and those associated with the organisation.
6. Monitoring and review – Commercial organisations must monitor, review and amend its procedures so as to ensure they are appropriately designed to prevent bribery by persons associated with the organisation.

The OECD peer-review process had previously criticised the United Kingdom for its failure to reform its antiquated anti-corruption legislation. However, future OECD peer reviews of the new Bribery Act 2010 (UK) will help determine whether this Act has superseded the FCPC as the international gold standard of anti-corruption legislative regimes.

The peer-review process adopted by the Working Party has enabled the OECD Secretariat to work with countries such as Chile and the representative

OECD countries to develop Chilean legislation to conform to the Convention. The impact of this peer-review process has been such that Spain, Turkey and Chile have each engaged in significant legal reform of their antiquated anti-bribery laws. The introduction of a new Penal Code in Spain on 9 June 2010, for example, included the introduction of a more workable definition of foreign bribery, introduced the concept of criminal liability for corporations who engage in corruption, provided for enhanced sanctions, increased limitation periods and broadening of the scope of directors duties and liabilities. However, the Spanish Penal Code maintains its narrow jurisdictional limits, and fails to hold parent companies responsible for the corrupt behaviour of their agents, subsidiaries and joint venturers.

An example of the domestic implementation of the Convention may be attributed to the Tax Recommendation that encourages States Parties to 'explicitly disallow the tax deductibility of bribes to foreign public officials' and review 'the effectiveness of its legal, administrative and policy frameworks as well as practices for disallowing tax deductibility of bribes to foreign public officials' (OECD 2009: 1–2). Further, it recommends that each States Party, in accordance with their legal system, 'establish an effective legal and administrative framework and provides guidance to facilitate reporting by tax authorities of suspicions of foreign bribery arising out of the performance of their duties' (ibid.: 2). In Australia, for example, section 26-52 of the *Income Tax Assessment Act 1997* (Cth) ('ITAA') prohibits the tax deductibility of payments of bribes by foreign public officials. However, section 26-52(4) of the ITAA excludes facilitation payments from this restriction by stating that 'an amount is not a bribe to a foreign public official if it is incurred for the sole or dominant purpose of expediting or securing the performance of a routine government action of a minor nature.' This exclusion is consistent with the clarification of Article 1 of the Convention as set out in paragraph 9 of the Commentaries. Further, section 70.4(1) of the Australian *Criminal Code*, set out in the schedule to the Criminal Code Act 1995 (Cth), expressly exempts facilitation payments whereby:

> (1) A person will not be deemed guilty … if (a) the value of the benefit was of a minor nature; and (b) the person's conduct was engaged in for the sole or dominant purpose of expediting or securing the performance of a routine government action of a minor nature; and, (c) as soon as practicable after the conduct occurred, the person made a record of the conduct … .

Part 3 The Civil Case Against Bribery

The Working Group considers 'active enforcement' to be an adequate deterrent to foreign bribery whereas 'moderate enforcement' denotes inadequate deterrence (Transparency International 2010b: 7). These classifications are based upon the number and importance of cases and investigations actively being pursued in the State (taking into account the volume of exports of the given State) (ibid.: 7).

The Working Group and Transparency International have each catalogued most of these cases and investigations (OECD 2010c; Transparency International 2010b). While not re-canvassing this well-trammelled territory, Part 3 considers the scope of the civil law cases relating to bribery in many of the OECD countries and describes the most resilient of the defences to the continued practice of bribery and corruption.

3.1 Civil Law Cases Relating to Bribery

The notion that bribery is unacceptable conduct stems from ancient times. For instance, in 1500 BC, the Egyptian pharaoh Harmhabs issued an edict that judges 'shall not take money from one party and decide without hearing the other; for how could you sit as judges upon other men's deeds when one among you is himself committing an offence against justice? The penalty for such an offence shall be death' (Wigmore 1992: 15–16). Bribery is an offence against justice, as Pharaoh Harmhabs stated, because its outcome is the oppression of the weak (Driscoll 1984–85: 24). Bribery deprives the principals, without their knowledge or informed consent, of the disinterested advice which they may expect from their agents or representatives (*Ross River Ltd* v *Cambridge City Football Club Ltd* [2007] EWHC 2115 (Ch) 204, 205). Bribery is viewed as improper conduct and as such, attracts both civil and criminal penalties. This part considers civil actions against bribery, and then discusses arguments raised by commentators and lawyers around the world in support of the practice of bribery.

In most countries around the world, bribery is viewed as a serious civil wrong, because it involves an element of betrayal whereby people who are in a position of trust and confidence—such as agents, partners, directors, or employees—abuse this trust. Such people, as fiduciaries, owe a duty not to profit from this position of trust. To accept a bribe is a breach of this duty and the court may impose a number of civil remedies in order to vindicate the rights of the beneficiary. For example, in *Attorney-General of Hong Kong* v *Reid* [1993] 3 WLR 1143, Mr Reid, while acting as a prosecutor for the government of Hong Kong, received payments to interfere in the prosecution of certain people. He used the money received to acquire a number of properties in New Zealand. The Hong Kong government commenced proceedings against him claiming that the properties he purchased with the payments were held on constructive trust for the Hong Kong government. The Privy Council observed that victims of a bribe are entitled to any monies constituting a bribe and to trace that money into property acquired by those monies. Accordingly, the Privy Council found that the New Zealand properties were held on constructive trust for the benefit of the Hong Kong government.

In civil law, when a bribe is established, there is an irrefutable presumption that its purpose is to induce the agent to act in favour of the briber. For instance, in *Hovenden and Sons* v *Millhoff* (1900) 83 LT 41, 43, Romer LJ stated:

> If a bribe be once established to the court's satisfaction, then certain rules apply. Amongst them the following are now established, and, in my opinion, rightly established, in the interests of morality with the view of discouraging the practice of bribery. First, the court will not inquire into the donor's motive in giving the bribe, nor allow evidence to be gone into as to the motive.

Similarly, Justice Slade in *Industries & General Mortgage Co* v *Lewis* [1949] 2 All ER 573, 574, stated that for the purposes of civil law, a bribe is defined as:

> … the payment of secret commission, which only means (i) that the person making the payment makes it to the agent of the other person with whom he is dealing; (ii) that he makes it to that person knowing that that person is acting as the agent of the other person with whom he is dealing; and (iii) that he fails to disclose to the other person with whom he is dealing that he has made that payment to the person whom he knows to be the other person's agent. Those three are the only elements necessary to constitute the payment of a secret commission or bribe for civil purposes.

The victim of a bribe may not only take civil action against the recipient of the bribe, but also against the payer of the bribe. As noted in *Panama and South Pacific Telegraph Company* v *India, Rubber Gutta Percha and Telegraph Works Co* [1875] LR 10 Ch App 515, 517, the court may provide the victim with any remedy it deems adequate to deal with the facts of the case. For instance, the victim may take action against the briber for damages for fraud and unlawful interference with the victim's business. Further, assuming that a contract entered into between the briber and the victim was the result of the bribe, the victim has a personal claim against the briber for restitution of an amount equal to the bribe. For example, in *Hovenden and Sons* v *Millhoff* (1900) 83 LT 41, 43, Romer LJ stated:

> … if the agent be a confidential buyer of goods for his principal from the briber, the court will assume as against the briber that the true price of the goods as between him and the purchaser must be taken to be less than the price paid to, or charged by, the vendor by, at any rate, the amount or value of the bribe.

The victim may also rescind the contract which is the subject of the bribe. For example, in *Logicrose Ltd* v *Southend United Football Club Ltd* [1988] 1 WLR 1256, 1260, Millet J noted:

> It is well established that a principal who discovers that his agent in a transaction has obtained or arranged to obtain a bribe or secret commission from the other party to the transaction is entitled, in addition to other remedies which may be open to him, to elect to rescind the transaction *ab initio* or, if it is too late to rescind, to bring it to an end for the future.

Further, as a result of the doctrine of knowing assistance, a number of other people may be liable to the victims of a bribe. This doctrine attaches liability to the people who assist in a breach of trust (*Barnes* v *Addy* (1874) LR 9 Ch App 244, 252). As a consequence, a person who is a stranger to a fiduciary relationship may be held liable if he or she, with actual knowledge, aids the fiduciary in a dishonest and fraudulent scheme (*Royal Brunei Airlines* v *Phillip Tan Kok Ming* [1995] 2 AC 378). Four elements must be present for a claim of knowing assistance to be successfully made out (Perell 1999–2000: 208):

- a trust or fiduciary relationship must exist between the victim and the person receiving the bribe;
- the trustee or fiduciary must fraudulently or dishonestly breach his or her equitable duties;
- the stranger to the fiduciary relationship must have actual knowledge of the misconduct, and
- the stranger to the fiduciary relationship must have assisted in the fraudulent or dishonest design.

As may be seen, victims of bribery are entitled to take civil action against a number of people, and they have a number of remedies available to protect their interests.

3.2 Cultural Relativism, Neo-colonialism and the Defence of Corruption

Cultural norms and values vary widely not only between countries but also within the customary practices of a single jurisdiction (Legvold 2009; Dix and Pok 2009; Smith 2009). In light of this diversity, the challenge of determining an international standard which recognises the limit of acceptable behaviours applicable to all countries beyond which an activity is not merely deemed to be corrupt, but unacceptably corrupt, is immense. A survey of international experience would likely record an infinitely abundant range of culturally relative practices which may cast bribery, *inter alia*, as an economic good, as an equivalent of tipping, as an ordinary occurrence in the usual course of dealings, as an activity which is analogous to the payment of a commission, or as a payment to be duly protected by the Act of State Doctrine. These examples of 'culturally relative practices' are often offered in defence to the transmission of a bribe.

Implicit within each of the examples offered in defence of corruption may be the charges of cultural relativism and neo-colonialism – charges levelled against those who would enforce transnational efforts to stem the frequency of such practices in international business transactions (Grundman 1980: 258; Mayer 1994: 383; Orentlicher and Gelatt 1993: 102; Nichols 1999: 80). Such charges may constitute 'an iteration of the argument that a multilateral regime proposed by the industrialized nations is nothing more than a form of moral colonialism imposed on less wealthy countries' (Nichols 1999: 80). To this end, many of those who argue that corruption is 'culturally relative' would likely condemn aspects of the

Convention as an embodiment of incongruent western individualism at odds with the cultural norms of their particular society (Sanyal 2005). Nichols, however, has suggested that this argument may be too facile. Instead, he suggests that it may be more accurately stated that 'less wealthy countries are being told which of their existing laws they must enforce' (Nichols 1999: 80) and further, that the choice of which laws a society may choose to enforce over others is perhaps more indicative of their particular cultural norms and values than is the complete register of laws and regulations enacted by that State (Arnold 1932: 14).

Transparency International has argued for the end to facilitation payments by taking the view that such payments are detrimental to the countries in which they are made and that such payments may lead to the payment of larger bribes (2010b: 14). However, facilitation payments are explicitly allowed by the laws and policies of Australia, Canada, Denmark, Germany, Japan, South Korea, The Netherlands, New Zealand and the United States. These jurisdictions often dismiss incidences of Petty Corruption as minor, if not irrelevant, expressions of permissible cultural norms (Joint Standing Committee on Treaties: OECD Convention on Combating Bribery 1998). This view is frequently based upon the argument that the payments are of relatively small amounts of money which are paid to secure a right that is legitimately due and, as such, do not damage nor distort the health of the host country's trade or economy (Salbu 2000; Ellis 2001). However, the World Bank (2000) has stated that the cost of corruption is essentially borne by the poorest of a society who rely upon publicly provided services which are reduced in the face of economic decline. However, the sympathetic view of facilitation payments has been facilitated by the OECD itself. For example, paragraph 9 of the Commentaries clarifies the scope of bribery prohibited in Article 1 as follows:

> Small 'facilitation' payments do not constitute payments made 'to obtain or retain business or other improper advantage' within the meaning of paragraph 1 and, accordingly, are also not an offence. Such payments, which, in some countries, are made to induce public officials to perform their functions, such as issuing licenses or permits, are generally illegal in the foreign country concerned. Other countries can and should address this corrosive phenomenon by such means as support for programmes of good governance. However, criminalisation by other countries does not seem a practical or effective complementary action.

Paragraph 9 of the Commentaries, while not absolving States of their responsibility to combat Petty Corruption, constitutes an acknowledgement of cultural difference and accords the officials within a given State the flexibility to determine what is to be deemed customarily acceptable and what activity is to constitute a violation of the domestic cultural norm or value. While the flexibility may be empirically useful in that it may facilitate cross-cultural comparison, too much flexibility may render the definition of corruption too broad to permit enough precision to be empirically useful (Gillespie and Okruhlik 1991: 77). Further to this, it is an unfortunate and ironic consequence of this flexibility that facilitation may be deemed illegal where paid domestically to a public official, but legal if the same bribe were to be paid to an internationally based public official. In recognition of the strain between prohibiting Grand Corruption while permitting Petty Corruption to continue where condoned or required by local custom, Paragraph VI of the 2009 Further Recommendation entreats States Parties to 'undertake to periodically review their policies and approach on small facilitation payments in order to effectively combat the phenomenon'.

While this concessional flexibility within the Convention may be justifiably interpreted as a worthy recognition of cultural difference, there are many who have disagreed with the ongoing sanction of this culturally devised distinction and have argued that Petty Corruption can be just as economically and socially debilitating as Grand Corruption (Bayley 1966; Nichols 1997; Ellis 2001). Consistent with this more restrictive and cautionary interpretation is the observation that every country in the world has rendered illegal the bribing of its own officials (Nichols 1999; Heimann 1994). Likewise, the 2007 APEC Code of Conduct for Business, which recognises that facilitation payments are prohibited under the anti-bribery laws of most countries and, as such, enterprises should eliminate them, strives to provide businesses with the power to exert 'a real impact on efforts to eradicate corrupt practices, leading to stronger economies and further trade liberalisation' (APEC 2007). However, the lack of consensus as to the correct characterisation of facilitation payments is not debilitating, as the apologistic principle of 'functional equivalence' remains at the core upon which the Convention was conceived. Regardless, it has been generally accepted that Grand Corruption is 'an evil practice which threatens the foundation of any civilised society' (*Attorney-General of Hong Kong* v *Reid* [1994] 1 All ER 1, 4).

While the debate over cultural relativism and neo-colonialism is contested, there must be explicit recognition of the limits ascribed to Petty Corruption. That is, it must be recognised that 'cultural relativism ends where the Swiss bank account enters the scene' (Transparency International 2010a). While corrupt practices may reflect the cultural norms within a given society, this should not make its continued presence any less of an anathema.

3.3 Defence to Bribery: Economic Benefit

Among economists, debate exists regarding the impact that bribery may have on the economic growth of a country. Some authors have suggested that bribery may improve economic growth. For example, Leff considered that bribery may have a positive impact on society because it can encourage entrepreneurship, especially in countries where governments are hostile to entrepreneurs. Further, bribery may enable individuals to avoid bureaucratic delays (Leff 1964: 10), quicken the pace of an inefficient regulatory process, and contribute to economic growth (Huntington 1968; Lui 1985).

Beck and Maher (1986) recognised that bribery is a common alternative to competitive bidding in developing countries. In most jurisdictions, however, such conduct is prohibited. For instance, the United States passed legislation in 1977 prohibiting American firms and individuals from paying bribes to foreign governments. In the United Kingdom, such conduct became illegal in 2002. More recently, in 2010, Slovakia passed a law imposing liability on Slovak companies who bribe foreign public officials. OECD Secretary-General Angel Gurria commented that the introduction of this law 'sends a strong message of commitment to the fight against corruption and helps create a level playing field for firms competing internationally' (OECD 2010a). However, Beck and Maher observed that there is a fundamental isomorphism between competitive bidding and bribery. They determined that in Third World countries the same supplier will win the contract with or without the bribe (Beck and Maher 1985: 1, 5).

In contrast to these views, Mauro (1995; 2004) found that bribery and corruption have a negative impact on economic growth. A number of other studies have reported similar effects (for example, Gyimah-Brempong 2002; Sashs and Warner 1997; Li, Xu and Zou 2000). Still other studies have found that bribery and corruption may increase the costs of conducting business (World Bank 2002; Kaufmann 2004: 88). This imposes a high burden on businesses and may in turn impact on entrepreneurship, because the exorbitant cost of setting up a business may dissuade people from investing in new ventures (Kestenbaum 2010). Further, by distorting competition, bribery can create a barrier to profitability and growth (Association of Chartered Certified Accountants 2007: 16). Bribery may also reduce the flow of foreign investments (Wei 2000). For example, Mauro found that if Bangladesh improved the integrity and efficiency of its bureaucracy, the number of private investments would drastically rise (Mauro 1995: 683).

In view of the abundant literature finding that bribery and corruption may have a negative impact on economic growth, the economic arguments in defence of bribery cannot be sustained. The legalisation of bribery would ultimately disadvantage businesses which seek to act as moral and ethical entities (Bushell 2000: 435).

3.4 Defence to Bribery: Tipping

Donaldson and Dunfee noted that for some people 'bribery is just like tipping' (1999: 45). Consequently, in such situations a bribe may be viewed as a payment for services rendered. For example, in dialogue between Socrates and Crito, Crito informed Socrates that the jailer allowed him access to Socrates' prison cell prior to visiting hours because he gave him a tip (Plato 360 BC, 2008: 1). As a tip, the conduct was acceptable. But is it really acceptable conduct?

Tips have been used in different contexts. In certain situations, tips may be viewed as a gratuitous unidirectional gift. In such instances, they improve social solidarity and increase individual utility. When a tip is provided as a reward for services well rendered, the likely intention is the reinforcement of behaviour of good service (Udoidem 1987: 616). Consequently, tips are acceptable.

Tips, however, are not always voluntary. In certain instances, they may be imposed on a person. While such exploitation may be morally questionable, the courts have deemed that the payment of tips as a forced gratuity is legitimate. In *Searle* v *Wyndham International Inc.* (2002) 102 Cal App 4th 1327, for example, Mr Searle alleged that the billing practice of Wyndham International Inc. in stating that 'a 17% service charge and applicable State Tax will be added. In Room Delivery Charge $3' was misleading and unfair because it compelled a gratuity which should be strictly voluntary. The Court of Appeal of California held that such charges were not misleading or unfair. It was up to the hotel to itemise its charges as it saw fit and its clients had the right not to use a service if they were unhappy with the price. Accordingly, the court did not consider that these tips were a form of an organised 'rip-off' (See also *Jeffrey Michaelson* v *The Ritz-Carlton Hotel Company LLC* (Unreported Judgment, Court of Appeal of California, 22 March 2004)).

While the practices of bribing and tipping may be viewed as 'twin practices' (Udoidem 1987: 614), it is important to distinguish between them because their purposes are different. A bribe, unlike a tip, is the payment of money to a person in a position of trust in order to influence his or her judgement or behaviour. Consequently, when a tip is attempting to induce or influence an action from its rightful and legitimate course, it is nothing more than a bribe.

3.5 Defence to Bribery: Course of Dealings

Although bribery is abhorred in all cultures, businesspeople may view the payment of bribes as an 'unavoidable sin' (Udoidem 1987: 615). They may refer to it as the payment of commission or gifts that are essential for the promotion of their business because, without them, business cannot be procured (Wilton 1906–07: 370). As such, a businessperson may argue that these payments should be allowed especially in Third World countries, where bribery is standard practice and a business is unlikely to be able to operate without 'kick-backs'.

For example, in *World Duty Free Company Ltd* v *The Republic of Kenya* (ICSID Case No ARB/00/7), Mr Nassir Ibrahim Ali, the Chief Executive Officer of World Duty Free, stated that when World Duty Free wished to establish duty-free complexes in Nairobi and Mombasa airports, he was advised that the protocol in Kenya required making a donation to the president of Kenya. If this is so, should such payments be allowed? Is it a defence to say that a payment is not a bribe but follows common practice in the particular country and, as such, is legal?

World Duty Free argued that such payments were routine practice when doing business in Kenya. It also claimed that such practices have cultural roots and formed part of the local system of custom ('Harambee'). Harambee originates from the African culture whereby societies make 'collective contribution toward individual or communal activities' (*World Duty Free Company Ltd* v *The Republic of Kenya* (ICSID Case No ARB/00/7), [134]). Kenyan sociologist, Dr Pius Mutie, stated that donations in Kenya were viewed as gifts. Exchange of such gifts 'irrespective of their worth is customarily sanctioned and failure to comply with those customary practices is indicative of either extreme poverty, meanness or rebellion against cultural norms' (as cited in Chatham House 2007).

Such gifts are not just common in African culture. Gift giving is also a common social custom in China, for example, and in certain circumstances gift giving may be perceived as a bribe by foreigners, when its real purpose is to allow people to be part of a network of personal relationship (Steidlemeier 1999: 121). In such instances, giving a gift cannot automatically be classified as a bribe. It is important to keep an open mind toward the different ethics and customs that may exist in different countries (Donaldson and Dunfee 1999).

However, there is a fine line between bribery and acceptable gift-giving practices. For example, a report of the Task Force on Public Collections or Harambees presented in 2003 to the Minister of Justice of Kenya noted that 'over the years, the spirit of Harambee has undergone a metamorphosis which has resulted in gross abuses. It has been linked to the emergence of oppressive and extortionist practices and entrenchment of corruption and abuse of office' (cited in *World Duty Free Company Ltd* v *The Republic of Kenya* (ICSID Case No ARB/00/7), [134]).

In *World Duty Free Company Ltd* v *The Republic of Kenya* (ICSID Case No ARB/00/7), the International Centre for the Settlement of Investment Disputes acknowledged that gifts were often exchanged as a protocol, but deemed that the payment made by the CEO of World Duty Free was a bribe, because its aim was not only to obtain an audience with the president of Kenya but also to acquire during that meeting the president's approval of the contemplated investments (*World Duty Free Company Ltd* v *The Republic of Kenya* (ICSID Case No ARB/00/7), [136]).

When determining if a payment is a bribe the customs of a country will be taken into account. If such payments are customary, a payment will not be viewed as a bribe. However, if the payment is made in order to gain a business benefit, the courts may regard the payment as a bribe and the conduct will be considered illegal. Accordingly, the fact that the payment of bribes is common practice in a country will not prevent a determination that a particular payment is illegal. Payment to officials of money to expedite a transaction is considered bribery and, as such, is prohibited because it ultimately harms the 'honest man' (ICC Case No 1110, [19]–[20]).

3.6 Defence to Bribery: Payment of a Commission as Common Practice

Another argument that has been raised in defence of bribery is that the payment of bribes is analogous to the payment of commission. The law has acknowledged that the payment of commission is allowed and will not be synonymous with bribery as long as it can be honestly justified. For example, in *Baring* v *Stanton* [1872] 3 Ch D 502, Mr Stanton, an American shipowner, had for several years an account with Messrs Baring Brothers and Co. Messrs Baring effected for him an insurance on his ships and they charged him full premiums for the services provided. Mr

Stanton was not aware that the merchants were retaining a commission from the premiums. When he discovered this, he did not wish to allow the merchants to retain the commission and took legal action against the firm regarding this matter. Bacon VC held that there was clear evidence that Messrs Baring Brothers and Co had carried on their business in that way for a number of years. The practice was not unreasonable, and as such the commission was deemed as usual. Mr Stanton could not raise an objection in relation to the matter because it was a common practice.

Similarly, in *Great Western Insurance Company* v *Cunlife* [1869] 9 Ch App 525, a marine insurance company, Great Western Insurance Company, appointed the firm of merchants, Pickersgill and Son, as their agents for settling claims in England and for effecting reinsurance. According to the custom between underwriters and brokers, the firm of merchants, in its capacity as agent, was allowed by the underwriters 5 per cent commission on each reinsurance and 12 per cent at the end of the year on the profit between underwriter and broker for the year. Great Western Insurance Company became aware of the payment of the 12 per cent commission in 1866, but did not object to it until 1868. In 1869, it took action against the firm of merchants for, among other matters, an account of the 12 per cent commission. The Court held that Pickersgill and Son were entitled to retain the 12 per cent commission because Great Western Insurance Company became aware of the payment in 1866 but did not directly object to the payment or stop their dealing with the firm of merchants. It was only after two years that action was taken regarding this matter.

However, if the payment of a commission cannot be honestly justified, such commission may be viewed as a bribe. For instance, in *Turnbull* v *Garden* [1859] 38 LJ Ch 331, a woman hired an army agent to provide her son with a military uniform. Purchase of the different articles forming part of the uniform was made by the army agent, who then charged his client the full invoice prices charged by the tradesmen while he himself had been provided with a discount. When the client became aware of this, she took action against the army agent. The Court directed the army agent to account for the profit he made as a result of the transaction. James VC observed (at 335): 'What appears in this case shows the danger of allowing even the smallest departure from the rule that a person who is dealing with another man's money ought not receive anything in the nature of a present or allowance without the full knowledge of the principal that he is so acting.'

Increasingly, contemporary commercial regulatory practice requires disclosure of commission payments within the financial services industry. For example, in Australia, section 1013D of the Corporations Act 2001 (Cth) requires product disclosure statements issued by financial services providers to disclose, among other things, any commission that may be paid as a result of the sale of the product. Further, the Australian government is currently considering passing legislation regarding the banning of the practice of the payment of commissions to financial advisers (Hawley 2010).

3.7 Defence to Bribery: Doctrine of Act of State

It has also been argued that the act of state doctrine may provide a defence to a charge of bribery. The doctrine originates from the case of *Underhill* v *Hernandez* (1897) 168 US 250, in which the United States Supreme Court decided (at 252) that 'every sovereign state is bound to respect the independence of every other sovereign state, that the courts of one country will not sit in judgment on the acts of the government of another done within its own territory.' The act of state doctrine accordingly prohibits American courts from declaring invalid the official act of a foreign country performed within its own territory. However, can the doctrine be used as a defence for bribery?

In *W S Kirkpatrick and Co v Environment Tectonics* (1990) 493 US 400, Mr Kirkpatrick was contracted by the Nigerian government to construct and equip an aero-medical centre. There was an agreement between the parties that Mr Kirkpatrick would pay a commission to two Panamanian entities in order to be awarded the contract. In turn, these two entities would give the money to Nigerian officials as a bribe. Mr Kirkpatrick tried to use the act of state doctrine as a defence. The court unanimously held that the act of state doctrine did not apply because the lawsuit did not require the court to declare invalid the official act of a foreign country. Additionally, the Nigerian government prohibited the payment and receipt of bribes.

Similarly, in the *United States* v *Giffen* (2004) 326 F Supp 2d 497, Mr Giffen bribed the president of Kazakhstan to facilitate six oil deals, including Mobil's purchase of a stake in Kazakhstan's Tengiz oilfield. Mr Giffen first sought to rely upon the act of state doctrine as a defence to a subpoena in a United States Grand Jury investigation (*In re Grand Jury Subpoena I* (2002) 218 F Supp 2d 544, 556). He argued that since the doctrine prevented the court from questioning the decisions of foreign governments, the documents held by him relevant to the bribery charges were not subject to legal proceedings because they were linked to the affairs of Kazakhstan. Judge Chin rejected this argument and noted that even if the documents originated from Kazakhstan, they were the records of an American company based in New York and, as such, they could be the subject of a subpoena (at 556).

In 2004, Mr Giffen again tried to raise the doctrine as a defence by claiming that he was an official of the Kazakhstan government. He claimed that he paid the bribes in his capacity as a foreign government official and, as such, the doctrine would apply to him and protect him from further legal action (*United States* v *Giffen* (2004) 326 F Supp 2d 497, 502–3). Judge Pauley rejected this claim and found that the status or title of Mr Giffen was not relevant to the application of the doctrine. The central question was whether the payment of a gift or bribe is legal under the laws of Kazakhstan. It is the payment of gift or bribe that may constitute an 'act of state'. Since bribes were forbidden in the foreign country, Mr Giffen's defence failed (at 503). Further, Judge Pauley noted that the bribes did not take place in Kazakhstan, but in the United States and Switzerland. As such, the Act of

State Doctrine did not apply (at 503). Accordingly, the Act of State Doctrine has not been successfully used as a defence in bribery cases.

Regardless, the availability and utility of the defence of the Act of State Doctrine was greatly diminished by paragraph 8 of the Commentaries which states that conduct will not constitute an offence under Article 1 where 'the advantage was permitted or required by the *written law or regulation* of the foreign public official's country including case law' (emphasis added).

As has been observed, international experience records an abundant range of culturally relative practices which has sought to characterise bribery as an economic good, an equivalent of tipping, an ordinary occurrence in the usual course of dealings, an activity which is analogous to the payment of a commission, and as a payment to be duly protected by the Act of State Doctrine. For good or evil, each of these defences to the provision of bribes has persisted. In counterpoint, member states have pursued a myriad of domestic and international responses to the problem of corruption and have developed cooperative mutual legal assistance schemes (such as the Convention of European Union on Mutual Assistance in Criminal Matters or the London Scheme on Extradition of Fugitive Offenders) to deal with shared legal challenges. In addition to these cooperative schemes, many States share a common legal heritage or language which has aided in the development of a common approach to the fight against corruption in transnational business transactions.

Part 4 The Road Forward – Prospects for Reform

Corruption amongst high officials is antithetical to the norm of the rule of law and its continued presence generally renders governments unresponsive to domestic or international pressures to reform (Bowen 2010: 170). Yet, notwithstanding the numerous domestic and international responses to corruption, the bribery of foreign officials has remained endemic in most OECD countries since the inception of the Convention in 1997. Looking forward in consideration of the prospects for reform, the Working Group has embarked upon a new introspective phase ('Phase 3') of mutual evaluation and peer pressure (OECD 2010e). (The implementation and enforcement of the Convention has been monitored through a peer-review monitoring system. Phase 1 had examined the anti-corruption legislation of each member State and Phase 2, which concluded in 2007, focused upon implementation and enforcement). With Phase 3, the Working Party, between 2009 and 2014, has resolved to renew its commitment to the practice of mutual evaluation of signatory States' application of the Convention as well as to the ongoing perseverance with the mission of raising awareness about the phenomenon of bribery and the commitment to remedying breaches with due haste, commitment and vigilance (OECD 2010e; Pieth and Lelieur 2007). Inclusive of this objective is the review of the implementation of the

2009 Recommendation of the Council for Further Combating Bribery of Foreign Public Officials in International Business Transactions.

Peer assessment and individual State perseverance, while laudable pursuits, have thus far yielded minimal returns in the fight against corruption. This lack of significant progress, when observed in light of the World Bank's estimate that the combined OECD economies comprise nearly two-thirds of the world's exports (World Bank 2010), further highlights the importance of the pursuit of meaningful reform in the OECD's anti-corruption instruments and measures (Transparency International 2010b). Given the transnational nature of the bribery of foreign officials, it is essential for any reform initiative to focus upon the coordination and cooperation of each of the international enforcement systems resident in each States Party to the Convention. While the Convention already sets as objectives the need for mutual legal assistance and jurisdictional cooperation and coordination between States Parties, these are the areas the OECD must substantially improve through reform if it is to make good its commitment to effectively combat corruption. To sever the Gordian knot of corruption in international business transactions, reform measures must address the inadequacies in legal frameworks as well as the enforcement systems.

4.1 Mutual Legal Assistance

The mechanisms requiring international cooperation and coordination, or mutual legal assistance, are addressed in Articles 4 and 9 of the Convention. Mutual legal assistance is vital to the investigation and prosecution of transnational bribery for the simple reason that the evidence required for a successful prosecution is likely to be drawn from a number of different jurisdictions – irrespective of whether the offence is committed in whole or in part in its territory (Article 4.1), or whether the offence has been committed abroad (Article 4.2). While Article 9 of the Convention requires States Parties to 'provide prompt and effective legal assistance to another Party for the purpose of criminal investigations and proceedings', further reform may increase the capacities for cooperation.

Pieth and Lelieur note that the great length of time it frequently takes to execute international rogatory commissions often undermines the effectiveness of an investigation of corruption – especially in light of domestic limitation statutes and the need to preserve the accused's right to a trial within a reasonable time, a vital limb of the rule of law. In recognition of these challenges, Articles 6 and 7 of the European Convention on Mutual Assistance in Criminal Matters permits the circumvention of diplomatic channels, the usual forum for international relations, by providing for the expedited execution of letters rogatory. Applying a similar procedural simplification to the Convention 'would have the dual merits of accelerating and reinforcing relations among prosecutors who … are not always interested solely in facilitating execution of international rogatory commissions' (Pieth and Lelieur 2007: 3). Further to this, the OECD should consider further reform consistent with Article 13 of the European Convention on Mutual

Assistance, as well as Article 49 of UNCAC, which empower investigators and prosecutors to transcend traditional jurisdictional hurdles by providing for the joint cooperation of inter-State law enforcement authorities.

The chair of the Working Party has further suggested that 'the effectiveness of mutual legal cooperation could certainly be enhanced through close working relations between the national investigation and prosecution authorities' (ibid.: 3). This suggestion is an echo of paragraphs 30–32 of the 1997 Commentaries that recommend further exploration of methods to improve the efficiency of mutual legal assistance within States Party to the Convention such as the waiver of extradition and custody procedures as well as the relaxation of the requirement of dual criminality between jurisdictions.

The challenges of securing mutual legal assistance treble where one or more of the States is not party to the Convention, as Article 9 will apply only to parties to the Convention. In particular, a significant deficiency in the structure of the Convention is attributable to the failure of Article 9 to provide for mutual legal assistance between signatory and non-signatory States. This omission is particularly concerning as mutual legal assistance does not cover developing countries where foreign bribery of public officials is rife. Furthermore, irrespective of whether mutual legal assistance is afforded, the lack of dual criminality may altogether preclude prosecution.

Instead, a request for mutual legal assistance must proceed in accordance with multilateral or bilateral conventions, where they exist. While the offence of bribery of foreign public officials is subject to a classification within Article 1 of the Convention, it may well be that the act of bribery may not be a crime in all other States and, as such, a request for mutual legal assistance may be refused (see Article 9.2). Further, despite Article 9.3 specifically excluding the authority of a State Party to 'decline to render mutual legal assistance for criminal matters within the scope of the Convention on the ground of bank secrecy', States not party to the Convention which maintain banking secrecy laws may decline any request for legal assistance on this ground. However, as illustrated by the case of Pakistan, where the embezzlement of state funds by the political elite is strife, the establishment of domestic bodies such as the National Accountability Bureau (NAB) can be effective in accessing those funds held in secret bank accounts (Hafiez 2003). However, the reliability of this commitment is legally limited by the lack of domestic legislation and shifting political will – especially in a Third World country challenged by poverty, illiteracy and a chronically corrupt political administration (OECD 2002).

Irrespective of the significant differences in legal systems and practices between jurisdictions, it is imperative that a common governing principle that provides for legal assistance between jurisdictions is developed. Unlike the Convention, Article 43.2 of UNCAC provides that 'the condition of dual criminality is deemed fulfilled irrespective of whether the laws of the requested State describe the offence in the same way as the requesting State.' Further, Article 46.8 states that a State may not decline a request for mutual legal assistance due to domestic banking secrecy laws.

Conversely, the equivalent requirements in the Convention apply only to States Parties. While ratification of UNCAC by all parties to the Convention could serve to circumvent the deficiencies in the scope of the Convention, this would only be of minimal consequence, as 31 of the 33 OECD countries have already done so – only Iceland and Korea are not signatories (as of September 2010). Transparency International (2003a; 2010b) have suggested that the cooperation between judicial authorities of States Parties and non-parties could be further improved were periodic meetings to be organised between law enforcement officials from non-party States and States party to the Convention (Transparency International 2003a).

4.2 Determination of Jurisdiction

Multiple States may compete for jurisdiction, disavow sufficient jurisdiction (arguing that another jurisdiction has a superior obligation to commence an investigation or prosecution), or may assert that jurisdiction should be defeated by a claim to a supervening 'national interest'.

Parallel investigations, at first glance, may best ensure that the investigations and eventual prosecutions of alleged corruption are thorough and reliable. However, this can only occur where the jurisdictions maintain close and constant contact and provide for ongoing mutual legal assistance during the investigative phase. Article 4.3 of the Convention provides that 'When more than one Party has jurisdiction over an alleged offence, [the Parties must] consult with a view to determining the most appropriate jurisdiction for prosecution.' That is, once the evidence is sufficiently compiled, steps should be taken to ensure that multiple and concurrent prosecutions in different States do not proceed. At the very least, once a definitive ruling is released, the other State(s) should immediately abandon its action so as to avoid violating the principle of double jeopardy (Pieth and Lelieur 2007). While Article 4.3 recommends that these initiatives be pursued, the logistical framework for achieving such cooperation is ad hoc, at best. Perhaps, with the Working Party taking leadership, a transnational network of prosecutors and investigators could be formed to establish a reciprocal system of information exchange. Moreover, the Working Party is ideally situated to consider the advocacy, monitoring and facilitation of transnational joint investigative teams to ensure that resources are efficiently and beneficially expended.

While all material and formal conditions to the request for mutual legal assistance may be satisfied, assistance may still be refused for political or other reasons. As was seen in *R (on the application of Corner House Research and others)* v *Director of the Serious Fraud Office* [2008] UKHL 60, the decision of the director of the Serious Fraud Office to discontinue a criminal investigation into the transnational payment of an alleged bribe by BAE Systems to facilitate an arms deal, perceived to necessary to safely balance the public interest and the rule of law, was upheld by the House of Lords. Although sections 108–110 of the Anti-terrorism, Crime and Security Act 2001 (UK), which gave effect to its obligations under the Convention, made it an offence triable in the United Kingdom for one of its citizens or companies to bribe a foreign public official, the 'national interest' rendered irrelevant the satisfaction of jurisdiction.

Where only one State Party has claim to jurisdiction, the refusal to investigate means the Convention will cease to play a role in combating corruption. However, the investigation may continue if a second State is also able to claim jurisdiction. Where this is possible, the second State may well benefit from a conferral of information from the first State. However, it is likely that such an exchange of information will be inhibited by the lack of political will or by an ongoing claim to national security on behalf of the first State. In these circumstances, the Working Group may be best situated to act as arbiter to determine the appropriate jurisdiction upon which the investigation may best proceed.

4.3 The Inadequacy of Dissuasive Sanctions for Foreign Bribery

Article 3 of the Convention permits a range of 'effective, proportionate and dissuasive' penalties to hold companies to account for foreign corruption. In particular, Article 3.3 states that the proceeds and value of the bribe should be subject to 'seizure and confiscation or that monetary sanctions of comparable effect' should be applicable. However, while the US FCPA provides for a penalty of up to US$2 million per violation per corporation and business entities and the Bribery Act 2010 (UK) provides for 'unlimited fines' for corporations that engage in the bribery of foreign officials, the sanctions employed across each of the jurisdictions of States Parties are insufficiently dissuasive.

In South Korea, for example, Transparency International has argued that the main inadequacy in the legal framework is that 'sanctions for foreign bribery remain inadequate, as the fines cannot exceed KRW20 million [about US$15,500], except where the proceeds are greater than KRW10 million' (2010b: 43). As a result, in South Korea's first case of corporate liability for its foreign bribery offence, the fine imposed amounted to less than 25 per cent of the total amount of the bribes (Moulette 2010; OECD 2007). As the Convention does not set appropriate limits to monetary sanctions, the Convention also provides measures to ensure that the bribe and its proceeds are subject, in the alternative, to seizure and confiscation. Relevantly, paragraph 21 of the Commentaries states that 'proceeds' of bribery, as used in Article 3.3 of the Convention, includes 'the profits or other benefits derived by the briber from the transaction or other improper advantage obtained or retained through bribery'. Paragraph 22 of the Commentaries provides that 'confiscation' includes forfeiture and extends to permanent deprivation of property. However, the Working Group has observed that there have been insufficient incidences of confiscation to enable an assessment of the effectiveness of confiscation as a dissuasive sanction (Moulette 2010). Regardless, it is clear that the imposition of relatively minor monetary sanctions alone is an ineffective remedy to corruption.

The Convention also encourages jurisdictions to impose additional civil and administrative penalties such as the placement of offending corporations under judicial supervision, the imposition of winding-up applications and the exclusion from entitlement to public benefits. In this vein, Patrick Moulette (2010) claims that the scope of the Bribery Act may include the possibility that a corporate conviction for foreign bribery could result in the permanent exclusion from all government (and European Union) contracts. Unfortunately, these aggressive sanctions are atypical. In deference to the notion of functional equivalence, the imposition of these additional sanctions has been neither universal nor consistent. In the case of South Korea, it could be argued that the payment of such a sanction offers little deterrence where the benefits of the bribe remain largely undisturbed. In the estimation of Transparency International, deficiencies in the securing of adequate sanctions occurs in 16 of the States Parties to the Convention (2010b).

4.4 Awareness of the Anti-corruption Regulatory Framework

One of the most significant obstacles to combating transnational corruption has been the low level of awareness of the existence and scope of the international anti-corruption regulatory framework. To gauge the level of awareness among legal professionals, the International Bar Association surveyed its membership in order to explore the level of awareness of the risks of corruption amongst the legal profession and to examine the role of bar associations, law societies and law firms in ensuring the legal profession is equipped to engage effectively in the international fight against corruption (International Bar Association 2010). The survey recorded that nearly 40 per cent of the respondents indicated that they were not aware of the existence of the Convention, nor any of the other anti-corruption instruments listed in Part 2.3. More extraordinary was the result that more than half of all respondents were not aware of instruments to which their jurisdiction was a party (ibid.: 16). In particular, despite the enforcement of the FCPA in the United States resulting in the highest number of prosecutions for bribery of foreign public officials in international business transactions, not one of the respondents from that country was aware of the FCPA itself (ibid.: 19). However, 38.5 per cent of respondents were aware of the Convention and 35.7 per cent were aware of UNCAC. Other significant findings of this April 2010 survey included:

- Nearly half of all respondents stated corruption was an issue in the legal profession in their own jurisdiction. The proportion was even higher – over 70 per cent – in the following regions: CIS, Africa, Latin America, the Baltic States and Eastern Europe.
- More than a fifth of respondents said they have or may have been approached to act as an agent or middleman in a transaction that could reasonably be suspected to involve international corruption. Nearly a third of respondents said a legal professional they know has been involved in international corruption offences.
- Nearly 30 per cent of respondents said they had lost business to corrupt law firms or individuals who have engaged in international bribery and corruption.

Interestingly, when these legal practitioners were surveyed as to whether they believed refusing to pay bribes would reduce the chances of securing foreign business in their country, respondents from emerging countries including Russia (60 per cent), India (62.5 per cent) and China (71.4 per cent) indicated: 'certainly', 'very likely', or 'likely'. Conversely, respondents from advanced economies tended to respond 'unlikely' or 'definitely not' to the same survey question: Sweden and Switzerland (100 per cent), Canada and Norway (95 per cent), and the United States and the United Kingdom (84 per cent) (ibid.: 12). Further to this, approximately 20 per cent of the respondents stated that they had been, or were likely to have been, approached to act as an agent in a transaction which could be reasonably suspected of involving corruption (ibid.: 13). However, a more revealing survey result was contained in the admission of 28 per cent of respondents in Africa and CIS countries that they believed more than half of the legal practitioners in their jurisdiction would knowingly engage in transactions that could be corrupt. This compares to only 1.5 per cent of respondents in the more developed regions of North America, the European Union and Australasia, who believed more than half of legal practitioners in their jurisdiction would engage in corrupt behaviour (ibid.: 14).

This lack of awareness of the international anti-corruption instruments among the legal profession reveals the scope of the failure of these measures to influence those best placed to combat corrupt practices in international business transactions. Nicola Bonucci has stated, 'The survey results are disappointing, so we need to do more to raise awareness of these instruments' (OECD 2010g). Similarly, Dmitri Vlassis, Head of the Corruption and Economic Crime Branch at United Nations Office on Drugs and Crime (UNODC), stated, 'UNODC supports the initiative because of its potential to equip the legal profession with the tools it needs to perform its crucial mission. We were taken aback by the lack of crucial knowledge among legal practitioners of key international instruments against corruption' (ibid.). In anticipation of the findings of the International Bar Association, Paragraph II (i) of the Further Recommendation had called for each States Party to examine its 'awareness-raising initiatives in the public and private sector for the purpose of preventing and detecting foreign bribery'.

From a reform perspective, the International Bar Association's survey reveals that legislation and regulation alone are insufficient anti-corruption measures. The deficiencies in awareness of the relevant international and domestic anti-corruption instruments and obligations must also be more prominently addressed by legal firms, law schools, bar associations and legal societies of each jurisdiction, with each doing more to increase awareness and understanding of the various domestic and international anti-corruption instruments and obligations. The International Bar Association, in cooperation with the OECD and UNODC, has released its *Anti-Corruption Strategy for the Legal Profession* which seeks both to initiate training sessions for the legal profession and to develop anti-corruption modules for the curricula law schools (International Bar Association 2010: 25). As with the OECD *Good Practice Guidance on International Controls, Ethics and Compliance* (see Part 2.3), this policy initiative must lead to development of further compliance programmes for the legal profession.

Part 5 Conclusion

Fourteen years after the advent of the Convention, 31 of the 38 States Parties are falling well short of their anti-corruption commitments. *In toto*, the collective States Parties have achieved only moderate success in their progressive goal of eradicating foreign bribery in international business transactions within their economic, legal and political jurisdictions. This lack of demonstrable success is attributable as much as to the flagging commitment to the ambitious goals of the Convention as it is to the considerable complexities of corruption. What is certain is that the collective response of States Parties, which has steadfastly ensured that the Convention has remained in jeopardy, is close to becoming a complete failure should existing support erode even further.

What appears certain is that the true extent of any deficiencies in the anti-bribery instrument are being masked by the lack of political will among the States which have ratified the Convention. While accountability and transparency have been described as antidotes to the perpetuation of corruption, corruption will continue to flourish within the OECD where the governmental and corporate ruling class fails to act to reduce corrupt practices within their respective jurisdictions (Rotberg 2009b: 341–58; Heineman 2009: 359–88). Indeed, a truer sense of the impact of the instrument could be more readily discerned were each member of the Convention to pursue their obligations in good faith and in consistency with the spirit of intendment that had welcomed the Convention at its birth. Given the transnational nature of the bribery of foreign officials, it is essential for any reform initiative to focus upon the Working Party's objective of enhancing the cooperative opportunities for mutual legal assistance and jurisdictional coordination between States Parties, as these are the areas the OECD must substantially improve through reform if it is to make good its commitment to effectively combat corruption.

The extraordinary lack of transnational awareness of the international anti-corruption instruments among the legal profession reveals the scope of the failure of these measures to influence those best placed to combat corrupt practices in international business transactions. The lack of political will demonstrates itself in the lack of adequate funding and staffing of the various enforcement mechanisms as does the more direct political obstruction of investigations and prosecutions. Should the Convention wish to address this lack of political will, it must be forcefully confronted not only by the Working Group and the OECD Secretary-General but within the leadership of every jurisdiction. Only with such an escalation can adequate pressure be placed upon laggard nations. Peer assessment and individual State perseverance, while laudable pursuits, have thus far yielded minimal returns in the fight against corruption. This lack of significant progress, when observed in light of the World Bank's estimate that the combined OECD economies comprise nearly two-thirds of the world's exports, further highlights the importance of the pursuit of meaningful commitment and meaningful reform in the OECD's anti-corruption instruments and measures. While the Convention advocates for the need for mutual legal assistance and jurisdictional cooperation and coordination between States Parties, to sever the Gordian knot of corruption in international business transactions, reform measures must address the inadequacies in political commitment and legal frameworks, as well as the enforcement systems.

References

Arnold, Thurman W. 1932. 'Law Enforcement – An Attempt at Social Discretion' *Yale Law Journal* 42: 1.

Asia Pacific Economic Cooperation 2007. 'APEC Code of Conduct for Business: Business Integrity and Transparency Principles for the Public Sector'. 6 September ,http://www.apec.org/apec/news___media/2007_media_releases/060907_aus_bizcodeconduct.html>.

—— 2007. 'APEC Tackles Corruption with Code of Conduct for Business'. News Release, 6 September ,http://www.apec.org/apec/news___media/2007_media_releases/060907_aus_bizcodeconduct.html>.

Association of Chartered Certified Accountants 2007. *Bribery and Corruption: The Impact on UK SMEs* <http://www.accaglobal.com/pubs/general/activities/library/small_business/sb_pubs/tech-ms-bac.pdf>.

Bayley, D.H. 1966. 'The Effects of Corruption in a Developing Nation', *Western Political Quarterly* 19(4): 719–32.

Beck, P. and M. Maher 1986. 'A Comparison of Bribery and Bidding in Thin Markets', *Economics Letters* 10: 1–5.

Bonucci, Nicola and Patrick Moulette 2008. 'The OECD Anti-Bribery Convention 10 Years On', *OECD Observer*, 264/265 (December 2007–January 2008).

Bowen, Rachel 2010. 'International imposition and Transmission of Democracy and the Rule of Law: Lessons from Central America', in Donald W . Jackson, Michael C. Tolley and Mary L. Volcansek (eds), *Globalizing Justice: Critical Perspectives on Transnational Law and the Cross-Border Migration of Legal Norms*, Albany: State University of New York Press.

Bushell, S. 2000. 'UK's Anti-Corruption Law- Filling in the Gaps', *International Business Lawyer* 28: 435–8.

Chatham House 2007. *World Duty Free v The Republic of Kenya: A Unique Precedent?* <http://www.chathamhouse.org.uk/files/9129_il280307.pdf>.

Cockcroft, Laurence 1996. 'Transnational Bribery: Is It Inevitable?', *Business Strategy Review* 7(3): 30–39.

Cragg, W. and W. Woof 2002. 'The US Foreign Corrupt Practices Act: A Study of its Effectiveness', *Business and Society Review* 107(1): 98–144.

Darrough, Masako N. 2010. 'The FCPA and the OECD Convention: Some Lessons from the US Experience', *Journal of Business Ethics* 93: 255–76.

Dix, Sarah and Emmanuel Pok 2009. 'Combating Corruption in Traditional Societies: Papua New Guinea', in Robert I. Rotberg (ed.), *Corruption, Global Security, and World Order*, Cambridge, MA: Brookings Institution Press.

Dobel, P.J. 1978. 'The Corruption of a State', *American Political Science Review* 72(3): 958–73.

Donaldson, T. and T. Dunfee 1999. 'When Ethics Travel: The Promise and Peril of Global Business Ethics', *California Management Review* 41(4): 45–63.

Driscoll, L.R. 1984–85. 'The Illegality of Bribery: Its Roots, Essence, and Universality', *Capital University Law Review* 14: 1–42.

Ellis, E.J. 2001. 'Globalisation, Corruption and Poverty Reduction' *Development Bulletin* 55: 26–9, July, Transparency-International-Australia and Blake Dawson Waldron <http://devnet.anu.edu.au/online%20versions%20 pdfs/55/8Ellis55.pdf>.

Friedrich, C.J. 1966. 'Political Pathology', *Political Quarterly* 37(1): 70–85.

Getz, K.A. 2006. 'The Effectiveness of Global Prohibition Regimes: Corruption and the Antibribery Convention', *Business & Society* 45(3): 7–30.

Gillespie, Kate and Gwenn Okruhlik 1991. 'The Political Dimensions of Corruption Cleanups: A Framework for Analysis' *Comparative Politics* 23: 77.

Grundman, V.R. 1980. 'The New Imperialism: The Extraterritorial Application of United States Law', *International Law* 14: 257.

Gyimah-Dempong, K. 2002. 'Corruption, Economic Growth and Income Inequality in Africa', *Economics of Governance* 3: 183–209.

Hafiez, Munir (Lt Gen.) 2003. 'Mutual Legal Assistance and Repatriation of Proceeds – Pakistan's Experience', in *Controlling Corruption in Asia and the Pacific*, Papers Presented at the 4th Regional Anti-Corruption Conference of the ADB/OECD Anti-Corruption Initiative for Asia and the Pacific, Organisation for Economic Co-operation and Development and Asia Development Bank, Kuala Lumpur, Malaysia, 3–5 December.

Hawley, Susan, 2000. 'Exporting Corruption: Privatisation, Multinationals and Bribery', *The Corner House*, June.

Heidenheimer, A.J. 1970. 'Introduction', in Heidenheimer (ed), *Political Corruption: Readings in Comparative Analysis*. New Brunswick, NJ: Transaction Books, pp. 2–28.

Heimann, Fritz F. 1994. 'Should Foreign Bribery be a Crime?', *Transparency International* (Berlin).

Heineman Jr, Ben W. 2009. 'The Role of the Multi-National Corporation', in Robert I. Rotberg (ed.), *Corruption, Global Security, and World Order*. Cambridge, MA: Brookings Institution Press.

Heller, Nathaniel 2009. 'Defining and Measuring Corruption: Where Have We Come From, Where Are We Now, and What Matters for the Future?', in Robert I. Rotberg (ed.), *Corruption, Global Security, and World Order.* Cambridge, MA: Brookings Institution Press.

Huntington, Samuel. 1968. 'Modernisation and Corruption', *Political Order in Changing Societies*. New Haven, CT: Yale University Press.

International Bar Association, Organisation for Economic Co-operation and Development and the United Nations Office on Drugs and Crime 2010. *Risks and Threats of Corruption and the Legal Profession: Anti-Corruption Strategy for the Legal Profession*, Survey.

Johnston, M. 1996. 'The Search for Definitions: The Vitality of Politics and the Issue of Corruption', *International Social Science Journal* 149: 321–35.

Joint Standing Committee on Treaties 1998. OECD Convention on Combating Bribery, Official Hansard Report, 9 March: 7 (Senator Amanda Vanstone).

Kaikati, J.G. et al. 2000. 'The Price of International Business Morality: Twenty Years Under the Foreign Corrupt Practices Act', *Journal of Business Ethics* 26(3): 213–22.

Kauffmann, D. 2004. 'Corruption, Governance and Security: Challenges for the Rich Countries and the World', in *The Global Competitiveness Report 2004/2005* <http://web.worldbank.org/WBSITE/EXTERNAL/WBI/EXTWBIGOVANTCOR/0,,contentMDK:20788416~pagePK:64168445~piPK:64168309~theSitePK:1740530,00.html>.

Kestenbaum, D. 2010. *Bribery in India: A Good Thing?* <http://www.npr.org/templates/story/story.php?storyId=126199094>.

Kurer, Oskar 2005. 'Corruption: An Alternative Approach to its Definition and Measurement', *Political Studies* 53: 222–39.

Leff, N. 1964. 'Economic Development through Bureaucratic Corruption', *American Behavioral Scientist* 8: 8–14.

Legvold, Robert 2009. 'Corruption, the Criminalized State, and Post-Soviet Transitions', in Robert I. Rotberg (ed.), *Corruption, Global Security, and World Order*. Cambridge, MA: Brookings Institution Press.

Li, H., L. Xin and H. Zou 2000. 'Corruption, Income Distribution and Growth', *Economics and Politics* 12: 51–181.

Lui, Francis. 1985. 'An Equilibrium Queuing Model of Bribery', *Journal of Political Economy* 93: 760-81.

Mauro, P. 2004. 'The Persistence of Corruption and Slow Economic Growth', *International Monetary Funds* 51(1): 1–18.

—— 1995. 'Corruption and Growth', *Quarterly Journal of Economics* 110: 681–712.

Mayer, A.E. 1994. 'Universal versus Islamic Human Rights: A Clash of Cultures or a Clash with a Construct?', *Michigan Journal of International Law* 15: 307.

Ministry of Justice 2011. 'The Bribery Act 2010 – Guidance about procedures which relevant commercial organisations can put into place to prevent persons associated with them from bribing (section 9 of the Bribery Act 2010)', Kenneth Clarke (Secretary of State for Justice), March <www.justice.gov.uk/guidance/bribery.htm>.

Moody-Stuart, G. 1994. 'The Costs of Grand Corruption', in Moody-Stuart (ed.), *Grand Corruption in Third World Development*, prepared for the UNDP Human Development Report (Berlin: Transparency International).

Moulette, Patrick 2010. Seminario Internacional: Responsabilidad Penal de las Personas Juridicas en Chile y Experiencias Comparadas, Panel 1: Modelos Comparados de Responsabilidad Penal de las Personas Juridicas, Speaking Notes, Santiago, 19–20 July.

Nicholls, Colin, Tim Daniel, Martin Polaine and John Hatchard 2006. *Corruption and Misuse of Public Office*. Oxford: Oxford University Press.

Nichols, Philip M. 1999. 'Outlawing Transnational Bribery Through the World Trade Organisation', Research Paper, Legal Studies Department, Reference 96-9-031 <http://knowledge.wharton.upenn.edu/paper.cfm?paperID=280>.

—— 1997. 'Outlawing Transnational Bribery Through the World Trade Organisation', *Law and Policy in International Business* 28: 305–11.

Nye, J.S. 1967. 'Corruption and Political Development: A Cost Benefit Analysis', *American Political Science Review* 61(2): 417–27.

OECD 2011a. 'Press Release – TI Calls on OECD Leaders to Reinvigorate Fight Against Corruption: New Report Shows Progress on Enforcement of OECD Anti-Bribery Corruption has Stalled' (24 May) <http://www.transparency.org/news_room/latest_news/press_releases/2011/2011_05_24_oecd_progress_report>.

—— 2011b. 'Working Group on Bribery: 2010 Data on Enforcement of the Anti-Bribery Convention' (April) <http://www.oecd.org/dataoecd/47/39/47637707.pdf>.

—— 2010a. 'Anti-Corruption: OECD Welcomes Slovak Move to Make Firms Liable for Foreign Bribery' <http://www.oecd.org/document/33/0,3343,en_2649_34855_45521313_1_1_1_37447,00.html>.

—— 2010b. 'Fighting Foreign Bribery: An Initiative to Raise Awareness' <http://www.oecd.org/dataoecd/52/12/45791299.pdf>.

—— 2010c. 'OECD Working Group on Bribery Data on Enforcement of the Anti-Bribery Convention, June 2010' <http://www.oecd.org/dataoecd/11/15/45450341.pdf>.

—— 2010d. 'Accession: Estonia, Israel and Slovenia invited to join OECD' <http://www.oecd.org/document/57/0,3343,en_2649_201185_45159737_1_1_1_1,00.html>.

—— 2010e. 'Phase 3 Country Monitoring of the OECD Anti-Bribery Convention' <http://www.oecd.org/document/31/0,3343,en_2649_34859_44684959_1_1_1_1,00.html>.

—— 2010f. 'Corruption: OECD Working Group on Bribery Recognised as Anti-Corruption Leader' <http://www.oecd.org/documentprint/0,344,en_2649_34855_45997563_1_1_1_37447.html>.

—— 2010g. 'Corruption: New Survey of Legal Professionals on Awareness and Impact of Bribery and Corruption' <http://www.oecd.org/documentprint/0,344,en_2649_34855_46137917_1_1_1_1,00.html>.

—— 2009. 'Recommendation of the Council on Tax Measures for Further Combating Bribery of Foreign Public Officials in International Business Transactions' <http://www.oecd.org/dataoecd/18/15/43188874.pdf>.

—— 2007. 'OECD Working Group on Bribery, Phase 2 Follow-up Report, 2 March 2007' <www.oecd.org/dataoecd/15/45/38239569.pdf>.

—— 2002. 'Documentation of the National Anti-Corruption Strategy' <www1.oecd.org/_daf/asiacom/countries/Pakistan>.

—— 1997. 'OECD Convention on Combating Bribery of Foreign Public Officials in International Business Transaction', adopted by the Negotiating Conference on 21 November <http://www.oecd.org>.

Orentlicher, D.F. and T.A. Gelatt 1993. 'Public Law, Private Actors: The Impact of Human Rights on Business Investors in China', *Journal of International Law and Business* 14: 66.

Overington, Caroline 2007. *Kickback: Inside the Australian Wheat Board Scandal*, Sydney: Allen & Unwin.

Perell, P. 1999–2000. 'Remedies for the Victims of a Bribe', *Advocates Quarterly* 22: 198–216.

Pieth, Mark 1999. 'Making the OECD Initiative Work', presented at the 9th International Anti-Corruption Conference, Durban, South Africa, October.

—— and Juliette Lelieur 2007. 'Strengthening International Coordination and Cooperation', Expert Meeting of the OECD Anti-Bribery Convention: The Road Ahead, Rome, 21 November.

——, Lucinda A. Low and Peter J. Cullen (eds) 2007. *The OECD Convention on Bribery: A Commentary*. Cambridge: Cambridge University Press.

Plato 360 BC, 2008 edn. *Crito*, translated by Benjamin Jowett, Forgotten Books.

Rose-Ackerman, S. 1999. *Corruption and Government: Causes, Consequences and Reform*. Cambridge: Cambridge University Press.

—— 1978. *Corruption: A Study in Political Economy*. New York: Academic Press.

Rotberg, Robert I. 2009a. 'How Corruption Compromises World Peace and Stability', in Rotberg (ed.), *Corruption, Global Security, and World Order*. Cambridge, MA: Brookings Institution Press.

—— 2009b. 'Leadership Alters Corrupt Behaviour', in Rotberg (ed.), *Corruption, Global Security, and World Order*. Cambridge, MA: Brookings Institution Press.

Salbu, Steven R. 2000. 'A Delicate Balance: Legislation, Institutional Change and Transnational Bribery', *Cornell International Law Journal* 13: 657, 664.

Sanyal, R. 2005. 'Determinants of Bribery in International Business: the Culture and Economic Factors', *Journal of Business Ethics* 59: 139–45.

Sashs, J. and A. Warner 1997. 'Sources of Slow Growth in African Economies', *Journal of African Economics* 6: 335–76.

Scott, J.C. 1972. *Comparative Political Corruption*. Englewood Cliffs, NJ: Prentice Hall.

Shleifer, A. and R. Vishny 1993. 'Corruption', *Quarterly Journal of Economics* 108: 599–617.

Society for Advanced Legal Studies Anti-Corruption Working Group 2000. 'Banking on Corruption: The Legal Responsibilities of Those Who Handle the Proceeds of Corruption'. London: Society of Advanced Legal Studies.

Smith, Daniel Jordan 2009. 'The Paradoxes of Popular Participation in Corruption', in Robert I. Rotberg (ed.), *Corruption, Global Security, and World Order*. Cambridge, MA: Brookings Institution Press.

Steidlmeier, P. 1999. 'Gift Giving, Bribery and Corruption: Ethical Management of Business Relationships in China', *Journal of Business Ethics* 20: 121–32.

Transparency International 2010a. 'FAQs on Corruption' <http://www.transparency.org/news_room/faq/corruption_faq#faqcorr1>.

—— 2010b. 'Progress Report 2010: Enforcement of the OECD Convention on Combating Bribery of Foreign Public Officials in International Business Transactions' <http://www.transparency.org/publications/publications/conventions/oecd_report_2010>.

—— 2003a. 'Overcoming Obstacles to Enforcement of the OECD Convention on Combating Bribery of Foreign Public Officials', Report on Paris Meeting of 2–3 October <http://www.transparency.org/global_priorities/international_conventions/readings_conventions>.

—— 2003b. 'The Transparency International Global Corruption Barometer: A 2002 Pilot Survey of International Attitudes, Expectations and Priorities on Corruption' <http://www.transparency.org/surveys/barometer>.

—— 2002. 'Corruption Perceptions Index 2002' <http://www.transparency.org/pressreleases_archive/2002/2002.08.28.cpi.en.html>.

—— 2002. 'Transparency International Bribe Payers Index 2002' <http://transparency.org/cpi/2002/bpi2002.en.html>.

—— 2000. 'Transparency International Source Book 2000' <http://www.transparency.org/sourcebook>.

Udoidem, I. 1987. 'Tips in Business Transaction: A Moral Issue', *Journal of Business Ethics* 6: 613–18.

Underkuffler, Laura S. 2009. 'Defining Corruption: Implications for Action', in Robert I. Rotberg (ed.), *Corruption, Global Security, and World Order*. Cambridge, MA: Brookings Institution Press.

United Nations 2003. *United Nations Convention Against Corruption*, Doc. A/58/422, 31 October <http://www.unodc.org/unodc/en/treaties/CAC/signatories.html>.

U4 Anti-Corruption Resource Centre 2010. 'UNCAC in a Nutshell: A Quick Guide to the United Nations Convention Against Corruption for Embassy and Donor Agency Staff', *U4 Brief*, September: 6 <www.cmi.no/publications/file/3769-uncac-in-a-nutshell.pdf>.

von Alemann, Urlich 2004. 'The Unknown Depths of Political Theory: The Case for a Multidimensional Concept of Corruption', *Crime, Law & Social Change* 42: 25–34.

Wei, Shang-Jin 2001. 'Is Fighting Corruption the IMF's Business?', *Brookings Policy Brief*, April, 79.

—— 2000. 'How Taxing is Corruption on International Investors?' *Review of Economics and Statistics* 82: 1–11.

Weismann, Miriam F. 2009. 'The Foreign Corrupt Practices Act: The Failure of the Self-Regulatory Model of Corporate Governance in the Global Business Environment', *Journal of Business Ethics* 88(4): 615-661.

Weiss, David C. 2009. 'The Foreign Corrupt Practices Act, SEC Disgorgement of Profits, and the Evolving International Bribery Regime: Weighing Proportionality, Retribution, and Deterrence', *Michigan Journal of International Law* 30: 471–514.

Wigmore, J.H. 1992. *A Panorama of the World's Legal Systems – Volume 1*. Florida: Wm. W. Gaunt and Sons, Inc.

WikiLeaks 2010. 'Subject: Ambassador's Introductory Call on Opposition Leader Kim Beazley', Reference ID 06Canberra1366, Created 9/8/2000, Embassy Canberra <http://images.theage.com.au/file/2010/12/15/2096934/Cables.htm>.

Wilton, G.W. 1906–07. 'The Prevention of Corruption Act, 1906', *Juridical Review* 18: 370–85.

Wolf, Sebastian 2010. 'Assessing Eastern Europe's anti-corruption performance: views from the Council of Europe, OECD, and Transparency International', *Global Crime* 11(2): 99–121.

World Bank 2010. 'High Income: OECD'. Washington, DC: World Bank <http://data.worldbank.org/income-level/OEC>.

—— 2002. 'Kazakhstan: Governance and Service Delivery – A Diagnostic Report', Poverty Reduction and Economic Management Unit (ECSPE), Europe and Central Asia Region, Washington, DC: World Bank.

—— 2002. *Voices of the Firms 2000: Investment Climate and Governance Findings of the World Business Environment Survey*. Washington, DC: World Bank.

—— 2000. *Anticorruption in Transition: A Contribution to the Policy Debate*. Washington, DC: World Bank.

Chapter 6
Human Rights and International Environmental Governance

Laura Horn

Introduction

The quality of the Earth's environment is continuing to deteriorate and this global degradation indicates that the present system of international environmental governance is failing to protect the environment for present and future generations. This failure has led to debate about how the system of global environmental governance could be improved in order to develop more effective institutions and implementation mechanisms to promote environmental protection (Mori 2004: 157). Global governance can be defined as follows: 'Global governance is the multi-layered system of rules, practices, procedures, customs, values and activities through which influence is exercised and resources deployed to address broad issues and achieve objectives at a level beyond a single state or region' (Sanson 2008: 12).

Unfortunately, the time available to resolve major environmental threats, including climate change and loss of biological diversity, is rapidly running out so that some environmental harm may be irreversible if changes do not occur soon. The Millennium Ecosystem Assessment report (2005: 1) indicates that there has been an irreversible loss of biological diversity on the planet because of the changes humans have made to ecosystems to meet the demands of an increasing human population. According to the Secretariat of the Convention on Biological Diversity in a recent report, *Global Biodiversity Outlook 3*:

> The loss of biodiversity is an issue of profound concern for its own sake. Biodiversity also underpins the functioning of ecosystems which provide a wide range of services to human societies. Its continued loss, therefore, has major implications for current and future human well-being. (2010: 9)

The first section of this chapter considers the failure of the international legal system to provide adequate mechanisms for global environmental governance. Secondly, there is a discussion about some proposals for change to environmental governance that could flow from existing institutions and developments. Third, the development of a specialist environmental tribunal to resolve environmental disputes is discussed as a proposed change to environmental governance. The subsequent section covers the possible development of an international human right to a healthy environment, to provide an interim focus for changes to global environmental governance.

There is potential for more major modifications to governance to be considered such as the establishment of a global environmental organisation (GEO) that could be negotiated by the international community in the future. The key argument in this chapter is that a new global environmental institution could operate in the interests of the common concern of humankind to ensure that the global environment is protected. This argument is founded upon the view that international environmental governance should be in a process of transformation through innovation beyond traditional models of governance to consider how authority may be exercised in the broader interest of the international community to protect the global environment. This perspective of innovative governance questions the present reliance upon states to develop effective international institutions to deal with global environmental protection and raises the possibility of a new global environmental organisation that has a wider representation which includes non-state actors (Burris et al. 2008: 21).

In the final part of this chapter, the potential development of this GEO is discussed. However, the dilemma is that this change could take some time to occur and the threat to the environment is becoming critical. Thus it is arguable that interim changes such as the development of a human right to a healthy environment could assist to protect the global environment in the intervening period of time.

Current Deficiencies in Global Environmental Governance

There have been many attempts to deal with global environmental problems through international negotiations that have resulted in an increasing number of international conventions and agreements covering a range of environmental issues. Over three hundred global and regional treaties have been negotiated on environmental problems over the last three decades (French 2009: 259). This gives rise to many inconsistencies because of the large number of treaties that have been negotiated. Many of the provisions on environmental issues may be covered in global agreements as well as in other regional agreements and there may be discrepancies between them, or the standards in the agreements may differ. Another problem is the potential for conflict between provisions in international environmental conventions and agreements with other areas of international law such as trade (ibid.). So ascertaining the duties and responsibilities of a particular state on questions of international environmental law becomes difficult in circumstances where the issue may be affected by bilateral, regional and international agreements.

Clearly, the reliance by the international community on numerous international conventions on environmental issues has not effectively resolved environmental problems. In part, the difficulty is a failure to ensure that these agreements are rationalised. Another reason for this predicament is that some states may refuse to ratify international conventions on environmental protection, leading to a lack of international cooperation to resolve global environmental problems. Even if states agree to ratify multilateral conventions concerning the protection of the environment, the wording of some of the articles in these conventions may be unclear. The lack of specific language may result in ambiguous or indefinite provisions which do not impose any binding legal obligations on states. There is also a tendency for state consensus to be based upon the lowest standards of environmental protection in order to encourage more states to agree to the terms of the treaty and to ratify it. Unfortunately, due to these lower standards, the actual protection of the environment is sacrificed and the agreement may prove inadequate to prevent deteriorating environmental conditions.

In the circumstances where the provisions in treaties and conventions are not legally binding, they may provide some evidence of international customary law if there is *opinio juris* (the recognition by states that the conduct in question constitutes a legal obligation) and adherence to the proposition by state practice over time. However, rules of international customary law are difficult to distinguish and may not bind all states if the rule is considered regional rather than global, or in the circumstances where some states object to the development of the new customary rules.

The failure of current system of international law to develop effective environmental standards and enforceable measures that protect the environment has led to renewed emphasis on alternatives to the present system. Overall, progress to prevent further environmental deterioration has been slow and in addition to numerous environmental international agreements, there are also a number of different institutions that can add to the complexity of environmental governance at an international level. Some of these institutions include the following: United Nations Environment Programme (UNEP), other UN agencies such as the World Bank and UNESCO, intergovernmental organisations such as the International Whaling Commission, the International Maritime Organisation, regional joint commissions, and the Conference of the Parties (COPs) and Secretariats of multilateral environmental conventions.

The process of reform to global governance is likely to be gradual as the consensus of states is required to approve key changes to the international legal system before they can take place. Reform to the system of global governance is also hampered by the tendency for states to rely upon the traditional international law concept of sovereignty to maintain jurisdiction and control over activities within their territorial area. This reliance upon the traditional concept of sovereignty is outdated and, due to the serious environmental threats facing the international community, it is likely that modifications to international global governance will be implemented in the future. Clear signs that have indicated that the concept of sovereignty should not apply to global environmental problems are the development of new international environmental law concepts such as the common concern of humankind (CCH).[1] This concept is applied to areas such as climate change and biological diversity in the preambles of the United Nations Framework Convention on Climate Change (FCCC) and the United Nations Convention on Biological Diversity.

The CCH operates in these conventions to erode the concept of sovereignty by emphasising the need for the priority of protection for the environment for the benefit of the international community. So the CCH draws the source of the concern (even if the problem is within a state's jurisdiction and arguably within its exclusive sovereignty) to the attention of the international community (Horn 2001: 127). This concept implies that it is the duty of the international community to have concern for the global environment and that action is necessary on the part of states to act both jointly and individually to address the concern (Draft Covenant: 36).[2] The common concern of humankind functions as a concept encouraging states to take overriding responsibility for environmental issues because it emphasises the interest of states in global resources and their common responsibility to seek to achieve the sustainable development of these resources (Birnie et al. 2009: 130). However, the ambit of this concept remains unclear and should be further developed in international environmental agreements. Some of the proposals for change to governance are considered in the following sections.

Changes to International Environmental Governance in the Short Term

Global governance for the protection of the environment could be reformed in the near future in four key ways that are elaborated below. First, the role of key institutions such as UNEP and CSD could be improved. Secondly, non-governmental organisations (NGOs) could be permitted to participate in litigation concerning international environmental disputes and to have their views recognised by international environmental organisations. Third, the introduction of appropriate compliance and enforcement procedures could help to ensure that more effective action is taken by states to adhere to environmental conventions and treaties. Fourth, a specialist environmental tribunal should be established at the international level to resolve international environmental disputes.

Some proposals for reform to existing institutions include the strengthening of UNEP and changes to the operation of the UN Commission on Sustainable Development (CSD). However, neither of these reforms is likely to be adequate to achieve the expected widespread social changes needed to bring about a reversal

1 The common concern of humankind is the gender-neutral version of the common concern of mankind referred to in United Nations Framework Convention on Climate Change (FCCC) and the United Nations Convention on Biological Diversity.

2 The Draft International Covenant on Environment and Development Article 3 indicates that 'The global environment is the common concern of humanity'; however, this covenant is only a draft document and there is no present prospect of it becoming a treaty.

of the environmental degradation that is occurring. These two institutions and the proposals for change are considered in the following sections.

UNEP

UNEP is a United Nations (UN) programme which deals with environmental concerns and has encouraged the development of multilateral environmental agreements and promoted the implementation of environmental treaties as well as guidelines and standards. This organisation has been granted crucial environmental governance roles and has been reasonably successful at developing multilateral environmental agreements and coordinating treaty secretariats. However, the overall effectiveness of UNEP has been criticised because it is incapable of performing the large number of the functions that have been assigned to it, and as a result of these concerns, there have been proposals to reform this organisation. (Haas et al. 2004: 271).

Two groups have been organised to improve governance at UNEP: the Environment Management Group (EMG) and the Global Ministerial Environment Forum (GMEF). UNEP established the EMG as a UN coordination body; its membership includes the secretariats of multilateral environmental agreements and the aim of the EMG is to improve cooperation between agencies in international environmental and human settlement areas.[3] The second group, the GMEF, was established after the UN Task Force on Environment and Human Settlements created an annual forum where the members could review policy issues concerning the environment. The first session was held in 2000 as a special session of the UNEP Governing Council (Charnovitz 2005: 107). The participation of national environment ministers at forums can promote discussion and cooperative action; however, there are too many members for this forum to be a viable governing council (ibid.) and as this is a new forum, it is experimental and relatively untested.

There is some concern about whether these measures introduced by UNEP to improve global environmental governance are adequate to support the many complex environmental situations that occur globally, particularly in areas such as sustainable development, climate change and loss of biological diversity. The principal decision makers in UNEP are states; they also constitute the chief members of the global environmental institutions including the COPs and of key organisations such as the International Whaling Organization (French 2009: 261). As the influence of states is very powerful in UNEP, there are less likely to be major reforms such as those necessary to promote a more democratic structure and to make provision for greater funding support. UNEP could be further strengthened through changes to include broader membership of its Governing Council (other than states) and also through reforms aimed at increasing its status to that of a UN agency rather than a programme (ibid.: 266).

---

3 See <http://www.unemg.org>.

Thus UNEP continues to be a rather weak organisation in comparison to more dynamic organisations that deal with economic development, such as the IMF, the World Bank and the World Trade Organization (WTO). There are proposals that UNEP could be made a UN-specialised agency similar to the WTO (Birnie et al. 2009: 69), or that it could form part of a strong world or global environment organisation (Biermann 2000: 22). The advantages of establishing a more powerful body are that it could rationalise the system of international environmental governance and provide a clear strategy for sustainable development. A larger organisation could improve capacity building in developing countries and establish international environmental standards (ibid.). The deficiencies in the current system of international environmental governance have led to proposals that a global environmental organisation be established and these suggestions will be discussed at the end of this chapter. Another option that has been canvassed is to strengthen the role of the CSD to enable it to carry out more effective monitoring and supervision of sustainable development initiatives.

The Commission on Sustainable Development (CSD)

After the United Nations Conference on Environment and Development (UNCED), the CSD was established to implement the provisions in the international agreement called Agenda 21: Programme of Action for Sustainable Development (Agenda 21). This programme for action is a non-binding agreement that promotes the involvement of all social groups as crucial for the implementation of the objectives of sustainable development.

Sustainable development is difficult to implement because it is framed as an international objective, and many different elements of this goal are elaborated in Agenda 21. The governance and international cooperation involved in this programme have become very complex. The primary responsibility falls on the national governments of states to develop priorities for action on sustainable development, and guidance at the international level is also essential. The overall system of international governance for sustainable development can be summarised as including international organisations such as the United Nations General Assembly, United Nations Economic and Social Council (ECOSOC) and the CSD, amongst others. There are also regional organisations such as UN regional commissions and national and local organisations. The principal UN organisation responsible for international cooperation in economic and social concerns is ECOSOC. This organisation coordinates the UN system, supervises subsidiary bodies and also has responsibility for integrating UN policies and programmes promoting sustainable development.

Future Role of the CSD

The CSD was established by the General Assembly in 1992 as a subsidiary body of ECOSOC and its functions were set out in Agenda 21 and General Assembly Resolution 47/191. This Commission, made up of 53 member states (for a three-year term), assesses the implementation of Agenda 21 and the Declaration of the United Nations Conference on Environment and Development (Rio Declaration) and surveys the developments following the Johannesburg *Plan of Implementation*. The Division for Sustainable Development in ECOSOC indicates that the role of the CSD as a high-level forum on sustainable development focuses on the following activities:

- To review the progress of the objectives in Agenda 21 and the Rio Declaration
- To continue to develop policy guidelines after the *Plan of Implementation*
- To promote sustainable development partnerships.

The Johannesburg World Summit on Sustainable Development *Plan of Implementation* (WSSD *POI* para. 145) acknowledges that the CSD should continue as the high-level forum for discussion of the questions related to the integration of the dimensions of sustainable development and this plan also indicated that:

> … the Commission needs to be strengthened, taking into account the role of relevant institutions and organizations. An enhanced role of the Commission should include reviewing and monitoring progress in the implementation of Agenda 21 and fostering coherence of implementation, initiatives and partnerships.

This call for the CSD to be strengthened also noted that the CSD should 'review and evaluate progress and promote further implementation of Agenda 21' (WSSD *POI* para 147(a)). So the powers and functions of the CSD could be expanded, enabling it to focus on encouraging action on sustainable development. Clearly, the present broad responsibilities of the CSD are inadequate for effective implementation of the sustainable development objectives. Birnie, Boyle and Redgwell (2009: 125) suggest that the CSD could play a more significant role in the future:

> Although the Commission on Sustainable Development has a role in assessing national reports on implementation of Agenda 21, and in determining future policy, at present it is not the job of the Commission to answer the question whether any particular development is or is not sustainable, or to hold governments to account, although such a role may in time evolve.

This problem could be addressed by allocating more resources and improved functions to the CSD so that it can take an active role to ensure the implementation of action on sustainable development. Given that one of the key objectives is that natural resources be maintained for the use of both present and future generations, more emphasis could be paid to the question as to whether in fact, states are managing effective sustainable development policies and programmes.

Incentives to Encourage Compliance

The aim of compliance procedures is to motivate states to act in accordance with the provisions in a multilateral environmental convention that they have ratified. These procedures may also be applied to 'soft law', or non-binding legal agreements such as the Rio Declaration and Agenda 21. Neither of the latter two agreements has a compliance scheme; however, there are a number of provisions guiding the implementation in Agenda 21. Even though these sustainable development agreements do not set out binding legal obligations for states, there is an underlying assumption by the international community that in the circumstances where states opt to enter these international agreements, they do intend to observe the commitments that they have made. The introduction of compliance schemes could support these general propositions. Agenda 21 (para 39.8(a)) provides that states should consider implementation mechanisms and establish reporting systems in order to facilitate action on international legal agreements. Thus, states should adopt appropriate legislation to carry out action plans on sustainable development within their own jurisdictions at both national and local levels.

Action could also be taken at the international level to improve compliance with sustainable development agreements. Some procedures such as reporting, monitoring and inspection are useful when considering methods of compliance for these agreements. Monitoring of the environmental problem has an important role to play in soft-law regimes and can encourage state compliance with provisions in non-binding agreements which may later on develop into international customary law. Generally, the adoption of monitoring procedures leads to the establishment of a reporting agency in each national government that stirs up public consciousness about the dangers involved with the environmental hazard. The monitoring agency communicates with other agencies and identifies any problems that a state may encounter when trying to fulfil its commitments. So, more formal requirements for monitoring, information gathering and supervision of the activities of states who are engaging in sustainable development programmes would assist with the achievement of this objective. However, not all states have a good reporting record and in order to protect the environment, the reporting needs to be conducted in a careful and verifiable way so that adequate procedures and methods of auditing can be developed (Birnie et al. 2009: 243).

Monitoring

One option is to strengthen the monitoring role of the CSD and require all states to report annually on their action to achieve sustainable development. The CSD could be granted additional powers and funding so that it can establish an improved monitoring and compliance system together with inspection services in appropriate circumstances. This would encourage states that are failing to take effective action on sustainable development to comply. Experts from the CSD could provide assistance to these states with the implementation of sustainable development action plans and additional support could be available for developing countries to aid their efforts to undertake action on sustainable development.

The rationale for adopting compliance procedures is that it is preferable to help countries to adhere to their agreements rather than apply punishment for non-compliance. This is particularly relevant to international environmental problems because a failure to comply may result in irreversible environmental harm; it is advantageous to encourage preventative action rather than attempt to remedy environmental damage after it has occurred. Another approach is to offer constructive incentives to increase the likelihood of compliance by governments, industry, business organisations and individuals. These incentives could be in the form of education, which could range from diplomatic conversations amongst government representatives or other direct approaches to those responsible for the environmental harm or the development of seminars to inform industry (Mitchell 1996: 14). These approaches help to prevent non-compliance due to lack of information about environmental concerns. A positive incentive is to provide financial aid (or other assistance) and this may be additional to the assistance provided to developing countries. Other pressures may be placed on governments or businesses through the operation of the media and NGOs who can act as a 'form of international public conscience' (Birnie et al. 2009: 636) and publicise the failure to take effective environmental action. International media attention and disapproval of an activity carried out by a government that may harm the environment could lead to other action such as trade embargoes with that state or to a boycott of products.

Review and Compliance

Arguably, the role and functions of the CSD should be reconsidered and amendments made to the powers of this institution in order to ensure it can adequately protect the sustainability of natural resources. The performance of the CSD could be improved by granting it powers to review the actions of individual countries and their efforts to achieve sustainability. The CSD could have additional functions, including the responsibility for the evaluation of the adequacy of environmental treaties and international agreements. These reviews would assist compliance and could be based upon appropriate monitoring, peer review and inspections of the activities in order to ensure effective action was being undertaken. Countries could exchange information about activities that have been successful and methods of improving action in the future. It may be possible to extend the functions of the CSD further by establishing a compliance committee as occurred under the Convention on Access to Information, Public Participation in Decision Making and Access to Justice in Environmental Matters where members of the public and NGOs have the opportunity to take complaints to the non-compliance committee (article 15). The overall emphasis would be on preventative action to encourage compliance with implementation of sustainable development objectives. Thus action to expand the monitoring and supervision functions and to increase funding for the CSD could improve international environmental governance on sustainable development. NGOs may also play a role in global environmental governance and increasingly, the value of the views of environmental NGOs as representatives of civil society are beginning to be appreciated in some international environmental institutions.

The Role of NGOs

There is a movement towards the increased engagement of the UN with civil society through organisations such as NGOs that can represent the collective views of groups of individuals. The role of NGOs is important in international governance as part of the global development of civil society because these organisations are capable of representing international common concern for the environment. If granted standing in an international forum, they may be able to take legal action at an international level to challenge the powers of states and corporations when they are engaged in activities that pollute or degrade the environment. The other advantage of including NGOs in the policy development of global environmental governance is that they encourage business organisations and states to be more accountable and transparent (Mori 2004: 158). These two roles are considered below.

First, environmental NGOs can play an important role in public interest advocacy by bringing or supporting litigation on environmental issues if they have standing in a tribunal with international jurisdiction. Some environmental NGOs may also act as guardians on behalf of future generations by representing their interests in litigation or arbitration proceedings. The influence of NGOs as participants in global governance has substantially increased over the past few decades so that civil society can now be regarded as 'the third arm of global governance, alongside governments and IGOs' (intergovernmental organisations) (Sanson 2008: 121).

The problem is that there is a lack of accountability and transparency guidelines for these organizations (ibid.: 153). Indeed, the views of NGOs may not necessarily reflect those of concern for good global environmental governance and there should be a process to determine the accountability and veracity of their views, particularly in situations where they are considered to be representing the interests of present and future generations. Arguably, NGOs should adopt appropriate procedures and codes of conduct that comply with good governance principles before these organisations are chosen to make representations to international environmental organisations.

There is some difference between the attitudes of Northern NGOs from those of Southern NGOs on environmental matters and this would have to be taken into account (French 2009: 9). If the NGOs are carefully selected, their participation could be beneficial because of their expertise, the independence of their views and because they could also represent the views of other stakeholders in the international community, including those of future generations.

The second role carried out by NGOs is through participation at international conferences and contributions to environmental policy discussions. In some cases, NGOs with experience and concern for environmental issues have acted as observers at negotiations concerning environmental conventions. The involvement by NGOs in international environmental conferences may also be considered a necessary part of public participation in environmental decision making and there is support for the consideration of the views of NGOs in ECOSOC. In fact, Article 71 of the Charter of the United Nations provides for the involvement of NGOs as follows:

> The Economic and Social Council may make suitable arrangements for consultation with non-governmental organisations which are concerned with matters within its competence. Such arrangements may be made with international organisations and where appropriate, with national organisations after consultation with the Member of the United Nations concerned.

It was evident through the increased participation of NGOs at international conferences during the 1990s that ECOSOC has granted consultative status to NGOs. However, NGOs have tried to expand their role as negotiators in order to gain recognised consultative rights in the General Assembly and Security Council. These attempts have not been very successful due to some state governments' concern that an increased role for NGOs could impinge on state sovereignty and undermine the role of the state in international decision making. Other states have simply objected to any increase of NGO activity (Mori 2004: 160). These views prevent changes to governance in international environmental organisations and deter the development of positive action to prevent irreversible damage to the environment, as in the case of the threat of climate change. There should be continued progress towards ensuring adequate representation of the views of NGOs (that have demonstrated good governance) in international environmental organisations. These NGOs can draw attention to the interests of the international community and the common concern of humankind in the global protection of the environment. Two examples of involvement of NGOs in international environmental governance occur in the operations of the CSD and in the operation of the FCCC. These two examples will be considered in the following sections.

The CSD – NGO involvement

The role of NGOs is also considered vital to implement participatory democracy and, in fact, Agenda 21 points out that they should be recognised as partners in the implementation of Agenda 21 (Agenda 21 1992: 27.1). Paragraph 27.3 of Agenda 21 indicates that non-governmental organisations:

> … possess well-established and diverse experience, expertise and capacity in fields which will be of particular importance to the implementation and review of environmentally sound and socially responsible sustainable development, as envisaged throughout Agenda 21. The community of non-governmental organisations, therefore, offers a global network that should be tapped, enabled and strengthened in support of efforts to achieve these common goals.

The CSD has encouraged engagement by NGOs and an example of this participation occurs in the operation of the multi-stakeholder dialogue (MSD) where major groups and governments discuss issues concerning sustainable development. Key groups are usually involved in the MSD segments including businesses, trade unions, NGOs, local authorities and scientific bodies. The representatives of NGOs were selected by a steering group based on certain criteria such as gender, age and geography. This representation provides a means of enabling major groups to participate in reviewing the implementation of Agenda 21.

There has been some criticism of this process because of the lack of acknowledgement by governments of these contributions and the failure to take into account the recommendations of the stakeholders in the final decisions. There is also the potential in these discussions for the other participants from the business sector to be considered more influential than those of the NGOs and this may result in a failure to include the views of NGOs (Mori 2004: 164). So, efforts could be made to balance the contributions from the different organisations and provide sufficient weighting to the distinct views. Another area where NGOs have made significant contributions is through their involvement in climate change negotiations and some environmental NGOs are encouraged to contribute to the COP of the United Nations Framework Convention on Climate Change (FCCC).

The FCCC – NGO involvement

An example of NGO involvement in international environmental governance is illustrated through the participation of NGOs in the COP as observers (FCCC Article 7). COPs are the institutions established according to the provisions of the treaty in order to carry out specified roles such as monitoring the implementation of the convention. The States Parties to the treaty are represented in the COPs, so they continue to be the most influential members of these organisations. NGOs may be accredited as observers and attend meetings of the COP if they are legal entities and can show ability at dealing with matters concerning climate change.

This example illustrates a movement towards a greater consideration by member states of a variety of opinions from many different representatives on climate change issues. More than 3,000 representatives of NGOs and non-profit organisations have participated in meetings concerning the FCCC (Mori 2004: 166). One problem is that many diverse groups are grouped together as NGOs, even though there may be different major categories such as business, local government and environmental NGOs. As a result, there is no opportunity to advance the influence of major environmental NGOs over business and industry groups (ibid.: 166). This situation could be improved by permitting environmental NGOs to contribute a greater input in the discussion processes and also by indicating how these inputs from environmental NGOs can be included in the overall decision-making process to enhance the development of policy (ibid.: 172). It is also possible for some NGOs to attend official meetings of the FCCC if they are members of government delegations. However, this opportunity may restrict their independence because of the political constraints of these delegations (ibid.: 166).

The following section discusses the implementation of appropriate compliance and enforcement procedures that could be extended under other international multilateral conventions in order to improve international environmental governance. There have been two key changes to governance. First, the responsibilities of COPs has increased in some multilateral environmental agreements. Secondly, specific compliance and enforcement mechanisms that have been adopted for the purposes of the FCCC and the Protocol to the United Nations Framework Convention on Climate Change (Kyoto Protocol) could also be established in other international agreements.

The Role of COPs

Some developments in international environmental law that could lead to changes in global governance on environmental issues depends upon the leadership role of COPs in the future and the extent to which the compliance and enforcement procedure are more widely adopted by states.

One example is the increasing responsibilities of the COP and the Secretariat in many multilateral environmental agreements. These bodies are usually required under the relevant treaty or convention to regularly meet, review reports, coordinate and facilitate the exchange of information and to access financial resources in order to implement the objectives of the Convention. Indeed, some commentators have described the role of these bodies as autonomous institutions because their approach to compliance is versatile and some of the norm creation engaged in by these COPs is very novel (Churchill and Ulfstein 2000: 2). The specific arrangements for COPs and secretariats depends upon the provisions in the particular convention and the responsibilities and voting arrangements within these bodies will also differ according to what has been agreed upon.

Other new developments in environmental treaties have included the introduction of compliance committees. One example occurs in the operation of the Kyoto Protocol, where compliance and enforcement committees were introduced in order to strengthen reporting obligations and monitor the transparency of accounting methods used by the parties to this protocol. The Compliance Committee has been established so that it can make appropriate decisions in cases where parties fail to comply with their commitments and its members are elected by the parties to the protocol. NGOs cannot be members of the Compliance Committee; however, they may submit data to it and information is also likely to be submitted by expert review teams (Birnie et al. 2009: 249). This committee has two branches: the facilitative branch and the enforcement branch. The facilitative branch can make recommendations about implementation and offer assistance such as technology transfer and capacity building. The party that is non-compliant is permitted a public hearing on this question by the enforcement branch. Decisions made in the enforcement branch must be based upon evidence with reasons and this body also has powers to impose penalties on a non-complying party, such as the suspension of treaty rights. The aims of these compliance programmes are to achieve implementation of the convention rather than relying on other options under international law such as traditional dispute-resolution methods that, in some cases, have not proved effective at resolving environmental issues in the past.

An example of litigation that failed to resolve the issues of the dangers of nuclear testing is the legal challenge in 1995 that was brought by New Zealand against France. New Zealand brought the 1995 *Nuclear Tests* case in order to apply to the International Court of Justice (ICJ) to reopen the earlier 1974 decision. The ICJ delivered its judgment on 22 September 1995 and decided on a narrow view of the proceedings: that while it had jurisdiction to open the original matter, France had not violated the 1974 order of the court. So the ICJ failed to fully investigate important environmental arguments concerning nuclear testing that were raised by New Zealand. These arguments were based upon the scientific evidence, the precautionary principle, the international customary principle not to cause harm to another country, obligations to inform another country of potential dangers to their environment and obligations to conduct an environmental impact assessment.

These novel developments concerning the role of COPs and compliance committees could have a significant impact on future environmental governance; however, it is possible for some states to take issue with these developments and decide not to adhere to the modifications to state obligations by these organisations, given that they infringe on state sovereignty and do not have widespread state agreement. Other states may be persistent objectors and fail to join in multilateral conventions on key global environmental issues such as climate change. These states have been described as 'free riders' because they gain the advantages of the environmental benefits obtained under the Convention but they do not agree to cooperate by making adjustments required in the multilateral agreement within their own jurisdiction. As a consequence of the ability of some states to undermine these reforms by relying upon the traditional view of state sovereignty, there should be a continued movement away from this concept in international environmental law and further development of the concept of the common concern of humankind. Obviously, more effective changes to international governance will be necessary in order to protect the global environment in the ensuing decades.

The international legal dispute resolution system has also been criticised as failing to provide adequate standing before the ICJ and because of the lack of flexible speedy remedies for cases concerning international environmental disputes. This has led to suggestions that a specialised international environmental tribunal could be established in the future.

An International Environmental Tribunal

States may choose one of a number of different dispute resolution procedures to resolve international disputes with other states. The Charter of the United Nations (UN) gives priority to the peaceful settlement of disputes and Article 33 indicates that the parties may 'seek a solution by negotiation, enquiry, mediation, conciliation, arbitration, judicial settlement, and resort to regional agencies or arrangements, or other peaceful means of their own choice'. So the option of litigation before the ICJ is only one of a number of possible procedures for international dispute resolution. There are some limitations to litigation on environmental protection issues before the ICJ because 'Only states may be parties before the Court', according to Article 34(1) of the Statute of the International Court of Justice. Other parties that are concerned about the global environment (including indigenous groups and NGOs) do not have standing to bring proceedings before this court. Unfortunately, there is no avenue for ensuring the representation of future generations before the ICJ, even though they could be impacted by the judgment of this Court on environmental issues.

The ICJ introduced a separate chamber to resolve environmental matters; however, the chamber has not been popular and may not be used in the future because the Court decided in 2006 not to conduct elections for the bench of this chamber.[4] Indeed these alterations to the ICJ provided few incentives for states to access this environmental chamber. There were no major changes to costs or procedures and there was no requirement that judges should be experts in international environmental law or experts in scientific and technical matters relevant to the dispute (Birnie et al. 2009: 255).

The current international legal system does not offer adequate solutions for the resolution of disputes concerning protection of the environment, or for speedy redress for individuals or groups affected by environmental degradation (Rest 2004: 19). Clearly, these inadequacies indicate that reform is required and there have been suggestions that the establishment of an international environmental court or a tribunal with mandatory jurisdiction would help individuals, states and

4 See <http//www.icj-cij.org/court/index.php?p1=1&p2=4>.

public interest groups to resolve international environmental disputes and those affecting the global commons (ibid.: 9). Some changes to the Permanent Court of Arbitration (PCA) provide more flexible methods of resolving international environmental disputes however this court does not have mandatory jurisdiction. Even though access to the PCA is optional, this forum may be appropriate for international environmental dispute resolution, as it has a range of dispute resolution methods available including mediation, conciliation, arbitration and inquiry, and also provides a broader basis for participation by all interested parties.

The Optional Rules for Arbitration of Disputes Relating to Natural Resources and/or the Environment of 19 June 2001, include modifications specifically aimed at facilitating the resolution of environmental issues (ibid.: 23). These rules were drafted in order to assist states, parties to multilateral environmental agreements that become involved in environmental disputes and may apply to all parties who agree to adopt them. They could be applicable to states, NGOs, intergovernmental organisations (IGOs), private legal entities such as companies and incorporated environmental interest groups and to individuals. At the option of the parties, a panel of environmental scientists may provide expertise to the arbitral tribunal and it is possible to nominate a panel of arbitrators with environmental law expertise or expertise in natural resources law. The tribunal has powers to order interim measures to prevent serious harm to the natural environment and this remedy is essential in cases involving environmental disputes in order to stop the damage before it occurs. These rules permit arbitration in a short time period and enable the tribunal to be constituted quickly in the circumstances where a speedy resolution is required to prevent serious environmental harm.

Another option for those involved in an international environmental dispute is to adopt conciliation as a method of dispute resolution through the PCA. The Optional Rules for Conciliation of Disputes relating to Natural Resources and/or the Environment apply to disputes involving the conservation of natural resources or the protection of the environment. These rules may apply to states or to private parties, or to international organisations or to other entities recognised under national or international law. This conciliation procedure provides an effective means of settling disputes concerning the environment and natural resources before an arbitration dispute resolution procedure is adopted, and has the advantage of flexibility because it allows many different actors to seek conciliation and is not limited to states.

The benefits of establishing a specialist environmental tribunal with mandatory jurisdiction are that there would be an opportunity to resolve disputes in cases where a state may permit serious environmental degradation within its jurisdiction that could affect other nearby states or the international commons. Multiparty environmental disputes could be accommodated and a panel of scientific and environmental technical experts would be available to assist with the resolution of disputes. This facility would also provide a means of resolving environmental conflicts as a last resort, where other procedures have failed and there is persistent non-compliance with international environmental conventions.

Decisions of a specialist environmental tribunal could possibly influence the development and progress of national environmental law and provide guidance about the implementation of international environmental agreements. There could be wider access so that environmental NGOs, interest groups, indigenous peoples and individuals could have standing to bring environmental claims and a range of flexible remedies that could be enforced against states, corporations and other entities. Unfortunately, one of the key difficulties with this suggestion is that state agreement is necessary to establish a new international environmental tribunal, and a number of states may find submission to the jurisdiction of a new tribunal politically unacceptable. It is likely that they would rely upon the concept of state sovereignty to try to prevent the development of this new tribunal or to withdraw from the jurisdiction of a new tribunal in the event that one is established. Clearly, the necessity to ensure effective international environmental dispute resolution processes indicate that there must be a movement away from reliance on sovereignty and renewed focus on the common concern of humankind in order to move towards the innovative development of a new institution to protect the global environment.

This discussion has indicated that there have been a number of reforms in international environmental governance that could be further developed to improve the present regime. First, the role of NGOs could be enhanced in international environmental conferences and discussions on the development of international policy on key environmental issues. Secondly, the independence of the COPs and their law-making functions could be encouraged, together with support for newly developed compliance and enforcement regimes in multilateral conventions. NGOs could provide input into some of these compliance regimes. Third, the changes to the Permanent Court of Arbitration could be followed by the introduction of a specialist international environmental tribunal with mandatory jurisdiction covering international environmental disputes that cannot be resolved by other dispute resolution procedures.

Major long-term reform to global governance institutions could be undertaken to ensure that states and corporations take responsibility for fulfilling their obligations in international environmental agreements and their commitments to take action towards the achievement of sustainable development. In the meantime, it may be preferable to reconsider the development of an international human right to a healthy environment because this human right offers opportunities to facilitate environmental protection in an earlier time-frame than would be available for more complex governance reforms. An appropriate international environmental tribunal could also be established that would be competent to deal with environmental human rights disputes in accordance with current developments in international environmental law. Thus the focus on human rights environmental protection and the development of an international human right to a healthy environment could be progressed in the near future.

An International Human Right to a Healthy Environment

Presently, there is an absence of direction about the relationship between international environmental law and human rights law, although clearly the two areas are related. The Rio Declaration refers to the role of humans and sustainable development in very general terms and fails to draw direct conclusions about the protections of human rights in relation to action on sustainable development. Principle 1 of the Rio Declaration indicates that 'Human beings are at the centre of concerns for sustainable development. They are entitled to a healthy and productive life in harmony with nature.'

The lack of emphasis in the Rio Declaration on human rights shows the uncertainty in international environmental law about the relationship between this area of law and human rights law. In other developments, the Meeting of Experts on Human Rights and the Environment has recognised 'that respect for human rights is broadly accepted as a precondition for sustainable development' (para. 12) and a substantial body of case law has acknowledged that violation of human rights has either caused or resulted in environmental degradation (para. 8).

In 1994, the UN Sub-Commission on the Prevention of Discrimination and Protection of Minorities carried out an investigation of 'Human Rights and the Environment' and recommended the recognition of a right to a satisfactory environment (Ksentini Report 1994). The Draft Declaration of Principles on Human Rights and the Environment annexed to the Ksentini Report included provision for an international human right to a healthy environment in Principle 2: 'All persons have the right to a secure, healthy and ecologically sound environment. This right and other human rights, including civil, cultural, economic, political and social rights, are universal, interdependent and indivisible.'

However, no significant progress on the development of this international right has occurred since this report was released. There was also very little support from the relevant institution at that time, the Commission on Human Rights[5] (Francioni 2010: 45). One problem is the uncertainty about what the essential requirements for a healthy environment are. The second main difficulty is how to clearly define this human right. There is also some criticism of this objective if it promotes an anthropocentric view of environmental issues, rather than fostering an appreciation of the intrinsic value of the environment. However Birnie, Boyle and Redgwell (2009: 280) point out that it is arguable that a human right put in such broad terms is not predominantly anthropocentric if the human rights focus is on environmental protection and sustainable use of natural resources.

The advantages of establishing a human right to a healthy environment are that it would benefit communities and provide the basis for litigation action to be taken by individuals. It could also open up opportunities for NGOs to bring or provide

5 In 2006, the Human Rights Council replaced the Commission on Human Rights – see Resolution on the Human Rights Council GA Res 60/251(3 April 2006).

support for legal action against governments or organisations that are failing to take effective action to achieve sustainable development.

Even though there is no internationally recognised distinct human right to a healthy environment, international human rights law can support sustainable development because of existing human rights, such as the right to life and to health, and the availability of dispute resolution mechanisms (through judiciaries and human rights commissions) and other institutions that can monitor sustainable development commitments. The New Delhi Declaration recognised the General Assembly's request for further development and codification of international law on sustainable development and considered 'that the realization of the international bill of human rights, comprising economic, social and cultural rights, civil and political rights and peoples' rights is central to the pursuance of sustainable development' (Preamble). This non-binding Declaration also indicates that states should observe human rights and emphasises the importance of integration as a means of ensuring the consideration of human rights issues (para. 7.1):

> The principle of integration reflects the interdependence of social, economic, financial, environmental and human rights aspects of principles and rules of international law relating to sustainable development as well as of the interdependence of the needs of current and future generations of humankind.

The advantage of the emphasis on the principle of integration is that both of the areas of human rights and environmental protection can supplement the goals of the other field. So, in the circumstances where the decision maker has the appropriate access to information and expertise from the other disciplines, effective integration of these areas is possible. Some means of ensuring that environmental interests of present and future generations are represented in environmental disputes is also essential. The common concern of humankind has a temporal dimension that takes into account the effects of the environmental degradation in the long term (Draft Covenant: 38), and the word 'humankind' applies to the protection of the global environment for both present and future generations. So a focus on this concept indicates that the interests of future generations in a healthy global environment should be included when environmental disputes are determined.

At the present time, the international community is focusing on the further development of international law to protect the environment and also on the cooperation of states to implement effective legislation on sustainable development within their own jurisdictions. Presumably, as these actions have not been effective, this leaves open the possibility of adopting a human right to a healthy environment as an international human right or a new declaration concerning human rights and the environment. As a consequence of these developments, litigation on human rights violations could be effective at focusing international attention on states, corporations and other enterprises that fail to adhere to their responsibility to protect the environment. A specialist environmental tribunal could also provide a mechanism for the resolution of disputes concerning an international human right to a healthy environment, if this right is introduced.

Another suggestion is that an institution such as a Planetary Rights Commission could be established that could carry out the role of ensuring conservation of the global environment in a similar way to that of human rights institutions at international law (Weiss 1989: 111). There could be a High Commissioner for the Environment to cover the situation of breaches of environmental human rights (for example, in the future many people could become displaced by climate change) and this would be a similar role to a High Commissioner for Human Rights and Refugees. Environmental NGOs could be involved and could help to draw attention to failures by states and companies to fulfil environmental responsibilities in a similar way to the role of Amnesty International (Haas et al. 2004: 278). An important avenue for long-term change to international environmental governance is the development of a major global environmental institution that could possibly be established if there is enough state agreement to develop this new institution.

A Global Environmental Organisation

A Global Environmental Organisation (GEO) could be established where the primary function of this body would be to operate as an umbrella institution to protect the global environment. The main reasons for establishing this organisation are the failure of the current system to prevent the degradation of the global environment and the need for rationalisation of international environmental governance (Charnovitz 2005: 102). Rationalisation could help to overcome some of the deficiencies of the current international system by addressing issues such as weak treaties, lack of coordination amongst the COPs of multilateral environmental agreements and fragmented coverage of environmental issues. It is crucial that the overall global environmental position is effectively monitored so that joint action by the international community can be taken to protect on areas at risk. Obvious advantages of establishing a GEO are that this organisation could assist with environmental capacity building in developing countries and it could coordinate the development of new treaties and stipulate clear international environmental standards (Biermann 2000: 22).

The current problem with international environmental governance is that the situation is not improving and is likely to continue as it has done in the past with even more proliferation of international environmental agreements and a failure to remove ineffective institutions (Charnovitz 2005: 102). In fact, in order to address this decline, more institutions have been created, including the Global Ministerial Environment Forum and the Environmental Management Group. Unfortunately, these new institutions are unlikely to overcome the defects in the system of global environmental governance due to their lack of independence from states. So, the establishment of a new coordinating institution that could rationalise the different environmental priorities would be preferable to the continued development of numerous institutions with overlapping functions. At the Belgrade Process, the second meeting of representatives on international environmental governance considered that the governance structures for the environment are the weakest. These representatives considered that governments would need to contemplate more widespread reforms, as in the case of a specialised agency such as a world environment organisation, and that there should be further consultations on this issue.[6]

If a global institution is established in the future, it should not solely be governed by states (Mori 2004: 157), because the focus of a global environmental organisation should be to maintain a healthy global environment. So a broader representation of other members of civil society should be included in the structure of the governing council of the GEO. Wider, more democratic representation could lead to improvements in global environmental governance and to increased protection for areas that are not within state jurisdiction, such as the global commons areas of the high seas and the atmosphere. Clearly, more research could be carried out into the structure and role of this new institution. If the new institution is solely governed by states, this could result in a lack of cooperation and the risk that the political influence of state governments could lead to self-interested actions rather than focusing on the common concern of humankind and the legal protection of the global environment.

This proposal for major institutional reform has been raised by some governments and academic commentators, amongst others (Biermann 2000: 22). However, if there is a lack of political will by states to introduce these major reforms, they may not take place. States may be reluctant to agree to proposals that threaten their territorial sovereignty and certain states carrying out economic activities that damage the environment would also be unwilling to cooperate. There has also been some scepticism about the ability of a new institution to make a significant difference to the current governance situation. According to Birnie, Boyle and Redgwell (2000: 70–71):

> There may well be efficiencies to be gained from a 'clustering' of secretariat services and non-compliance procedures within UNEP. Certainly, there is a need for a system that can ensure the integration of environmental and development objectives in a more balanced and efficient manner, but a more centralized, bureaucratic, and entrenched institution may be less likely to influence the system as a whole, or to facilitate the cross-sectoral integration that Agenda 21 seeks to promote.

In spite of these criticisms, it is possible to develop new systems of governance at an international level which do not rely on state authority but which reflect the interests of broader international community and can operate in accordance

---

6 See <www.unep.org/environmentalgovernance/LinkClick.asp?filetiacket=2G652fbt8U%3&tabid=2227&language=en-US>.

with the common concern of humankind. In order for the GEO to focus on the goal of protection of the global environment, it should be established within the framework of existing United Nations organisations. International cooperation to provide environmental protection at a global level requires efforts on the part of all members of the community and at all levels: global, regional, national and local. As the UN has already established a number of institutions that promote 'good ecological stewardship' (Charnovitz 205: 106), the United Nations system is best placed to provide the universality required. In any event, there should be opportunity for participation in the new GEO by NGOs and other sectors of civil society, as this has already occurred in key environmental institutions such as the CSD. Broader representation by regional organisations, as well as local environmental groups, could also be considered. These representatives could be chosen based upon their environmental qualifications and their demonstrated commitment to environmental interests of the international community and to instigating environmental change in communities around the world. The major goal of the GEO would be to persuade states and other organisations that adherence to the international treaties and conventions on protection of the environment is both in their own best interests and necessary for the future well-being of the international community.

There are some advantages to retaining UNEP within the structure of the new institution and two possible options about restructuring UNEP within the GEO have been suggested. One suggestion is that the GEO is created as a Specialized Agency of the UN under Article 59 of the UN Charter. This change would lead to UNEP becoming a major division of this institution. The other proposal advocates that UNEP is originally incorporated into the GEO but, over time, UNEP will lose its identity within this organisation (Charnovitz 2005: 106).

Another controversial point is how to establish an effective governance relationship between the GEO and the COPs of all of the multilateral environmental agreements. At present, only some of these multilateral environmental agreements are coordinated by UNEP. One proposal is that the GEO could supervise a reorganisation of international environmental agreements to remove duplication and conflicting provisions and it may also be possible to design a uniform approach to governance for all multilateral environmental agreements. An alternative approach would be to divide multilateral environmental agreements into groups of those dealing with similar issues and to design an umbrella convention to apply to individual clusters of these agreements. (ibid.: 111–12). The latter approach may be preferable as it appears that COPs are presently operating in an innovative and autonomous fashion and these developments should not be stifled by any reorganisation process.

The GEO could promote compliance rather than focus on dispute settlement and could operate in tandem with an international environmental tribunal or together with the Permanent Court of Arbitration and its environmental facility. In order to alleviate adverse environmental impacts resulting from WTO decisions, a GEO could influence environmental trade disputes in the WTO by providing rosters of international environmental lawyers to take part on WTO panels (Haas et al. 2004: 278), so that environmental issues are given adequate consideration in trade disputes.

Another related question is whether it is preferable to have a global environmental organisation or a global sustainable development organisation. A sustainable development organisation would cover a broader range of issues including developmental and environmental programmes; however, because of the potential inclusion of many areas such as trade, WTO and the World Bank, it is unlikely that such an organisation is viable or politically acceptable (Charnovitz 2005: 114).

Conclusion

The problem for international environmental governance is that there is no independent global institution with responsibility for coordination of numerous multilateral environmental agreements. Clearly, it would be appropriate to establish an independent body to rationalise the international agreements and to encourage states, business entities and local and regional communities to adhere to these agreements. Until such a time as this development takes place, it would be preferable to rely upon the potential development of an international human right to a healthy environment, as this right could facilitate efforts to protect the global environment until more long-term governance changes can be negotiated by states. An international environmental tribunal could determine the resolution of disputes concerning potential and actual violations of this human right. This tribunal would permit NGOs and other groups acting in the public interest to have standing to bring legal action to prevent states, corporations and other organisations from carrying out activities that cause serious environmental harm that could affect the territory of other states and the global commons.

Gradually, there appears to be an indication amongst some academic commentators and government representatives that there should be a movement away from reliance upon the present system of international environmental governance towards ongoing consultation about reform, including the possible establishment of a GEO. The introduction of a GEO based upon a more democratic system with representation from civil society, together with improved compliance procedures monitored by panels of independent environmental experts and representatives from civil society, could facilitate the accountability of states and corporations and encourage more effective environmental action. However, this development is uncertain and will depend upon the willingness of states to agree to the establishment of a new global environmental organisation at some time in the future – and the risk for the international community is that this agreement may never be forthcoming.

References

Book References

Birnie, P., A. Boyle and C. Redgwell. 2009. *International Law and the Environment*. 3rd edn. Oxford: Oxford University Press.

Bradnee Chambers, W. and J. Green. 2005. *Reforming International Environmental Governance: From Institutional Limits to Innovative Reforms*. New York: United Nations University Press.

Kanie, N. and P.M. Haas. 2004. *Emerging Forces in Environmental Governance*. New York: United Nations University Press.

Weiss, E.B. 1989. *In Fairness to Future Generations: International Law, Common Patrimony, and Intergenerational Equity*. Tokyo: United Nations University Transnational Publishers.

Sanson, M. 2008. *International Law and Global Governance*. London: Cameron May Ltd.

Book Chapters

Charnovitz, C. 2005. 'A world environment organization', in W. Bradnee Chambers and J. Green (eds), *Reforming International Environmental Governance: From Institutional Limits to Innovative Reforms*. New York: United Nations University Press, pp. 93–123.

Gleckman, H. 2004. 'Balancing TNCs, the states, and the international system in global environmental governance: A critical perspective', N. Kanie and P.M. Haas (eds), in *Emerging Forces in Environmental Governance*. New York: United Nations University Press, pp. 203–15.

Haas, P.M., N. Kanie and C.N. Murphy. 2004. 'Conclusion: Institutional design and institutional reform for sustainable development', in Kanie and Haas (eds), *Emerging Forces in Environmental Governance*. New York: United Nations University Press, pp. 157–75.

Mitchell, R. 1996. 'Compliance theory: An overview', in J. Cameron, J. Werksman and P. Roderick (eds), *Improving Compliance with International Environmental Law*. London: Earthscan, pp. 3–28.

Mori, S. 2004. 'Institutionalization of NGO involvement in policy functions for global environmental governance', in N. Kanie and P.M. Haas (eds), *Emerging Forces in Environmental Governance*. New York: United Nations University Press, pp. 157–75.

Journal Articles

Andromecca, M. 1997. 'Discovering and enforcing a human right to environmental protection', *Journal of Natural Resources and Environmental Law* 13: 123–47.

Biermann, F. 2000. 'The case for a world environment organization', *Environment* 42(9): 22–32.

Bodansky, D. 1999. 'The legitimacy of international governance: A coming challenge for international environmental law', *American Journal of International Law* 93: 596–624.

Burris, S., M. Kempa and C. Shearing. 2008. 'Changes in governance: A cross-disciplinary review of current scholarship', *Akron Law Review*, 1–48.

Churchill, R. and G. Ulfstein. 2000. 'Autonomous institutional arrangements in multilateral environmental agreements: A little-noticed phenomenon in international law', *American Journal of International Law* 94: 623–59.

Francioni, F. 2010. 'The human dimension of international law, "progress of stagnation": A symposium in honour of Antonio Cassese', *European Journal of International Law* 21: 41–55.

French, D. 2009. 'Finding autonomy in international environmental law and governance', *Journal of Environmental Law* 21: 255–89.

Rodriguez-Rivera, L.E. 2001. 'Is the international right to environment recognized under international law? It depends on the source', *Colorado Journal of International Environmental Law and Policy* 12: 1–45.

Salazar-Duran, O.O. 2009. 'A human rights approach to corporate accountability', *University of San Francisco Law Review* 43: 733–60.

Shelton, D. 2006. 'Human rights and the environment: what specific environmental rights have been recognised?', *Denver Journal of International Law and Policy* 35: 129–71.

Rest, A. 2004. 'Enhanced implementation of international environmental treaties by judiciary – access to justice in international environmental law for individuals and NGOs: efficacious enforcement by the permanent court of arbitration', *Macquarie Journal of International and Comparative Environmental Law* 1: 1–28.

Wolfe, K.E. 2003. 'Greening the international human rights sphere? An examination of environmental rights and draft declaration of principles on human rights and the environment', *Journal of Environmental Law and Practice* 13: 109–29.

International Agreements and Cases

1992 *Agenda 21: Programme of Action for Sustainable Development.* The final text of agreements negotiated by Governments at the United Nations Conference on Environment and Development (UNCED) 3–14 June 1992, Rio de Janeiro, Brazil.

United Nations Publications.

Agenda 21: Programme of Action for Sustainable Development UNCED 1992. New York: United Nations Publication. GA Res S-19/2 <http://www.un.org/esa/dsd/agenda21/res_agenda21_00.shtml> (referred to as *Agenda 21*).

Convention on Access to Information, Public Participation in Decision Making and Access to Justice in Environmental Matters 38 ILM (1999) 517 (entered in force 29 October 2001).

Declaration of the United Nations Conference on Environment and Development (14 June 1992) UN Doc A/CONF.151/26 (Volume 1), 31 ILM 874 (referred to as *Rio Declaration)*

General Assembly Resolution UN GA A/RES/ 47/191 Institutional Arrangements to follow up the United Nations Conference on Environment and Development (22 December 1992).

Ksentini, F.Z. 1994. *Human Rights and the Environment.* Final report prepared by Mrs Fatma Zohra Ksentini, Special Rapporteur, 13 September 1994, Economic and Social Council, E/CN.4/Sub/21994/9.

Nuclear Tests Cases(New Zealand v *France)* Request by New Zealand for an Examination of the Situation [1995] ICJ Reports 288.

Protocol to the United Nations Framework Convention on Climate Change opened for signature 11 December 1997, 37 ILM 22 (1998) (entered into force 16 February 2005) (referred to as *Kyoto Protocol*).

Universal Declaration of Human Rights. GARes on the Universal Declaration of Human Rights, 217A (III) (10 December 1948) UN Doc A/810.

United Nations Convention on Biological Diversity opened for signature 5 June 1992, 1760 UNTS 79 (entered into force 29 December 1993).

United Nations Framework Convention on Climate Change opened for signature 9 May 1992, 1771 UNTS 107 (entered into force 21 March 1994) (referred to as *FCCC*).

Internet Sites

Consultative Group of Ministers or High-level Representatives on International Environmental Governance Rome, 26–29 October 2009. Second meeting. Developing a set of options for improving International Environmental Governance Available at <www.unep.org/environmentalgovernance/LinkClick.asp?filetiacket=2G652fbt8U%3&tabid=2227&language=en-US> (referred to as *The Belgrade Process*).

Draft International Covenant on Environment and Development. Available at <http://www.i-c-e-l.org/english/EPLP3IEN_rev2.pdf> (referred to as *Draft Covenant*).

Permanent Court of Arbitration. Available at <http://www.pca-cpa.org>.

ECOSOC Division for Sustainable Development Available at <http:// www.un.org/esa/dsd/csd/csd_mandate.shtml>.

Meeting of Experts on Human Rights and the Environment, 14–15 January 2002 Available at <http://www2.ohchr.org/english/issues/environment/environ/conclusions.htm>.

Horn, L. *The Common Concern of Humankind and Legal Protection of the Global Environment*, PhD digital thesis, University of Sydney 2001. Available at <http://hdl.handle .net/ 2123/6188>.

Millenium Ecosystem Assessment 2005. *Ecosystems and Human Well-Being: General Synthesis.* Washington, DC: Island Press. Available at <http://www.milleniumassessment.org/documents/document.356aspx.pdf>.

International Law Association (ILA) New Delhi Declaration of Principles of International Law Relating to Sustainable Development, 2 April 2002 Available at <http://www.springerlink.com/content/v52m 758047k73q41/> (referred to as *New Delhi Declaration*).

Secretariat of the Convention on Biological Diversity 2010. *Global Biodiversity Outlook 3*. Available at <http://www.cbd.int/GBO3>.

United Nations Report of the World Summit on Sustainable Development. Available at <http://daccess-ddsny.un.org/doc/UNDOC/GEN/NO2/639/93/PDF/NO263693.pdf?OpenElement> (referred to as WSSD).

Chapter 7
Global Governance Implications of Terrorism: Using UN Resolutions to Justify Abuse of Basic Rights

Michael Head

Introduction: 9/11 and the United Nations

From a purely formal standpoint, the response of the United Nations to the terrible events of 11 September 2001 constituted a triumph for transnational governance. The UN Security Council took unprecedented action following the terrorist attacks, seemingly demonstrating its capacity to act decisively as the global instrument for collective action. Within 24 hours, United Nations Security Council Resolution 1368 had been adopted, unanimously condemning the attacks and sanctioning military responses. Two weeks later, Resolution 1373 obligated all member states to take far-reaching legislative and executive action in order to combat terrorism. Never before since its establishment after the Second World War had the Security Council ordered all countries to undertake a course of action, a nominally unified course of action, to deal with a perceived common threat – in this instance, that of international terrorism.

In reality, it will be argued, quite opposite conclusions should be drawn. The response to 9/11 demonstrated that the UN functioned as a conduit for the strategic and economic interests of the major powers, notably the United States. Indeed, the twin resolutions effectively paved the way for military unilateralism, starting with the US invasion of Afghanistan, and for equally self-interested domestic responses, with governments seizing upon the declared 'war on terrorism' – and the lack of any definition of terrorism by the UN – to introduce repressive measures that served their own political purposes.

Under the thinly-veiled threat of potential retribution from Washington if they failed to cooperate – US President George W. Bush had declared in an address to a joint session of Congress on 20 September 2001 that 'Either you are with us, or you are with the terrorists' (White House 2001) – governments of all stripes around the world complied with the UN resolutions, while often utilising them to deal with their own political foes. Thus, for example, China cracked down on dissent, including by the banned Falun Gong spiritual movement and Uighur people (Head 2005: 84–91), and Indonesia introduced authoritarian measures reminiscent of the Suharto dictatorship on the pretext of targeting Islamic fundamentalists (ibid.: 77–84).

Numerous writers have commented on the obvious contradiction between the fact that the UN has formally compelled member states to adopt measures to fight terrorism, while not being able to agree on how to define the phenomenon. Most observers, however, have depicted this dichotomy as one capable of being remedied by the UN, rather than as an inherent exposure of the character of the UN itself. Some have warned the UN that it risks losing credibility. One study cites the advice offered by a group of practitioners: 'Action in the absence of an agreed-upon definition exposes the United Nations to the charge of double standards, thus undermining the very legitimacy and universality that are among its most precious assets' (O'Neill 2003, cited in Boulden and Weiss 2004: 4)

Rather, the dichotomy reflects the reality that the UN remains dominated by the five veto-wielding powers that emerged victorious from the last world war and that it is constituted by nation-states, each of which has its own political, commercial and strategic interests to protect. Resolution 1368, passed the day after 9/11, recognised 'the inherent right of individual or collective self-defence' as a legitimate response to terrorism for the first time. By doing so, the Security Council effectively removed itself from further decision making about the legitimacy of the use of military force by the US and its partners in Afghanistan under the banner of combating terrorism. Given Washington's adoption of a pre-emptive intervention doctrine that asserted a sweeping right to act unilaterally, the US seemed to be handed a 'carte blanche' (Boulden and Weiss 2004: 11–12).

Resolution 1373, adopted two weeks later, appeared to offer a contrast. It detailed requirements that necessitated significant actions by member states, including legislative changes, making the Security Council arguably intrusive in domestic affairs. The resolution left open the definition of terrorism, however, allowing a wide latitude for interpretation – in effect, another *carte blanche*. Various states have used the international legitimacy conferred by Resolution 1373 and other UN provisions to de-legitimise political opponents and demonise them as terrorists. Thus, the terrorist label has been attached to Uighur separatists (China), Chechen rebels (Russia), Kashmir militants (India), Papuan separatists (Indonesia) and Palestinians (Israel). A Maldives opposition politician was sentenced to ten years' imprisonment on terrorism charges for peacefully protesting against rights violations by the government, and in Uzbekistan, 15 men were convicted of terrorism offences for organising public demonstrations (Saul 2006: 50–51).

On the one hand, member states were ordered to criminalise all terrorist-related acts, and were instructed to provide compliance reports within three months. Some 117 reports were submitted on time – 'by all historical standards, a remarkable response' – and by December 2002 this number had increased to 175 (Oudraat 2004: 162). On the other hand, the lack of any agreed definition of terrorism was amplified by another issue: despite the establishment of a Counter Terrorism Committee (CTC) to assess compliance with the resolution, there was no specified enforcement mechanism. Paragraph 8 of Resolution 1373 expressed the council's 'determination to take all necessary steps in order to ensure the full implementation of this resolution'. The absence of any compliance procedure, however, opened the door to unilateral responses both internally and externally. The US was not alone in asserting its right to attack a supposedly non-complaint state. Russia threatened to intervene against Georgia for its 'glaring violation' of Resolution 1373 in failing to halt rebel raids into Chechnya (ibid.: 163–5).

Until the aftermath of September 11, the lack of a common international definition of terrorism was largely legally inconsequential, in the sense that no state or government was obliged by international law to provide for specific punitive provisions against terrorism. Since 2001, however, the Security Council has required states to implement measures against terrorists and terrorist acts, attaching to those terms serious legal consequences, without even defining them (Saul 2006: 5).

The United States is widely credited with initiating Resolution 1373, which was adopted unanimously on 28 September 2001, after a Council meeting that officially lasted just three minutes (SC Res. 1373, 28 September 2001, S/RES/1373 (2001)). The resolution was adopted under Chapter VII of the United Nations Charter, and is therefore binding on all UN member states. It marks a shift in international law, which was previously presumed to be valid only if a state had voluntarily signed the relevant international treaty; whereas the Security Council imposed Resolution 1373 on all member states.

Resolution 1373 obliges governments to ensure that terrorist acts are established as serious criminal offences in domestic laws and regulations, and that the seriousness of such acts is duly reflected in sentences served. It further requires all states to prevent and suppress the financing of terrorism, as well as criminalise the wilful provision or collection of funds for such acts. The funds, financial assets and economic resources of those who commit or attempt to commit terrorist acts or participate in or facilitate the commission of terrorist acts and of persons and entities acting on behalf of terrorists must also be frozen without delay. Further, states must prohibit their nationals or persons or entities in their territories from making funds, financial assets, economic resources, financial, or other related services available to persons who commit or attempt to commit, facilitate, or participate in the commission of terrorist acts.

States must also refrain from providing any form of support to entities or persons involved in terrorist acts; take the necessary steps to prevent the commission of terrorist acts; deny safe haven to those who finance, plan, support, or commit terrorist acts and provide safe havens as well. Moreover, states must prevent those who finance, plan, facilitate, or commit terrorist acts from using their respective territories for those purposes against other countries and their citizens. Perhaps, most significantly of all, states must ensure that anyone who has participated in the financing, planning, preparation, or perpetration of terrorist acts or in supporting terrorist acts is 'brought to justice'.

States were also required to afford one another the greatest measure of assistance for criminal investigations or criminal proceedings relating to the financing or support of terrorist acts, and to prevent the movement of terrorists or their groups by effective border controls. States were obliged to intensify and accelerate the exchange of information regarding terrorist actions or movements; forged or falsified documents; traffic in arms and sensitive material; use of communications and technologies by terrorist groups, and the threat posed by the possession of weapons of mass destruction. States were also called on to exchange information and to cooperate to prevent and suppress terrorist acts and to take action against the perpetrators of such acts. States were instructed to become parties to, and fully implement as soon as possible, the relevant international conventions and protocols to combat terrorism.

The Security Council's CTC monitored implementation, including through mandatory state reporting. This process became increasingly demanding, with governments under pressure to take ever greater actions to prove compliance. In 2002, the CTC chairman, UK Ambassador Jeremy Greenstock, stated, 'Do not expect us to declare any member state compliant, because 1373 is open-ended, and the threats posed by various forms of terrorism will evolve' (Saul 2006: 237).

As a result of these processes, it is suggested, during the first decade of the twenty-first century, in jurisdictions around the world, counter-terrorism laws and prosecutions became some of the most prominent measures directed against perceived threats to the social order and the interests of the state itself. As will be seen, long-standing legal principles, including habeas corpus, the presumption of innocence and freedom of thought and association, were overridden or eroded. Novel concepts, such as 'preventative' punishment, offences of 'praising' or 'glorifying' terrorism (itself defined in broad terms) and detention without trial were introduced.

Notorious Problems of Definition

Anti-terrorism legislation has been officially justified as being aimed at protecting members of society against violent acts. However, it is almost invariably targeted at conduct that is motivated by a political, ideological, or religious purpose in a manner that either challenges, disturbs, or seeks to change the established order. Nearly all legal definitions of terrorism refer to such motives, even if the inherently political character of such classifications has prevented any commonly agreed international definition.

Anti-terrorism measures suddenly rose to centre stage this century, following the 9/11 attacks, yet terrorism was hardly a new trend. It had been a feature of conflicts, both civil and military, for centuries. The recorded history of terrorism goes back at least to Sicarii Zealots – a Jewish extremist group fighting Roman rule in Judaea Province at the first century AD. The term 'terrorism' itself was originally used to describe the actions of the Jacobin Club during the 1790s in its period of rule by terror following the French Revolution. Ironically, this was an instance of state-sponsored terrorism, a practice that is excluded from the official contemporary legal definitions of terrorism (Tigar 2007: 12–13). One of the first reported usages of the term in its modern context was by Sergey Nechayev, who founded the anti-Tsarist Russian People's Retribution in 1869, describing himself as a 'terrorist' (Hoffman 1998: 83–167; Chaliand 2007: 56–68).

The classification of 'terrorist,' like that of 'saboteur' or 'traitor', is notoriously susceptible to abuse for political purposes. African National Congress leader Nelson Mandela, for example, was sentenced to life imprisonment and was imprisoned for 27 years for conduct that would probably today fall under anti-terrorism law. He was convicted on four charges of sabotage for planning armed actions against the apartheid regime, before being released in 1990 to enter negotiations with the regime, leading to a power-sharing political and economic system. Mandela was later awarded a Nobel Peace Prize. Other groups, when involved in an armed struggle, have been labelled 'terrorists' by Western governments or media, only to be later called 'national leaders', 'statesmen', 'heroes', or even 'peace-makers'. Another example, and Nobel Peace Prize laureate, was Menachem Begin, a Zionist anti-British terrorist who later became an Israeli prime minister (Coady et al. 2002).

Today's primary 'terrorist' targets – Al Qaeda-linked groups – were yesterday's 'freedom fighters' in the eyes of the Western powers and mass media during the guerrilla war against the Soviet-backed regime in Afghanistan. Billions of dollars were siphoned into Osama bin Laden's Islamic fundamentalist movement by the Carter, Reagan and George Bush senior administrations until the early 1990s (Blum 2002: 155). Likewise, ousted Iraqi president, Saddam Hussein, was also once a close ally of Washington, particularly during the fratricidal Iran–Iraq war of the 1980s (ibid.: 133–4, 145–6).

All legal definitions of terrorism exclude what has been termed 'state terrorism', that is, acts of violence or intimidation organised, supported, or sanctioned by governments or government agencies. These may include wars of aggression, military interventions, coups, assassinations, renditions and torture. Past practices of this variety were conducted by the Nazi regime in Germany, and by the US-backed dictatorships of Suharto in Indonesia and Pinochet in Chile. Intensive, but unsuccessful, efforts were to bring some of those allegedly responsible, including General Augusto Pinochet and former US Secretary of State Henry Kissinger, to justice (Tigar 2007: 27–74). Considerable evidence has been produced of such crimes being committed by the US government and its allies since 2001. In some instances, lawsuits seeking to prosecute or obtain redress for such actions have been dismissed by courts on various grounds, including 'state secret' doctrines invoked by the government allegedly responsible (see below).

Another problem is that the terminology of the terrorism provisions is generally so broad that it is difficult to predict the precise circumstances in which police, intelligence and prosecuting authorities will decide to proceed against political or religious groups or individuals. The extent of the discretions entailed in making these law-enforcement decisions is so great that there is considerable scope for selective and discriminatory interventions and prosecutions. It is particularly necessary to examine this area of law from the standpoint of the political circumstances and context in which it has been activated in numbers of criminal cases.

Legally defining terrorism has proved controversial, precisely because the term has become so politically, as well as emotionally, charged. Various legal systems and government agencies use different definitions. International agencies such as the UN have been unable to formulate a universally agreed upon, legally binding definition. A 1988 study counted 109 definitions of terrorism that covered a total of 22 different definitional elements (Schmid et al. 1988: 5–6). Another, in 1999, listed over a hundred definitions and concluded that the 'only general characteristic generally agreed upon is that terrorism involves violence and the threat of violence' (Laqueur 1999: 6). Yet, this fails to distinguish terrorism from many other crimes, and indeed from such activities as global diplomacy, not to speak of war and military interventions to topple governments.

According to one review of international and regional treaties, the so-called international community has – despite efforts since the 1920s – never been able to reach consensus on a generic definition of terrorism. At the UN level, the draft Comprehensive Convention on International Terrorism, which includes a generic definition, has not progressed further than the drafting stage; the most important issues of contention are the exclusion from the definition of struggles for self-determination and the application of the Convention to state armed forces and situations of foreign occupation (Saul 2006: 168–90).

Some of the definitional difficulties relate to distinguishing between what is seen as legitimate resistance to oppression, including national oppression, and what is classified as criminally reprehensible behaviour. A briefing paper for the Australian Parliament noted, 'During the 1970s and 1980s, the United Nations attempts to define the term foundered mainly due to differences of opinion between various members about the use of violence in the context of conflicts over national liberation and self-determination' (Martyn 2002). Sami Zeidan, a Lebanese diplomat and scholar, explained some of the political reasons underlying the definitional difficulties as follows:

> The difficulty of defining terrorism lies in the risk it entails of taking positions. The political value of the term currently prevails over its legal one. Left to its political meaning, terrorism easily falls prey to change that suits the interests of particular states at particular times. The Taliban and Osama bin Laden were once called freedom fighters (mujahideen) and backed by the CIA when they were resisting the Soviet occupation of Afghanistan. Now they are on top of the international terrorist lists. (Zeidan 2006: 491–2)

UN Security Council Resolution 1566, adopted unanimously on 8 October 2004, sought to spell out what the Security Council regarded as terrorism:

> … criminal acts, including against civilians, committed with the intent to cause death or serious bodily injury, or taking of hostages, with the purpose to provoke a state of terror in the general public or in a group of persons or particular persons, intimidate a population or compel a government or an international organization

> to do or to abstain from doing any act, which constitute offences within the scope of and as defined in the international conventions and protocols relating to terrorism, are under no circumstances justifiable by considerations of a political, philosophical, ideological, racial, ethnic, religious or other similar nature.

Although this conception has operative effect for the purposes of Security Council action, it does not represent a definition of terrorism that binds all states in international law. That is a task which could only be achieved by way of agreeing to an international treaty under the auspices of the UN General Assembly. A Comprehensive Convention was negotiated in draft form, but agreement to its exact terms, most particularly the definition of terrorism, has remained elusive. This lack of legal precision was compounded by Security Council Resolution 1624 of September 2005 (SC Res. 1624, 14 September 2005, S/RES/1624 (2005)), which called on states to 'prohibit by law *incitement* to commit a *terrorist act*', without defining either term. [italics added]

Significantly, suggestions that terrorism be defined as a threat to democratic governance have run into the objection that democracy is not an accepted international value. Indeed, autocratic and totalitarian regimes have embraced the 'war on terrorism' and exploited Resolution 1373 for repressive purposes. Most regional instruments, too, present terrorism as a crime against the state and its security and stability, sovereignty and integrity, rather than as an anti-democratic crime. Even in the European Union, ostensibly a community of democracies, terrorist offences are defined in terms of motives to damage or destroy the political, economic, or social structures of a state (Saul 2006: 37–8).

Of course, states that are allies can also disagree, for reasons of history, culture and politics, over whether or not members of a certain organisation are terrorists. For many years, some branches of the US government refused to label members of the Irish Republican Army (IRA) as terrorists, even though they were branded as such by the British government. This was highlighted by *Quinn* v. *Robinson* (783 F.2d 776, 54 USLW 2449), where a US federal court determined that an IRA member could not be extradited to the UK to face charges of murder and conspiracy to cause explosions, because of the 'political offence' exception, an international law principle that had been incorporated in the relevant US–UK extradition treaty.

Susceptibility to Political Abuse

Numerous studies have pointed to the pejorative political content of the label 'terrorist' (for example, Hoffman 1998: 32; Saul 2006: 3). Because of its symbolic potential, the terrorism concept is open to abuse and, to some extent, uncontainable:

> … terrorism will always exceed the limits of our efforts to hold the line on what really constitutes it. In part that is because it is a contested concept, which is

> inseparable from disagreements about the legitimacy of violence in particular contexts. But in part it is also because terrorism is a justificatory concept, the distinctiveness of which lies in its capacity to exploit fears and mobilise support for the introduction of laws and procedures that would otherwise be unacceptable. (Marks and Clapham 2005: 358)

The greatest concern with the counter-terrorism legislation is that all the various definitions adopted since 2001 are so broad and vague, and politically loaded, that they have given governments and their security agencies considerable scope to persecute and criminalise political dissenters and government opponents. Legitimate protests, acts of civil disobedience and industrial action could be targeted under these provisions. Although the measures were initially used against alleged Islamic fundamentalists, supporters of other causes not favoured by the Western powers have found themselves accused of terrorism, including Kurdish and Sri Lankan Tamil separatists.

In 2010, some leading US politicians called for WikiLeaks founder Julian Assange to be treated as a 'terrorist' for disseminating leaked diplomatic cables that revealed US involvement in illegal spying, wars of aggression, coup plots, assassinations and other crimes. A wider range of groups could be subjected to prosecutions in the future, particularly in the event of intense unrest and protests over austerity measures imposed because of the global financial crisis that began in 2008.

In most Western states, notably the participants in the United States-led 'Coalition of the Willing' that invaded Iraq in 2003, the alleged threat of terrorism has been used, particularly since September 2001, as a pretext to make far-reaching inroads into basic democratic rights, including free speech, freedom of political association protections against arbitrary detention, and the right to open and public trial for any serious offence. Despite criticisms by civil liberties groups, both the British and American governments introduced an array of measures, including detention without trial and proscription of organisations (Hancock 2002: 2–8). Amnesty International condemned the Bush administration for breaching the International Covenant on Civil and Political Rights and other international protocols against arbitrary detention and inhuman treatment of prisoners (Amnesty International 2002). In Australia, legislation has been introduced to substantially increase the surveillance, detention and proscription powers of the government and its security and intelligence agencies. Like its US and UK counterparts, the Australian legislation has four fundamental features. It (1) defines terrorism in vague terms, (2) permits the banning of political groups, (3) allows for detention without trial, and (4) shrouds the operations of the intelligence and police agencies in secrecy and provides for semi-secret trials (Head 2002; 2004).

The Indefinite 'War on Terror': Some Contradictions

Under President George W. Bush's doctrine, the 'war on terror' is an endless state of war. 'Terrorism' is not a tangible enemy, nor even an ideological or political cause. It is, at most, a set of tactics, to which resort can be had by a multitude of disaffected political currents.

Moreover, the collapse of the reasons used to justify the United States-led invasion of Iraq – 'weapons of mass destruction', and Saddam Hussein's supposed links to Al Qaeda-backed terrorism – suggest that lies were told to divert attention away from the real motives of the 'war on terror', both domestically and internationally. The Middle East and Central Asia, as is well known, contain the largest proven concentrations of oil and natural gas reserves in the world. The outrages in New York and Washington provided the pretext for the implementation of plans prepared much earlier – during the 1990s – for the conquest of Afghanistan and Iraq (Bacevich 2002).

The report of the US national commission investigating the terrorist attacks of 11 September was filled with criticisms of the Bush and Clinton administrations and the performance of the government agencies responsible for intelligence and national security emergency response. But the commission attributed all of these failures to incompetence, mismanagement, or 'failure of imagination'. The fundamental premise of its investigation was that the CIA, the FBI, the US military and the Bush White House acted in good faith (The 9/11 Commission 2004). The report thus excluded, *a priori*, the most important question raised by the events of 9/11: did US government agencies permit – or even assist – the carrying-out of this terrorist atrocity, in order to provide the Bush administration with the necessary justification to carry out its programme of war in Central Asia and the Middle East and a huge build-up of forces of state repression at home?

For all their claims to be introducing democracy to the Middle East by removing governments in Afghanistan and Iraq, Washington, and its allies have for decades financially, diplomatically and military propped up dictatorships like the Saudi monarchy and Gulf kingdoms, in the interests of controlling access to the region's oil wealth (Shalom 1993: 63–88). Equally, the claims of exporting democracy are belied by the erosions of legal and democratic rights at home, as will be seen from examining aspects of the counter-terrorism legislation in Britain, the US and Australia.

The inroads into basic rights include the creation of extensive surveillance over citizens. In 2010, the *Washington Post* conducted an investigation into the scale of the US domestic intelligence apparatus built up since the 9/11 terrorist attacks. The project concluded that the federal government was carrying out the collection and integration of personal information on hundreds of thousands, and potentially millions, of Americans, most of whom had committed no criminal offence and were not engaged in anything that could reasonably be considered 'terrorism'. A total of 4,058 federal, state and local organisations had 'counter-terrorism' functions, with one-quarter of these either newly created since 9/11 or involved in counter-terrorist activities for the first time since then. US police agencies were deploying technologies tested on the battlefields of Iraq and Afghanistan and using them to monitor and target American citizens. State and local police agencies were monitoring legal political activities, including protests over environmental, immigration and other issues, and filing reports with counter-terrorism 'fusion centers' in the 50 states. The *Washington Post* report drew attention to an aspect of the connection between the foreign and domestic features of the 'war on terrorism'. It noted, 'The special operations units deployed overseas to kill the al-Qaeda leadership drove technological advances that are now expanding in use across the United States' (Priest and Arkin 2010).

Some of the troubling issues raised by the anti-terrorism measures can be illustrated by reviewing several key provisions and terrorist trials in three Western jurisdictions.

Britain

The main UK legislation is spread over several acts, including the Terrorism Act 2000, Anti-terrorism, Crime and Security Act 2001, Prevention of Terrorism Act 2005, Terrorism Act 2006 and the Counter-Terrorism Act 2008.

This legislation has significantly altered the criminal law as it relates to police investigations, police powers and prosecutions in terrorist offences. Many new offences have been created, police powers have been expanded, and the relationship between the state and the individual has been in many cases fundamentally altered. The legislation raises many significant issues relating to freedom of speech, freedom of association and the right to a fair trial.

The concerns about how these provisions and powers can be used for political purposes are all the greater because of the string of 'miscarriage of justice' cases of the 1970s to the 1990s, including the Birmingham Six, Guildford Four and Maguire Seven. The Birmingham Six were sentenced to life imprisonment in 1975 for the Birmingham pub bombings. Their convictions were declared unsafe and overturned by the Court of Appeal in 1991. After spending 16 years behind bars, the six men were later awarded compensation ranging from £840,000 to £1.2 million. The Guildford Four and the Maguire Seven were two sets of people whose wrongful convictions for the Guildford pub bombings were also eventually quashed. In 1975 and 1976, the Guildford Four were convicted of bombings, apparently carried out by the IRA, and the Maguire Seven were convicted of handling explosives found during the investigation into the bombings. Both groups' convictions were declared 'unsafe and unsatisfactory' and reversed after they had served 15 years in prison. When the convictions of the Maguire Seven were quashed in 1991, the court held that members of the London Metropolitan Police had beaten some of the defendants into confessing to the crimes and withheld information that would have cleared them (Blom-Cooper 1997).

The Guildford bombings were most likely the work of the 'Balcombe gang', members of which publicly claimed responsibility at their own trial for other IRA-related murders and bombings. They were sentenced to life imprisonment, but were released under the terms of the 1998 Good Friday Agreement, which essentially established a power-sharing arrangement between the IRA, the Northern Ireland Loyalists and the British government (Moysey 2008). That settlement provided another example of the transformation of officially designated 'terrorists' into politically acceptable figures in the eyes of the government, the establishment and mainstream media.

British terrorism legislation contains numerous features of note, including a wide definition of terrorism, sweeping provisions directed against 'encouraging' or signifying support for terrorism, and broad executive powers to proscribe organisations. Other key provisions expand the scope of the measures, include those relating to possession of terrorist-linked materials, failure to disclose information to the authorities, fund-raising and preventative detention. The Terrorism Act 2000 defined terrorism broadly as follows:

> (1) In this Act 'terrorism' means the use or threat of action where:
>
> (a) the action falls within subsection (2),
>
> (b) the use or threat is designed to influence the government or to intimidate the public or a section of the public and
>
> (c) the use or threat is made for the purpose of advancing a political, religious or ideological cause.
>
> (2) Action falls within this subsection if it:
>
> (a) involves serious violence against a person,
>
> (b) involves serious damage to property,
>
> (c) endangers a person's life, other than that of the person committing the action,
>
> (d) creates a serious risk to the health or safety of the public or a section of the public or
>
> (e) is designed seriously to interfere with or seriously to disrupt an electronic system.

For these purposes, 'action' includes action outside the UK (*Terrorism Act* section 1(4)(a)); a 'person' or 'property' refers to any person, or to any property, wherever situated (section 1(4)(b)); and 'the public' includes the public of a country other than the UK (section 1(4)(c)). The use or threat of action falling within head (1) that involves the

> use of firearms or explosives is terrorism, whether or not head (2) is satisfied (section 1(3)). This latter sub-section was applied in *R (on the application of the Islamic Human Rights Commission) v Civil Aviation Authority* ([2006] EWHC 2465 (Admin), [2007] ACD 5 at [43], [44]).

'The government' means the government of the UK, of a part of the UK, or of a country other than the UK (section 1(4)(d)). 'The government' is not limited to countries governed by democratic or representative principles, and can include a tyranny, dictatorship, military junta, or usurping, or invading power: *R* v *F* ([2007] EWCA Crim 243, [2007] QB 960, [2007] 2 All ER 193, [2007] 2 Cr App Rep 20). The Court of Appeal dismissed the appeal of F, a Libyan dissident who was being prosecuted for possession of a document or record 'likely to be useful' to a terrorist, namely a blueprint for setting up an underground organisation in Libya to oppose the government of Colonel Gaddafi. Thus, dissidents fighting any regime that is currently favoured by the UK government can be subjected to terrorism charges.

Moreover, the Terrorism Act 2006 amended the definition to include 'international governmental organisations' in addition to 'the government'. This extended the offence to cover acts directed against the UN and other international institutions. The Secretary of State can also make orders and regulations, and give directions, under the Terrorism Act 2000 (sections 123, 124).

Organisations can be outlawed by executive order. Schedule 2 to Part II of the Terrorism Act 2000 listed certain proscribed organisations. The list has been added to by the Home Secretary, and now includes Al Qaeda and the Egyptian Islamic Jihad among several others, and the Home Secretary retains the power to remove or amend names on the schedule. Organisations that unlawfully 'glorify' acts of terrorism can now be proscribed (Section 21, Terrorism Act 2006). The procedure for appealing against proscription is set out in sections 5–6.

Membership (or professing membership) of a proscribed organisation is an offence carrying a maximum penalty of ten years' imprisonment. It is a defence for a person to show that the organisation was not proscribed when he last joined, and that he has not taken part in any of its activities while it has been proscribed. It is an offence for a person to invite support for a proscribed organisation (section 12(1)); to arrange a meeting which he knows is to support a proscribed organisation (or to further its activities or to be addressed by a member of a proscribed organisation) (section 12(2)); and to address a meeting with the purpose of encouraging support for a proscribed organisation (section 12(3)). There are statutory defences. The maximum penalty for these offences is also ten years' imprisonment.

It is even an offence for a person to wear, in a public place, an item of clothing (or wear or display an article) in such a way as to arouse reasonable suspicion that he is a member or supporter of a proscribed organisation (section 13). The maximum sentence for this offence is 6 months' imprisonment. Under section 56 of the Terrorism Act, it is an offence, punishable by life imprisonment, for a person to direct, at any level, the activities of an organisation that is concerned in the commission of terrorist acts.

The possession provisions are highly problematic. Section 57 of the Terrorism Act created an offence for a person to possess an article in circumstances that give rise to a reasonable suspicion that the possession is for a purpose connected with the commission, preparation or instigation of terrorist acts. This offence partly reverses the onus of proof. It is a defence to prove that the possession was not for such a purpose. However, the effect of section 118 of the 2000 Act is that, if a defendant adduces evidence that raises an issue as to whether his possession of the article in question was for such a purpose, the burden shifts back to the prosecution of proving beyond reasonable doubt that the possession of the article was held for such purpose.

A court may assume possession if the article is found at premises at the same time as the person is present, or on premises that he controls (unless he proves he did not know of its presence or that he had no control over it). The maximum sentence for this offence is 15 years' imprisonment. Under section 58, it is an offence to collect or make a record of information of a kind likely to be useful to a person committing or preparing an act of terrorism, or to possess a document or record containing information of that kind.

Earlier efforts by the Court of Appeal to limit the scope of sections 57 and 58 were thrown into doubt by the House of Lords in *R* v *G; R* v *J* ([2009] 2 WLR 724, [2009] 2 All ER 409, [2009] 2 Cr App R 4, [2009] UKHL 13) in which both sections were re-examined. The House of Lords upheld the conviction of G, who had been in prison at the time of the alleged offence, even though he had collected the incriminating information precisely because he knew how 'this terrorism stuff' had 'really got on the nerves of the prison officers'. Lord Rodger said, 'On no view could a desire to wind up prison officers in this way be a reasonable excuse for collecting and recording the information' (*R* v *G; R* v *J* [2009] UKHL 13, [89]). By this interpretation, an accused could be convicted for possessing material linked to terrorism even if his or her purpose had nothing whatever to do with instigating an act of terrorism, but, for example, related to annoying law enforcement personnel.

There are extensive anti-fund raising measures. Section 15 of the Terrorism Act makes it an offence to invite a person to provide money or other property, intending that it should be used (or having reasonable cause to suspect it may be used) for the purposes of terrorism. Receiving money or property intending it should be used (or having reasonable cause to suspect it may be used) for terrorist purposes is also an offence, as is providing money or property knowing (or having reasonable cause to suspect) that it will or may be used for the purposes of terrorism. 'Providing' money or property means giving, lending, or otherwise making available, whether or not this is in return for something else.

The Terrorism Act 2006 created several new offences, some of which were controversial, and also significantly extended police powers in terrorist investigations. It further provided that certain offences can be prosecuted even if they are committed outside the UK (section 17). Several offences contradict the right to freedom of expression, by punishing the communication of ideas, rather than any actions.

'Encouragement of terrorism' is criminalised by section 1. The offence is committed if a person makes a statement that is likely to be understood by some or all members of the public to whom it is published as 'a direct or indirect encouragement or other inducement to them' to commit, prepare, or instigate acts of terrorism. The person must publish the statement intending members of public to be directly or indirectly induced by it to commit or prepare such acts. Alternatively, the person making the statement must be reckless as to whether members of the public will be directly or indirectly encouraged, and so on.

Statements 'likely to encourage' include a statement that 'glorifies' the commission or preparation of terrorist offences, where the public could reasonably be expected to infer that the conduct being glorified should be emulated by them. Where a person is charged with this offence, and it is not proved that he intended to encourage or induce acts of terrorism, it is a defence to show that it was clear that the statement did not express his views, and was not endorsed by him. Encouragement of terrorism carries a maximum sentence of seven years' imprisonment.

Preparation and training offences take the terrorism measures well beyond the traditional criminal law concepts of attempt and complicity, and provide for severe penalties of up to life imprisonment. Section 5 of the 2006 Act makes it an offence for a person who intends to commit or assist an act of terrorism, or to engage in any conduct in preparation in order to give effect to his intention. The maximum sentence is life imprisonment.

Police powers have been increased. Under section 43 of the Terrorism Act 2000, a police officer may stop and search a person whom he reasonably suspects to be a terrorist to discover whether he has in his possession anything which may constitute evidence that he is a terrorist. Any person arrested under suspicion of being a terrorist may also be searched. Items that the officer reasonably suspects may constitute evidence that the person is a terrorist may be seized.

Even more fundamentally, the principle of habeas corpus – no detention without trial – is overturned to allow a terrorist suspect to be held in police custody prior to charge for a maximum of 28 days. This power is also reminiscent of the measures used in relation to Ireland, where internment without trial was introduced during the 1970s. A person arrested under section 41 of the Terrorism Act 2000 (that is, on suspicion of being a terrorist) may be held initially by the police without charge for 48 hours. Since the passage of the Terrorism Act 2006, detention beyond 48 hours can be extended by a High Court Judge, at intervals of 7 days, to a maximum of 28 days.

The British courts have held this power to be potentially consistent with the European Convention on Human Rights, despite Article 5, which provides the right to liberty, subject only to lawful arrest or detention. In order to justify the detention of terrorist suspects, the British government derogated from that article by invoking Article 15 of the Convention, which permits justified, necessary and proportionate responses 'in time of war or other public emergency threatening the life of the nation'. In 2004, the House of Lords accepted that indefinite detention without trial of foreign national terrorist suspects, unable to be prosecuted or deported, could be permissible under the 'public emergency' clause, in the context of the 9/11 attacks in the United States (*A and others* v *Secretary of State for the Home Department* [2004] UKHL 56). However, the majority ultimately declared the particular circumstances to be discriminatory and disproportionate to the exigencies of the public emergency. In a dissent on the threshold issue of whether the threat of terrorism constituted a 'public emergency threatening the life of the nation', Lord Hoffman stated that the gravest threat to Britain arose not from potential terrorist attacks, but from legislation such as that resorted to by the government ([2004] UKHL 56 [86–97]).

None the less, the eight-to-one majority view was that the courts had to defer heavily to the executive government's assessment of national security. In the words of Baroness Hale:

> Assessing the strength of a general threat to the life of the nation is, or should be, within the expertise of the Government and its advisers ... If a Government were to declare a public emergency where patently there was no such thing, it would be the duty of the court to say so. But here we are considering the immediate aftermath of the unforgettable events of 11 September 2001. The attacks launched on the United States on that date were clearly intended to threaten the life of the nation. ([2004] UKHL 56, [226])

The potential for the terrorism legislation to be used against anti-war protestors was demonstrated by the 2008 trial of Juliet McBride, a member of the Aldermaston Women's Peace Camp, who was charged with a terrorist offence for conducting a peaceful 'no Trident replacement' protest at the Atomic Weapons Establishment (AWE) at Aldermaston in March 2007. It was first trial pursuant to the controversial provisions of section 128 of the Serious Organised Crime and Police Act 2005 (SOCPA) as amended by section 12 of the Terrorism Act 2006. The amendment created a 'strict liability' offence of trespass on a 'nuclear licensed site'. A prosecution could be brought only with the Attorney General's consent.

For more than twenty years, the Aldermaston peace camp group had held a monthly protest at the site against British-manufactured nuclear weapons. When section 128 was amended in 2006, the relevant minister assured Parliament that the Aldermaston women were not its target, and that peaceful protestors who had not gone substantially beyond the fence would not be prosecuted. On the day of her arrest, McBride had crossed the outer perimeter fence and was sitting on the inner fence holding a peace flag. Although she was peaceful at all times, had not entered the site, and her protest related to a political matter, the Attorney General agreed that she should be prosecuted.

Following a visit to the site itself and consideration of a series of conflicting maps detailing the site boundary, District Judge Sanders agreed that the Ministry of Defence and AWE Aldermaston had mistakenly assumed that the boundary of the nuclear-licensed site was marked by the outer perimeter fence. In fact, the correct boundary is the inner fence, and so McBride had not entered the licensed area when arrested and there was no trespass. The court awarded the defendant her costs (Doughty Street Chambers 2008).

For a case study of how various measures can be used to deprive an individual of liberty without trial for protracted periods, see *Secretary of State for the Home Department* v *Saadi* ([2009] EWHC 3390 (Admin)). Libyan national Faraj Faraj Hassan Al-Saadi, who had been under restriction for six years in the United Kingdom on terrorism charges, won a long court battle to have his control order revoked.

Faraj Hassan came to the UK in 2002, fleeing persecution in Libya. He was arrested shortly thereafter and spent 15 months detained without trial before being eventually charged under the Terrorism Act in 2003 and served with an Italian extradition warrant. Although the extradition order was ultimately suspended, he continued to be detained for another four years on the basis of secret evidence, with the government seeking to deport him to Libya. Whilst his deportation was ruled unlawful, he was then made the subject of a control order in addition to a UN financial sanction which prevented him from obtaining any income.

United States

Both federal and state anti-terrorism provisions exist in the US. Many of the federal measures are derived from the USA PATRIOT Act of 2001. They are primarily codified in Chapter 113B, entitled Terrorism, of Title 18 of the United States Code, which provides for criminal penalties ranging from ten years' imprisonment to the death penalty.

Section 2331(5) defines domestic terrorism as

> … activities that (A) involve acts dangerous to human life that are a violation of the criminal laws of the US or of any state, that (B) appear to be intended (i) to intimidate or coerce a civilian population, (ii) to influence the policy of a government by intimidation or coercion, or (iii) to affect the conduct of a government by mass destruction, assassination, or kidnapping, and (C) occur primarily within the territorial jurisdiction of the US.

Terrorism is also included in the definition of racketeering, and terms relating to 'cyber-terrorism' are redefined, including 'protected computer', 'damage' and 'loss'.

The USA PATRIOT Act authorised a vast array of measures to boost the powers of the domestic security services (Title 1), enhance controversial surveillance procedures, including to gather 'foreign intelligence information' from both US and non-US citizens (Title II), to facilitate the prevention, detection and prosecution of 'international money laundering' and the 'financing of terrorism' (Title III), and to expand the enforcement and investigative powers of the Immigration and Naturalization Service (Title IV).

Title VIII, entitled 'Terrorism criminal law', had many other provisions. New penalties were created to convict those who attack mass transportation systems. If the activity was undertaken while the mass transportation vehicle or ferry was carrying a passenger, or the offence resulted in the death of any person, then the punishment is life imprisonment. A number of measures penalised activities that are deemed to support terrorism. It was made a crime to harbour or conceal terrorists, and those who do are subject to imprisonment of up to ten years.

The potential for anti-terrorism laws to be used against organisations engaged in lawful advocacy, even those teaching about explicitly non-violent political lobbying, was underscored in 2010 when the US Supreme Court upheld 6–3 a provision of law making it a federal crime to 'knowingly provide material support or resources to a foreign terrorist organization', even if the 'support' consisted only of 'expert advice or assistance' for 'lawful, non-violent purposes'.

The challenged law was part of the Antiterrorism and Effective Death Penalty Act 1996 (AEDPA), signed into law on the first anniversary of the Oklahoma City bombing (18 U.S.C. Section 2339B(a)(1)). It provided that the US Secretary of State could designate any 'foreign organization' as 'terrorist' based on 'classified information' establishing that it 'engages in terrorist activity' which 'threatens the security of United States nationals or the national security of the United States'. As a result of the court's ruling, an individual can be sentenced to as much as 15 years' imprisonment if found to 'provide material support' for a designated organisation, even if only by means of engaging in discussions with it or speaking on its behalf. In effect, at the application of the Obama administration, the Supreme Court gave its imprimatur to the prosecution and imprisonment of US citizens for advocating support of organisations opposing the policies of the US government or its allies anywhere on the planet.

The plaintiffs in *Humanitarian Law Project* v. *Holder* (561 U.S. ____ (2010)) were a coalition of US-based human rights organisations, non-profit groups and citizens who obtained a lower court injunction to protect them from being criminally prosecuted for advising and assisting the separatist groups, the Partiya Karkeran Kurdistan (PKK) and Liberation Tigers of Tamil Eelam (LTTE). Both were designated as 'foreign terrorist organizations' by President Bill Clinton's Secretary of State Madeline Albright in 1997. The Obama administration's Attorney General, Eric Holder, appealed the injunction to the Supreme Court, where he was represented by Solicitor General Elena Kagan.

The injunction allowed the plaintiffs to 'train members of the PKK on how to use humanitarian and international law to peacefully resolve disputes', to 'engage in political advocacy on behalf of Kurds who live in Turkey', and to 'teach PKK members how to petition various representative bodies such as the United Nations for relief'. The plaintiffs also were allowed to 'train members of the LTTE to present claims for tsunami-related aid to mediators and international bodies', to 'offer their legal expertise in negotiating peace agreements between the LTTE and the Sri Lankan government', and to 'engage in political advocacy on behalf of Tamils who live in Sri Lanka'.

Rejecting plaintiffs' claims that the law unconstitutionally criminalised conduct protected by the First Amendment's guarantees of freedoms of speech and association, Chief Justice John Roberts, writing for the six-judge majority, stated that such actions:

> … meant to 'promot[e] peaceable, lawful conduct' … can further terrorism … Such support frees up other resources within the organization that may be put to violent ends. It also importantly helps lend legitimacy to foreign terrorist groups – legitimacy that makes it easier for those groups to persist, to recruit members, and to raise funds – all of which facilitate more terrorist attacks. (at 25)

Comparing the struggles of these nationalist movements against US allies Turkey and Sri Lanka to an all-out world war, Roberts wrote:

> If only good can come from training our adversaries in international dispute resolution, presumably it would have been unconstitutional to prevent American citizens from training the Japanese Government on using international organizations and mechanisms to resolve disputes during World War II. (at 33–4)

The judgment accorded great deference to Congressional findings regarding the PKK and LTTE and noted that money is fungible, thus supporting the conclusion that 'humanitarian aid' could ultimately serve violent activities. The majority also gave deference to the executive branch, quoting a State Department affidavit (at 28). While the majority acknowledged the court had an important role to play – writing 'we are one with the dissent' that national security considerations do not 'automatically trump' judicial obligations – the majority quickly emphasised the judicial 'lack of competence' in such matters. The majority chastised the dissent for failing to address 'the real dangers at stake' (at 33).

Associate Justice Stephen Breyer wrote the dissent, stating:

> I cannot agree with the Court's conclusion that the Constitution permits the Government to prosecute the plaintiffs criminally for engaging in coordinated teaching and advocacy furthering the designated organizations' lawful political objectives. That this speech and association for political purposes is the kind of activity to which the First Amendment ordinarily offers its strongest protection is elementary. (Dissent at 1)

Breyer concluded that the court had failed to 'examine the Government's justifications with sufficient care' and failed to 'insist upon specific evidence, rather than general assertion' (at 23).

Australia

The legislation introduced since 2002 in Australia contains several almost unprecedented features. They include secret interrogation and detention without trial, with those detained or questioned by the Australian Secret Intelligence

Organisation (ASIO) prohibited from informing anyone, even family members, of their disappearance or the reasons for it. There are also lengthy jail terms for refusing to disclose information requested by the authorities; powers to outlaw 'association' with a member or supporter of a proscribed terrorist organisation; and people charged with a 'terrorist' offence can be tried semi-secretly, partly on the basis of evidence that they are forbidden to view or hear. The legislation also defines terrorism in sweeping terms, capable of criminalising many traditional forms of protest and dissent; permits the banning of political groups by executive fiat, a power that the High Court rejected in the *Communist Party case (Australian Communist Party* v. *Commonwealth* (1951) 83 CLR 1); and shrouds the operations of the intelligence and police agencies in secrecy. (For full details, see Head 2002; 2004a; 2004b).

None of these measures were necessary to protect ordinary people from terrorism. The government and the police and security agencies had every power needed to detect, monitor, arrest and charge terrorists. Every conceivable terror act was already a serious crime – from murder to arson and hijacking. Furthermore, the criminal law amply covered all planning, preparing, conspiring, financing, supporting and attempting related to such activities. Moreover, ASIO and the state and federal police already possessed immense powers to infiltrate organisations, tap phones, bug premises, intercept mail, search homes and hack into computers (Head 2002).

Of particular concern is the exceptional range of the definition of 'terrorist act' given by section 100.1 of the Criminal Code Act 1995 (Cth). It specifies that:

> ***terrorist act*** means an action or threat of action where:
>
> the action falls within subsection (2) and does not fall within subsection (3); and
>
> the action is done or the threat is made with the intention of advancing a political, religious or ideological cause; and
>
> the action is done or the threat is made with the intention of:
>
> (i) coercing, or influencing by intimidation, the government of the Commonwealth or a State, Territory or foreign country, or of part of a State, Territory or foreign country; or
>
> (ii) intimidating the public or a section of the public.
>
> 2) Action falls within this subsection if it:
>
> (a) causes serious harm that is physical harm to a person; or

(b) causes serious damage to property; or

(c) causes a person's death; or

(d) endangers a person's life, other than the life of the person taking the action; or

(e) creates a serious risk to the health or safety of the public or a section of the public; or

(f) seriously interferes with, seriously disrupts, or destroys, an electronic system including, but not limited to:

(i) an information system; or

(ii) a telecommunications system; or

(iii) a financial system; or

(iv) a system used for the delivery of essential government services; or

(v) a system used for, or by, an essential public utility; or

(vi) a system used for, or by, a transport system.

(3) Action falls within this subsection if it:

(a) is advocacy, protest, dissent or industrial action; and

(b) is not intended:

(i) to cause serious harm that *is* physical harm to a person; or

(ii) to cause a person's death; or

(iii) to endanger the life of a person, other than the person taking the action; or to create a serious risk to the health or safety of the public or a section of the public.

Thus, terrorism extends to acts or threats that advance 'a political, religious or ideological cause' for the purpose of coercing or influencing by intimidation' any government or section of the public. 'Advocacy, protest, dissent or industrial action' is exempted but not if it involves harm to a person, 'serious damage' to property, 'serious risk' to public health or safety, or 'serious interference' with an information, telecommunications, financial, essential services or transport system.

This definition could cover a demonstration or strike in which a person was injured or felt endangered, given that the purpose of many protests and strikes is to apply pressure to ('coerce' or 'intimidate') a government, employer, or other authority. Nurses taking strike action that shuts down hospital wards in support of a political demand for greater health spending, for example, could be accused of endangering public health and thus be charged as terrorists.

In some instances, terrorist intent is not necessary. The legislation imposes jail terms ranging from life to ten years for preparing, planning, or training for terrorist acts, and for possessing documents or other objects used in the preparation of such acts. A person can be jailed for possessing such a 'thing' even if they did not know it would be used for terrorist purposes, but were merely 'reckless' as to that fact (Criminal Code sections 101.2, 101.4, 101.5, 101.6).

The various, related, terrorist offences could apply to a wide range of political activity, such as planning a protest outside government buildings or facilities where damage may occur. Demonstrators who prepared to block roads or entrances to financial institutions, such as the stock exchange, could be charged as terrorists, as could computer hackers. During questioning in a Senate committee hearing in 2002, the Attorney-General's representatives admitted that someone who cut through a fence at the Easter 2002 protest at the Woomera refugee detention centre or who marched into the Parliament building in Canberra during a 1996 trade union rally could have been charged with terrorism (Senate Committee 2002: 19). The officials acknowledged that a picketing striker who caused property damage or a person who possessed a mobile phone used to discuss a violent act could be prosecuted (ibid.: 14–15).

While citing the 9/11 attacks in the United States as its justification, the government adopted a definition of terrorism that went beyond the USA PATRIOT Act, which covered activity that was dangerous to human life and violated existing criminal laws. The Australian version is based on the British Terrorism Act 2000, but went further in specifying disruption to various communications systems (Hancock 2002: 2–8).

Four types of detention without trial have been introduced. (1) The Australian Federal Police (AFP) can detain someone for investigation of a terrorist offence under section 23CA of the Crimes Act 1914 (Cth). Although a person can ordinarily be held for questioning for only four hours, the Act enabled police to apply to a 'judicial officer' (a magistrate, justice of the peace, or bail justice), for an extension of the 'investigation period' of up to 24 hours. The police can also ask for a suspension of the questioning time limit for a non-exhaustive list of reasons, including to allow other 'authorities,' inside or outside Australia, 'time to collect information', and 'to collate and analyse information' from other sources. Initially, there was no time limit on how long the questioning clock could be stopped and no limit on the number of times a 'judicial officer' could approve such AFP requests. As became clear when Dr Mohameed Haneef was detained in 2007 (see below), the provisions were broad enough to permit almost indefinite detention. In the wake of the public outcry over Haneef's mistreatment, amendments in 2010 set a seven-day limit on the amount of time that can be specified by a magistrate and disregarded from the investigation period, effectively capping the total detention time at eight days.

(2) Amendments to the *Australian Security Intelligence Organisation Act 1979* (Cth) gave ASIO the power to detain and question people. ASIO and AFP officers can raid anyone's home or office, at any hour of the day or night, and forcibly take them away, interrogate and strip-search them and hold them incommunicado, effectively indefinitely through the issuing of repeated warrants. Detainees do not need to be suspected of a terrorist offence, or any other criminal offence. The Attorney-General can certify that their interrogation would 'substantially assist the collection of intelligence that is important in relation to a terrorism offence', even if no act of terrorism occurred. This power can be used to detain journalists and political activists, as well as the children, relatives, or acquaintances of terrorism suspects. Any detainee who refuses to answer ASIO's questions is liable to five years' imprisonment. Initial detention can last for up to seven days, including three eight-hour blocks of questioning over three days, but the Attorney-General can approve further seven-day periods, on the basis that 'additional to or materially different' information had come to light.

(3) Anyone whom police allege may be involved in a future terrorist act, or may have information about such an act, can be subjected to 'preventative detention' for up to 48 hours by federal police or 14 days by state police. The grounds for obtaining a preventative detention order are broad and effectively remove the burden of proof on the Crown to prove its case beyond a reasonable doubt. The Criminal Code Act 1995 section 105.4 provides for an 'issuing authority' – a judge, former judge, or magistrate operating in a 'personal capacity' (that is, not as a court, but as part of the executive) – to approve the internment in an initial '*ex parte*' hearing, that is without the 'suspect' being present. Suspects have limited rights to know why they are being detained. They may be held incommunicado and any conversations they hold with a lawyer can be monitored, violating lawyer-client privilege. Anyone – including family members, lawyers and the media – who reveals that the person has been detained, can be jailed for five years. These provisions are designed to ensure that no one knows how many people have been rounded up, or why, or in what conditions they are being held. The Australian Press Council pointed out in its submission to the Australian Senate Legal and Constitutional Legislation Committee:

> Even in circumstances where a person has been detained illegally or inappropriately, the media are unable to investigate or report upon the detention. If detainees have suffered torture or abuse during their detention, they cannot inform the media of this, and the media are prohibited from reporting the abuse. (Australian Press Council 2005)

(4) Specially designated 'issuing courts' may grant 'control orders' – which can include house arrest, the fitting of personal tracking devices and bans on

employment and all forms of communication-also without any initial notice or hearing. Like preventative detainees, those under house arrest can be barred from alerting anyone to their internment. The control orders can last 12 months and be renewed continuously. Detainees can only challenge them, possibly weeks or months later, in the same special courts. The grounds for granting a control order are equally as vague as for preventative detention, and lower the burden of proof to the 'balance of probabilities' (Criminal Code section 104.4).

Preventative detention and control orders can be imposed on top of each other. This is in addition to the investigation, questioning and detention provisions. The authorities could detain someone for a week of questioning, followed by eight days of investigation, then 14 days of 'preventative detention' and a year or more of virtual house arrest. These laws could allow governments and their security agencies to lock someone away based solely on what they allege the 'suspect' might be intending to do in the future. The legislation clears the way for practices commonly identified with totalitarian regimes. People can simply 'disappear' into police custody, without the media, or anyone else, being able to report it.

In 2005, the Australian federal, state and territory governments introduced Anti-Terrorism Bills that were self-evidently designed for use where the police and intelligence agencies can present no evidence of involvement in specific terrorist activity or planning. The Anti-Terrorism Bill (No. 1) changed the wording of many terrorist offences from 'the' terrorist act to 'a' terrorist act. In effect, it means that people can be convicted of planning or preparing for terrorism, and sentenced to life imprisonment, without evidence of a time, date, location, or method of the supposed attack. The prosecution need only establish that the accused's conduct related to 'a' terrorist act – that is, any potential act. In addition, a person can be convicted even if 'a terrorist act does not occur'. These provisions give the police wide powers to arrest people on vague charges of, for example, 'assisting', 'preparing', or 'supporting' an unidentified terrorist act that never takes place.

Another aspect of the 2005 legislation is its capacity to chill political dissent, and to replace the 'unlawful associations' provisions as a means of proscribing political groups. Any organisation that 'advocates' a terrorist act can be outlawed by the Attorney-General, exposing its members, supporters and financial donors to imprisonment as well. Section 102.1(1A) of the Criminal Code defined 'advocates' as 'directly or indirectly counseling or urging', or 'directly or indirectly providing instruction' on the doing of 'a terrorist act,' or 'directly praising' the doing of a terrorist act in circumstances where there is a risk that such praise might have the effect of leading a person to engage in a terrorist act.

'Praising' terrorism could extend to justifying or expressing sympathy for a hypothetical terrorist act, or even calling for an understanding of terrorism's social and economic roots. A 2010 amendment inserted the word 'substantial' before 'risk'. However, that leaves considerable discretion in the hands of the authorities and the courts as to the meaning of 'substantial'. The amendment also changed subsection 102.1(3) to extend the period of a regulation that proscribes a terrorist organisation from two to three years

Under section 102.1 of the Criminal Code, 'terrorist organisation' means 'an organisation that is directly or indirectly engaged in, preparing, planning, assisting in or fostering the doing of a terrorist act (whether or not a terrorist act occurs)', or an organisation listed in regulations. To list an organisation, the Attorney-General 'must be satisfied on reasonable grounds' that the organisation meets the above definition or 'advocates the doing of a terrorist act (whether or not a terrorist act has occurred or will occur)'. Any person who directs or provides support to the activities of a terrorist organisation, knowing it to be terrorist, can be jailed for 25 years or, if they are 'reckless' as to whether the organisation is terrorist or not, for 15 years. A member of a group banned under a regulation faces up to ten years' imprisonment. Membership is defined to include 'informal membership' or taking 'steps to become a member'. It is a defence to have taken 'reasonable steps' to cease membership 'as soon as practicable' after knowing the organisation was terrorist, but the burden of proof lies on the defendant.

The legislation also retains a backdoor method for banning organisations by freezing their funds, even if they have not been formally declared terrorist. The Attorney-General can freeze assets or proscribe groups if a UN Security Council freezing order has been issued. Either the Minister can 'list' an organisation by Gazette notice or the Governor-General may make proscription regulations. Anyone collecting or providing donations for the organisation can be jailed for five years. If the funds are used for terrorist purposes, the penalty is life.

The potential for the anti-terrorism laws to be abused, in combination with migration legislation, was demonstrated in the 2007 case of a young Indian Muslim doctor, Mohamed Haneef. AFP officers arrested Haneef at Brisbane airport, as he was about to leave the country. Sensational media claims were made that Haneef was secretly fleeing Australia in the wake of failed bomb plots in London and Glasgow several days earlier. Yet Haneef had obtained emergency leave from the Gold Coast Hospital where he worked to travel to India, where his newborn daughter was ill.

He was initially held for nearly two weeks without charge under the AFP's expanded Crimes Act investigation power, discussed above. The doctor was eventually charged under s 102.7 of the Criminal Code (Cth) with 'intentionally' providing support or resources to a terrorist organisation that would help it engage in terrorist activity, while being 'reckless' as to whether the organisation was terrorist. That offence carries 15 years' imprisonment. Police alleged that before he left the United Kingdom in 2006 to work in the Gold Coast Hospital, Haneef gave a mobile phone SIM card to his cousin Sabeel Ahmed. The card was allegedly found in the jeep driven by Ahmed's brother Kafeel that was used in the attack on Glasgow Airport. By this logic, anyone who sold petrol to the jeep driver, or provided any other resources, could also be charged. Ultimately, after media reports, police admitted that the SIM card was not in the jeep, and the Director of Prosecutions (DPP) dropped the charge.

In the meantime, Immigration Minister Kevin Andrews revoked Haneef's visa just after a magistrate had granted Haneef bail. The minister exercised a personal discretion vested in him by section 501 of the Migration Act 1958 (Cth) to cancel a visa if he considers that a person fails the 'character test'. Attorney-General Philip Ruddock then issued a Criminal Justice Certificate under section 145 of the Migration Act. The stated intended effect of the twin decisions was that Haneef would be held in immigration detention pending trial, rather than being released on bail. Haneef commenced an action in the Federal Court challenging the visa decision. Two weeks later, the minister announced that after seeking advice from the Commonwealth Solicitor-General David Bennett, he did not propose to change his decision, even though the DPP had withdrawn the charge against Haneef.

Section 501 empowers the minister to personally cancel a visa if he 'reasonably suspects that the person does not pass the character test' and he 'is satisfied that the refusal or cancellation is in the national interest'. To cancel Haneef's visa, Andrews relied upon a part of the character test which states that a person fails the test if 'the person has or has had an association with someone else, or with a group of organisation, whom the minister reasonably suspects has been or is involved in criminal conduct.'

The application for judicial review that Haneef lodged with the Federal Court argued that the decision was unlawful on several grounds, including that the minister had wrongly interpreted the word 'association' in section 501. The Migration Act did not define 'association'. Haneef alleged that the minister had unlawfully considered that any association, even a purely family one, was sufficient to fail the character test. In *Haneef* v *Minister for Immigration and Citizenship* ([2007] FCA 1271), Federal Court Justice Spender agreed, saying that 'completely innocent' people could be stripped of visas simply because they had a relative, friend, or even lawyer whom police suspected of criminal conduct. The Full Federal Court unanimously upheld Justice Spender's decision in *Minister for Immigration & Citizenship* v *Haneef* ([2007] FCAFC 203).

The outcome of the case, and the subsequent government inquiry conducted in 2008 by former NSW Supreme Court Justice John Clarke, left many unanswered questions about the Howard government's apparent role in orchestrating the witch-hunt against Haneef. There is considerable evidence that Prime Minister Howard and other senior ministers played a direct hand in instigating the legal proceedings against Haneef (Head 2009).

Equally troubling was the 2008 prosecution of Belal Khazaal. Essentially, he was tried in the New South Wales Supreme Court for advocating and writing about terrorism, not for being involved in terrorist acts, even in the most indirect manner. He was charged with 'knowingly collecting or making a document connected with terrorism', and 'inciting a person to commit a terrorist act'. The 'document' that Khazaal was accused of compiling had not been linked to any terrorist activity or planning. Nor was it published surreptitiously, an essential requirement of any terrorist plot. He posted on a publicly available Jihadist website an Arab-language book composed of material gathered from other identified sources already in the public domain.

It appears that the manuscript, whose title has been translated as *Provisions on the Rules of Jihad – Short judicial rulings and organisational instructions for fighters and Mujahideen against infidels*, offered inflammatory support and advice for an Islamic fundamentalist 'holy war'. It praised the terrorist attacks of 11 September 2001, hailing Al Qaeda's 'impressive success of the conquest of New York'. The media played up the prosecution's assertions that the book listed 'targets that should be assassinated', including US President George Bush and members of his cabinet, such as Donald Rumsfeld and Colin Powell, US generals and intelligence officials, along with 'infidels' in Arab countries. Other texts apparently provided a checklist for assassins, from organising budgeting and transport to checking wiring before using a time-bomb.

However, no specific terrorist act was outlined, and no evidence was produced in court suggesting that any assassination or other terrorist activity was committed or attempted as a result of someone reading the material, which was posted online in 2003. Once ASIO and the police raised objections to the book with Khazaal in 2004, he removed it from the Internet. Two months later, however, he was arrested and charged.

There is no doubt that the perspective advanced by Khazaal was repugnant. The September 11 atrocities, which involved the indiscriminate killing of nearly 3,000 innocent people, embodied Al Qaeda's contempt for ordinary working people. Nevertheless, Khazaal was exercising a basic democratic right when he expressed his views. The struggle for freedom of expression and other democratic rights has spanned centuries, precisely to protect the voicing of political, ideological and religious opinions, no matter how unpopular, dissenting, or abhorrent. Once a government is allowed to outlaw a particular point of view, the precedent can be used against any other.

Ultimately, a jury was unable to reach a verdict on the incitement charge, while finding him guilty of compiling a document that could be used to assist a terrorist attack. He was sentenced to 12 years' imprisonment (*R* v *Khazaal* [2009] NSWSC 1015). In June 2011, Khazaal's conviction was set aside on appeal and a new trial was ordered, but no judicial reasons were released for this reversal.

One further case highlighted the potential for the anti-terrorism laws to be used against supporters of overseas anti-government or separatist movements. In 2010, the federal Director of Public Prosecutions (DPP) abandoned nine terrorism charges against three prominent members of Australia's Tamil community. They had been accused of being members of the separatist Liberation Tigers of Tamil Eelam (LTTE) and providing funds to the LTTE, knowing it to be 'a terrorist organisation'.

However, the DPP said the three men – who all pleaded not guilty – would still be tried on five remaining charges of breaching the Charter of the United Nations Act 1945 by making money available to a 'proscribed organisation'. Aruran Vinayagamoorthy, Sivarajah Yathavan and Arumugam Rajeevan were arrested in 2007 as part of a series of police raids in Sydney and Melbourne, following a wave of similar arrests in the United States and France of alleged LTTE supporters, despite the LTTE not being listed as a terrorist organisation under the Australian anti-terrorism laws.

From the outset, the police admitted there was no evidence of any involvement in, or planning for, terrorist activity within Australia. Instead, they accused the three men of raising money for relief projects, including for victims of the 2004 Boxing Day tsunami, with the knowledge that some funds were going to the LTTE, which at that time controlled parts of the tsunami-affected north and east of Sri Lanka.

The Sri Lankan government immediately welcomed the arrests. While the Australian government insisted that the arrests and charges were purely a matter for the federal police and prosecution authorities, the case was part of an international operation against LTTE supporters. Similar police investigations were launched in Canada, Britain, The Netherlands, Germany and Italy.

The UN Charter Act effectively provides for outlawing organisations via ministerial regulations, which mostly rely on an ever-expanding UN Security Council list. If similar laws had existed in the past, people could have been jailed for giving money to the anti-apartheid movement in South Africa, Irish Republican causes, or East Timorese independence groups. The LTTE has been on the list since 2001, even though from 2002 until 2009 it was not outlawed in Sri Lanka itself because of a ceasefire agreement with the Sri Lankan government. Ultimately, the men were convicted, but given suspended sentences (*R* v *Vinayagamoorthy & Ors* [2010] VSC 148).

International Law and Human Rights

As mentioned earlier, in the 2004 English House of Lords decision in *A* v *Secretary of State for the Home Department*, the court, with Lord Hoffman dissenting, accepted that indefinite detention without trial of foreign national terrorist suspects, unable to be prosecuted or deported, could be permissible under the 'public emergency' clause of the European Convention on Human Rights and Fundamental Freedoms, as incorporated by the UK Human Rights Act 1998. However, the majority ultimately declared the provisions, as directed selectively against foreign nationals, to be discriminatory and disproportionate to the exigencies of the public emergency.

The ruling highlights the extent to which international law reserves to the national state the power to override basic legal and democratic rights in alleged emergencies or dire challenges to the stability of the state. In the Universal Declaration of Human Rights, the International Covenant on Civil and Political Rights (ICCPR), and other related instruments, such as the European Convention on Human Rights and Fundamental Freedoms and the UK Human Rights Act, the listed civil and legal rights are mostly subject to far-reaching exemptions, including 'national security' and 'public safety' – leaving considerable leeway for draconian measures, such as the forms of detention without trial and other provisions imposed in the name of fighting the 'war on terrorism'. Thus, Article 4 of the ICCPR states:

> 1. In time of public emergency which threatens the life of the nation and the existence of which is officially proclaimed, the States Parties to the present Covenant may take measures derogating from their obligations under the present Covenant to the extent strictly required by the exigencies of the situation, provided that such measures are not inconsistent with their other obligations under international law and do not involve discrimination solely on the ground of race, colour, sex, language, religion or social origin.
>
> 2. No derogation from articles 6, 7, 8 (paragraphs I and 2), 11, 15, 16 and 18 may be made under this provision.

These exceptions to derogation relate to killing, torture, slavery, trial by law and freedom of religion. Under the European Convention on Human Rights and Fundamental Freedoms, even the right to life is carefully circumscribed to permit killing by state forces in order to make arrests, prevent escapes from detention and quell riots and insurrections (Article 2). Governments can derogate from most obligations under the European Convention 'in time of war or other public emergency threatening the life of the nation' (Article 15). Particularly since the declaration of the 'war on terrorism' in 2001, courts have tended to give executive governments much leeway to use these provisions.

Thus, international human rights law provides little reliable protection against the application of offences against the state, regardless of any violation of basic democratic rights. In any case, because the nation-state system that still prevails globally, international law is not legally binding domestically unless it is incorporated into national legislation. Moreover, with some exceptions, such as the US Constitution's Bill of Rights and the Canadian Charter of Rights and Freedoms, domestic human rights measures are not constitutionally entrenched, and can therefore be abridged, amended or repealed by legislatures.

Some provisions simply require courts to interpret all legislation, where possible, consistently with enumerated human rights, generally drawn from the International Covenant on Civil and Political Rights. If the legislation under consideration cannot be interpreted consistently with a human right, the court may only declare that an incompatibility exists, and report the issue to the legislature. Such a declaration does not affect the validity of the legislation in question.

Furthermore, under provisions like the UK Human Rights Act, the courts are instructed to permit reasonable limits to human rights if the limit is 'demonstrably justified in a free and democratic society'. This proviso, which the English House of Lords judges have described as one of proportionality, leaves scope for governments to brush aside or whittle down democratic rights of minorities in the name of upholding the democratic rights of the majority.

State Terrorism

In the name of defending the state, governments or official security agencies may engage in unlawful acts of surveillance, harassment, violence, or intimidation. These may also include wars of aggression, military interventions, coups, assassinations, renditions and torture (Tigar 2007: 1–110). It appears that such practices increased in the first decade of the twenty-first century. Considerable evidence has been produced of such crimes being committed from 2001 onward, both domestically and abroad. It is not possible to investigate or review these operations here. But it is important to note that those allegedly affected by these crimes have faced considerable difficulties in bringing lawsuits seeking to prosecute or obtain redress for such conduct. Courts have dismissed legal actions on various grounds, including 'state secret' doctrines invoked by the government accused of being responsible. Two American cases decided in 2010 illustrate this development. One concerned the use of 'renditions' to secretly transport prisoners to locations in other countries where they could be tortured. The other involved the targeted assassination of people identified as terrorists.

In the first decision, the US Ninth Circuit Court of Appeals in a 6–5 *en banc* ruling dismissed a lawsuit by five victims of the Central Intelligence Agency's 'extraordinary rendition' programme against Jeppesen Dataplan, a unit of Boeing. The ruling relied upon the 'state secrets' doctrine advocated by the Obama administration. The American Civil Liberties Union brought the suit, charging that defence contractor Jeppesen Dataplan knowingly facilitated the renditions, also known as 'torture flights', by providing flight planning and logistical support to CIA personnel. The suit, *Mohamed* v *Jeppesen Dataplan, Inc.* (9th Cir. – Sept. 8, 2010), sought to expose a web of connections between top executives of defence corporations, foreign intelligence agencies and the US government.

The Ninth Circuit's ruling argued that 'there is precious little Jeppesen could say about its relevant conduct and knowledge without revealing information about how the United States government does or does not conduct covert operations.' On this basis, the court dismissed the case. Earlier, a three-judge panel of the Ninth Circuit had ruled against the Obama administration. Writing for the panel, Judge Michael D. Hawkins wrote that the 'state secrets' doctrine advocated by the administration 'has no logical limit'. The judge noted, 'As the Founders of this Nation knew well, arbitrary imprisonment and torture under any circumstance is a gross and notorious act of despotism.'

The panel's decision was overturned by the entire Ninth Circuit, in a judgment authored by Judge Raymond C. Fisher. While couching his opinion in the language of 'balancing' national security against individual liberties, Judge Fisher concluded, 'Courts must act in the interest of the country's national security to prevent disclosure of state secrets, even to the point of dismissing a case entirely' (Savage 2010).

In another 2010 decision, Federal District Judge John D. Bates dismissed a lawsuit that challenged the Obama administration's policy of targeted killings of individuals around the world, including US citizens. The administration had placed the name of US citizen Anwar Al-Aulaqi on a 'kill list', permitting any of the US government's military or intelligence agencies to carry out his assassination. Al-Aulaqi was reported to be in Yemen. The CIA had launched a cruise missile at a meeting Al-Aulaqi was attending there, but the intended victim survived.

In *Al-Aulaqi* v *Obama* (D.D.C. Dec. 7, 2010), the American Civil Liberties Union (ACLU) and the Center for Constitutional Rights (CCR) filed a lawsuit on behalf of Al-Aulaqi's father, Nasser Al-Aulaqi, challenging the targeted killing programme. The Obama administration argued that the president had the power to order the killing of an American citizen without a trial or judicial review, despite this being a clear violation of international law and the US Bill of Rights. The Fifth Amendment to the US Constitution states: 'No person shall be ... deprived of life ... without due process of law.' The administration further argued that the case should not be allowed to proceed because it threatened to reveal 'state secrets'.

Judge Bates, in his ruling, acknowledged that the case raised 'stark' and 'perplexing' questions. He asked (at 2): 'Can the Executive order the assassination of a U.S. citizen without first affording him any form of judicial process whatsoever, based on the mere assertion that he is a dangerous member of a terrorist organization?' However, Bates concluded that the case could not proceed because Anwar Al-Aulaqi's father, Nasser Al-Aulaqi, lacked legal standing to bring the case.

This ruling implies that in order for the targeted killing programme to be challenged, the persons marked for death must appear themselves in the courts of the country that is trying to assassinate them. Bates included in his opinion a passage suggesting that in light of Anwar Al-Aulaqi's political and religious views, he should not be entitled to the protections of the US Constitution. The judge wrote that Al-Aulaqi has 'decried the US legal system and suggested that Muslims are not bound by Western law'. Accordingly, Bates wrote, Al-Aulaqi would not 'likely want to sue to vindicate his US constitutional rights in US courts'.

Judge Bates dismissed Al-Aulaqi's claims under international law because the doctrine of 'sovereign immunity' prevents the government from being the target of certain lawsuits without its express consent. Bates held that a judicial evaluation of the Obama administration's assassination programme would involve a 'political question' not subject to judicial review. Bates indicated that in light of his other rulings dismissing the case, it was unnecessary to decide whether the 'state secrets' doctrine applied.

Conclusion

Rather than offering a new paradigm for global governance, the United Nations' response to 9/11 and the Bush administration's declaration of a 'war on terrorism' laid the basis for unilateral militarism and serious erosions of basic legal and democratic rights. On the surface, the UN displayed unprecedented unity and forcefulness, formally committing UN member states to concerted action to fight terrorism. In reality, the Security Council resolutions sanctioned military interventions by the major powers, especially the United States, and legitimised repressive domestic measures by governments around the world.

Governments of all kinds have utilised the UN resolutions, and exploited their lack of any definition of terrorism, to introduce far-reaching legislation and other measures that can be used to criminalise certain political activities and the expression of dissenting ideas. Sweeping definitions of terrorism have been adopted, vague offences of preparation, incitement and advocacy have been introduced and virtually unprecedented powers of surveillance and detention have been established.

Although Islamic fundamentalists have been the most prominent initial targets, others have already been affected, including anti-war activists, humanitarian groups and supporters of overseas anti-government organisations. At the same time, state terrorism has been legitimised and extraordinary steps taken to protect governments from accountability for violent actions, including renditions and assassinations. Finally, international human rights law has proven incapable of fundamentally restraining the abuses of civil liberties, not least because of the elasticity of doctrines such as 'national security', 'public safety' and 'emergency'.

References

Amnesty International. 2002. *Amnesty International's concerns regarding post September 11 detentions in the USA*. New York: Amnesty International

Australian Press Council. 2005. Submission. Available at <http://www.aph.gov.au/senate/committee/legcom_ctte/terrorism/submission/sub143.pdf>.

Bacevich, A. 2002. *American Empire: The Realities and Consequences of US Diplomacy*. Cambridge, MA: Harvard University Press.

Blom-Cooper, L. 1997. *The Birmingham Six and Other Cases*. London: Duckworth.

Blum, W. 2002. *Rogue State: a guide to the world's only superpower.* London: Zed Books.

Boulden, J. and Weiss, T. 2004. 'Whither Terrorism and the United Nations?', in Boulden and Weiss. *Terrorism and the UN – Before and After September 11*. Bloomington: Indiana University Press.

Chaliand, G. 2007. *The History of Terrorism: From Antiquity to al Qaeda*. Berkeley: University of California Press.

Coady, T., et al. 2002. *Terrorism and Justice: Moral Argument in a Threatened World.* Melbourne: Melbourne University Publishing.

Doughty Street Chambers. 2008. 'Victory for free speech and the right to protest – peaceful anti-nuclear protestor acquitted of terrorist offence'. Available at <http://www.doughtystreet.co.uk/news/news_detail.cfm?iNewsID=281>.

Hancock, N. 2002. *Terrorism and the Law in Australia: Supporting Materials.* Canberra: Parliament of Australia (Department of Parliamentary Library, Research Paper No. 13).

Head, M. 2009. 'What the Haneef Inquiry revealed (and did not)', *Alternative Law Journal* 35.

—— 2005. 'A Disturbing Convergence? Civil Liberties and the "War on Terror"', *Asia-Pacific Yearbook of International Humanitarian Law* 1: 63.

—— 2004a. 'Another threat to democratic rights: ASIO detentions cloaked in secrecy', *Alternative Law Journal* 29:127.

—— 2004b. 'ASIO, Secrecy and Lack of Accountability', *Murdoch University Electronic Journal of law* 11.

—— 2002. 'Counter Terrorism Laws: A Threat to Political Freedom, Civil Liberties and Constitutional Rights', *Melbourne University Law Review* 26:666.

Hoffman, B. 1998. *Inside Terrorism*. New York: Columbia University Press.

Laqueur, W. 1999. *The New Terrorism: Fanaticism and the Arms of Mass Destruction*. New York: Oxford University Press.

Marks, S. and Clapham, A. 2005. *International Human Rights Lexicon*. Oxford: Oxford University Press.

Martyn, A. 2002. 'The Right of Self-Defence under International Law – the Response to the Terrorist Attacks of 11 September'. Australian Law and Bills Digest Group. Canberra: Parliament of Australia.

Moysey, S. 2008. *The Road to Balcombe Street: The IRA Reign of Terror in London*. Binghamton, NY: Haworth.

O'Neill, W. 2003. Conference Report, in International Peace Academy. *Responding to Terrorism: What Role for the United Nations?* New York: International Peace Academy.

Oudraat, C. 2004. 'The Role of the Security Council', in Boulden and Weiss. *Terrorism and the UN – Before and After September 11*. Bloomington: Indiana University Press.

Priest, D. and Arkin, W. 2010. 'Monitoring America', *Washington Post*. Available at <http://projects.washingtonpost.com/top-secret-america/articles/monitoring-america/>.

Saul, B. 2006. *Defining Terrorism in International Law*. Oxford: Oxford University Press.

Savage, C. 2010. 'Court Dismisses a Case Asserting Torture by C.I.A.', *New York Times*. 8 September 2010. Available at <http://www.nytimes.com/2010/09/09/us/09secrets.html>.

Schmid, A., et al. 1988. *Political Terrorism: A New Guide to Actors, Authors, Concepts, Data Bases, Theories, and Literature*, New Brunswick, NJ: Transaction Books.

Senate Committee. 2002. Senate Legal and Constitutional Committee, 8 April 2002.

Shalom, S. 1993. *Imperial Alibis: Rationalizing US Intervention After the Cold War*. Boston, MA: South End Press.

The 9/11 Commission. 2004. *The 9/11 Commission Report*. Washington, DC: Government Printing Office.

Tigar, M. 2007. *Thinking About Terrorism. The Threat to Civil Liberties in Times of National Emergency.* Chicago, IL: American Bar Association.

White House. 2001. Address to a Joint Session of Congress and the American People. Available at <http://georgewbush-whitehouse.archives.gov/news/releases/2001/09/20010920-8.html>.

Zeidan, S. 2006. 'Desperately Seeking Definition: The International Community's Quest for Identifying the Specter of Terrorism', *Cornell International Law Journal* 36: 491–2.

Chapter 8

International Criminal Governance: Will the International Criminal Court be an 'Effective' Mechanism for Justice?

Steven Freeland

Introduction[1]

On 22 November 2010, the trial in the case of *The Prosecutor* v. *Jean-Pierre Bemba Gombo* commenced at the International Criminal Court (ICC or the Court) in The Hague. The accused is charged with criminal responsibility, as a person effectively acting as military commander within the meaning of article 28(a) of the Rome Statute of the International Criminal Court (Rome Statute),[2] for two crimes against humanity (murder and rape) and three war crimes (murder, rape and pillaging), allegedly committed in the territory of the Central African Republic during the period from approximately 26 October 2002 to 15 March 2003.[3]

This is the third trial to have formally commenced at the ICC,[4] but Bemba represents the Court's highest-profile accused brought before the Court thus far (he was at one time vice-president of the Democratic Republic of Congo (DRC) and a senator in the DRC Parliament). This trial also breaks new ground at the ICC, in that it is the first where evidence of sexual violence comprises a significant part of the Prosecution's case. It is also the first ICC trial to charge an accused for command responsibility for rape.

At a press conference held at the ICC coinciding with the commencement of the trial, the rights of the parties and participants in the proceedings before the Court were stressed. The ICC Registrar, Silvana Arbia, stated that 'only through a

1 This chapter is written and describes the current law and international situation as at December 2010.

2 2187 UNTS 3; 37 ILM 999 (Rome Statute).

3 See International Criminal Court, 'Warrant of Arrest for Jean-Pierre Bemba Gombo Replacing the Warrant of Arrest Issued on 23 May 2008', *The Prosecutor* v. *Jean-Pierre Bemba Gombo*, Case No: ICC-01/05-01/08, 10 June 2008 <http://www.icc-cpi.int/iccdocs/doc/doc535163.pdf> (accessed 25 November 2010).

4 The other two trials that are currently underway at the ICC relate to the situation in the Democratic Republic of the Congo. These are *The Prosecutor* v. *Thomas Lubanga Dyilo* and *The Prosecutor* v. *Germain Katanga and Mathieu Nqudjolo Chui.*

fair trial can the law play its proper role in establishing lasting peace and fighting effectively against impunity for crimes which are … of concern to the international community as a whole and which deeply shock the conscience of humanity'.[5]

These comments highlight important issues as to the function of the ICC, particularly in its role as the most significant mechanism of international criminal governance that has ever been established and representing, as it does, a very significant element of what is often referred to as the 'internationalisation of justice'.

Over the past two decades, a number of international and internationalised courts and tribunals have been created, each of which have, in general terms and within the specific framework of their respective jurisdictional limitations, been charged with the mandate to prosecute those persons who are accused of committing crimes that are regarded as having 'shock[ed] the conscience of humanity'.[6] This evolution of international criminal governance has seen *ad hoc* Tribunals established to deal with crimes committed in the Balkans,[7] Rwanda,[8] and various other situations where such crimes may have been committed.[9]

In addition, of course, the ICC, which (as part of this evolutionary process) is generally regarded as a more comprehensive mechanism of international criminal governance, has been operating since 2002 and is intended to deal with

---

5 International Criminal Court, 'Journalists in Bangui, Kinshasa and The Hague put questions to parties and participants in the trial of Jean-Pierre Bemba Gombo', Press Release, 22 November 2010 <http://www.icc-cpi.int/NR/exeres/7BA1991C-707F-414F-AC34-9F15830ACA96.htm> (accessed 22 November 2010).

6 See, for example, Rome Statute, preambular paragraph 2.

7 International Criminal Tribunal for the Former Yugoslavia (ICTY).

8 International Criminal Tribunal for the Prosecution of Persons Responsible for Genocide and Other Serious Violations of International Humanitarian Law Committed in the Territory of Rwanda and Rwandan Citizens Responsible for Genocide and Other Such Violations Committed in the Territory of Neighbouring States, between 1 January 1994 and 31 December 1994 (ICTR).

9 These are The Serious Crimes Panels for Timor-Leste, established in 2000 by the United Nations Transitional Administration in East Timor (UNTAET), pursuant to UNTAET Regulations 2000/11 and 2000/15 (6 March 2000 and 6 June 2000 respectively); The Special Court for Sierra Leone, established by an agreement between the United Nations and the Government of Sierra Leone dated 16 January 2002, pursuant to United Nations Security Council Resolution 1315 on the Situation in Sierra Leone, 14 August 2000; The Extraordinary Chambers for Cambodia, established by an agreement between the United Nations and the Government of Cambodia dated 6 June 2003, pursuant to United Nations General Assembly Resolution 57/228 B on Khmer Rouge Trials, 13 May 2003; The Special Tribunal for Lebanon – see United Nations Security Council Resolution 1664 on the Situation in the Middle East, 29 March 2006, and United Nations Security Council Resolution 1757 on the Situation in the Middle East, 30 May 2007. More recently, there have been some suggestions to establish another international Tribunal to try those persons detained at Guantánamo Bay: Guénaël Mettraux, 'A Nuremberg for Guantánamo', *New York Times*, 19 August 2009 <http://www.nytimes.com/2009/08/20/opinion/20mettraux.html?_r=1&emc=eta1> (accessed 24 August 2009), although this appears to be unlikely.

certain crimes that occur in the future, rather than just specific geographically or temporally restricted conflicts, as had been the case with the *ad hoc* Tribunals.

Yet, as this process continues to evolve, it is worthwhile reflecting on whether international criminal governance has been, is, or can ever be 'effective'. As the initiatives mentioned above might suggest, we have seen a very significant development in international criminal law over the past decade as a way of enforcing the rules of international humanitarian law. But how are we to determine whether this still evolving system of international criminal governance actually 'works'? Certainly, for example, with regard to the only internationalised Tribunal to have already completed its formal mandate – The Serious Crimes Panels for Timor-Leste – there had been many difficulties[10] that significantly limited its impact on the development of national law and contribution to the development of international criminal law.[11] Even more disconcerting, there remain widespread perceptions that the 'justice' the *ad hoc* Tribunal produced was neither conclusive nor comprehensive.[12]

Given that, with the establishment of a permanent court, the ICC, we have moved to a new phase of international criminal governance, these observations become even more relevant. How does/should one evaluate the 'success' of international criminal governance, and what does this tell us about the future prospects for the effectiveness (or otherwise) of the ICC? This chapter therefore seeks to examine the establishment of the ICC within the broader context of this process of the internationalisation of justice, and then proceeds to offer some reflections as to how the ultimate 'success' or otherwise of this justice mechanism might possibly be determined in the future.

An Evolving Process of the 'Internationalisation of Justice'

The establishment of the ICC represents the culmination, thus far at least, of a process that has seen a gradual internationalisation of criminal governance, involving the development of international justice mechanisms to address many of the situations in which (allegedly) international crimes have been perpetrated. This evolution has taken place over the twentieth century, and more particularly over

10 For a detailed description and analysis of the various problems associated with the operation of The Serious Crimes Panels for Timor-Leste, see Steven Freeland et al., 'Introduction – the Special Panels for Serious Crimes in Timor Leste', in Andre Klip and Goran Sluiter (eds), *Annotated Leading Cases of International Criminal Tribunals, Volume XIII, Timor Leste – The Special Panels for Serious Crimes, 2001–2003* (2008), pages 15-27.

11 C. Reiger and M. Wierda, International Center for Transitional Justice, 'The Serious Crimes Process in Timor-Leste: In Retrospect', March 2006, pp. 25–6.

12 See, for example, Karishma Vaswani, 'Still no justice in East Timor', *BBC News*, 27 August 2009 <http://news.bbc.co.uk/2/hi/asia-pacific/8223686.stm> (accessed 27 August 2009).

the past 60 years, and has witnessed some failed attempts, remarkable successes, long periods of inaction and, more recently, the establishment of a range of different mechanisms designed to enforce still evolving concepts of justice. It is convenient to categorise this process by various stages, each of which are briefly described below.

Prior to the Second World War

The first (unsuccessful) attempts to establish mechanisms of international criminal governance were made in the early part of the twentieth century. Once victory by the Allied and Associated Powers seemed likely during the First World War, they began to publicly call for the punishment of major war criminals through the processes of international law. For example, it was reported in *The Times* (London) and the *New York Times* (New York) in October 1918 that the French government, in response to a request by the Germans for an armistice, had declared that 'Conduct which is equally contrary to international law and the fundamental principles of all human civilization will not go unpunished ... the authors and directors of these crimes will be held responsible morally, judicially, and financially.'[13]

At the conclusion of the First World War, the Treaty of Versailles[14] provided for the prosecution of 'persons accused of having committed acts in violation of the laws and customs of war'.[15] More specifically, the Allied and Associated Powers publicly arraigned William II of Hohenzollern, formerly the German Emperor (Kaiser), 'for a supreme offence against international morality and the sanctity of treaties'.[16]

The Treaty of Versailles provided for a special international Tribunal to be constituted, comprising judges from the United States of America, Great Britain, France, Italy and Japan, to try the Emperor. The proposed Tribunal had the following sentencing powers:[17]

13 Quoted in Nina H.B. Jørgensen, *The Responsibility of States for International Crimes* (2000), p. 5.

14 Treaty of Peace between the Allied and Associated Powers and Germany, 112 BFSP 317 (Treaty of Versailles).

15 Treaty of Versailles, article 228.

16 Treaty of Versailles, article 227. On the first day of the First World War, the German Emperor had reportedly written in a letter to the Austrian Emperor: 'Everything must be drowned in fire and blood. It is essential to kill men and women, children and old men, not to leave standing a single house or a single tree. By these terrorist methods, the only methods capable of frightening such a degenerate people as the French, the war will be ended in less than two months: while if I take considerations of humanity into account, the war will last several years': see Nina H.B. Jørgensen, *The Responsibility of States for International Crimes* (2000), p. 4 and the corresponding footnote.

17 Treaty of Versailles, article 227.

> In its decision the tribunal will be guided by the highest motives of international policy, with a view to vindicating the solemn obligations of international undertakings and the validity of international morality. It will be its duty to fix the punishment which it considers should be imposed.

However, by the time the Treaty of Versailles was in force, the Emperor had already sought refuge in The Netherlands, which did not agree to surrender him for prosecution, instead regarding itself as a 'land of refuge for the vanquished in international conflicts'.[18] A trial *in absentia* was considered as futile and, as a result, the international Tribunal was not established. The Emperor remained in The Netherlands until his death in 1941.

The Treaty of Versailles also envisaged the establishment of other military Tribunals. Pursuant to article 228, the German government was deemed to have expressly recognised the right of the Allied and Associated Powers to bring persons accused of having committed acts in violation of the laws and customs of war before their own military Tribunals. In practice, however, the German leadership did not accept this, and a compromise was eventually reached by which the Germans themselves would try alleged war criminals. However, over time, it became increasingly clear that these trials fell far below the expectations of the Allied and Associated Powers, and that the sentences imposed were, in their opinion, grossly inadequate.[19]

In 1920, the Treaty of Sèvres,[20] which covered the terms of peace reached with Turkey, provided for war crimes trials to be held, not only in relation to the deaths of Allied soldiers or civilians in occupied territories, but also those of many thousands of Armenians that had taken place under the Ottoman Empire.[21] This

18 Nina H.B. Jørgensen, *The Responsibility of States for International Crimes* (2000), p. 7.

19 Between 23 May and 16 July 1921, a number of German War Crimes Trials were conducted under German national law in the Leipzig Criminal Senate of the Imperial Court of Germany. The Allied countries had prepared an initial list of some 900 persons to be tried by that court, which was over time reduced to about 40 individuals. In the end, 12 men were tried, with six being convicted. However, the conduct of these trials was 'very different from the trials expected by the public after the Armistice of 11th November 1918': Claud Mullins, *The Leipzig Trials: An Account of the War Criminals' Trials and a Study of German Mentality* (1921), p/ 23. The sentences delivered by the seven German Judges were widely regarded as being too lenient in the circumstances, and those who had been on trial were considered in Germany as being war heroes. As a result, in the following year, the Allied countries demanded that the Leipzig trials should not continue and that Germans accused of war crimes should instead be tried before an international Tribunal to be established under the Treaty of Versailles. As noted above, this Tribunal never came into existence.

20 1920 UKTS 11.

21 Article 230 of the Treaty of Sèvres provided for the establishment of a Tribunal to try persons responsible for 'massacres committed during the continuance of the state of war on territory which formed part of the Turkish Empire on August 1, 1914'.

treaty was not ratified by Turkey and never came into force. It was subsequently 'replaced'[22] in 1923 by the Treaty of Lausanne, which contained a 'Declaration of Amnesty' for all such offences committed between 1 August 1914 and 20 November 1922.[23]

In 1937, a treaty was adopted by the League of Nations that envisaged the establishment of an international criminal court.[24] However, this instrument was not widely supported and also never came into force. Thus, despite some attempts to do so, at the commencement, and during the course of the Second World War, there was yet to be established any international judicial mechanism that could prosecute those persons charged with having committed war crimes.

Immediately following the Second World War

This situation changed following the end of the Second World War. Two international military tribunals – the International Military Tribunal for the trial of the German major war criminals at Nuremberg (Nuremberg Military Tribunal) and the International Military Tribunal for the trial of the major war criminals in the Far East (Tokyo Military Tribunal) – were established by the Allied Powers, although the agreement to do so only came relatively late in the piece. With the exception of the United States, the Allies had initially been of the opinion that an international judicial process was not appropriate. This was only partially due to the fact that such an approach was unprecedented; it also stemmed from their more 'extreme' views as to how such persons should be brought to account. The British government had, for example, instituted a formal policy of 'summary execution' of enemy leaders in 1943, which remained in place until the end of the war.[25]

The terms of the document that established the Nuremberg Military Tribunal[26] were the subject of a series of negotiations involving the Allied Powers and were finalised in 1945 at the International Conference on Military Trials (London Conference). In the end, principally in line with the viewpoint of the United States, a public and (largely) transparent international judicial process was established

---

22 William A. Schabas, *An Introduction to the International Criminal Court* (2001), p. 4.

23 Treaty of Lausanne Between Principal Allied and Associated Powers and Turkey, 28 LNTS 11.

24 Convention for the Creation of an International Criminal Court, LN Doc C.547(I).M.384(I).1937.V (opened for signature 16 November 1937).

25 Richard Overy, 'The Nuremberg trials: international law in the making', in Philippe Sands (ed.), *From Nuremberg to The Hague: The Future of International Criminal Justice* (2003), 1, pp. 3–4.

26 Charter of the Nuremberg International Military Tribunal, annexed to the 1945 London Agreement for the Establishment of an International Military Tribunal, 8 August 1945, 82 UNTS 279 (Nuremberg Military Tribunal Charter).

involving Military Tribunals having a mandate and procedural framework that largely reflected 'Western notions of justice'.[27]

A number of fundamental principles of international criminal justice emerged from the jurisprudence of those Tribunals. What was perhaps most striking about this entire process, at least compared to any earlier attempts to criminalise acts committed during warfare, was that these Tribunals applied *international law* doctrines and concepts to judge the acts of those individuals brought before them. A formalised concept of *international* criminal governance had come to be accepted. It was recognised that those crimes for which the defendants in Nuremberg and Tokyo had been charged were actions that offended the values of the broader international community. Implicitly, there was an acceptance of the worth of a system of international criminal governance that incorporated and (in theory at least) enforced norms of international justice.

In December 1946, the United Nations General Assembly affirmed 'the principles of international law recognized by the Charter of the Nürnberg Tribunal and the judgment of the Tribunal' and directed the International Law Commission (ILC)[28] to formulate those principles for the purposes of codification.[29] The 'Nürnberg Principles' adopted by the ILC in 1950 – and subsequently considered as reflecting customary international law – confirmed the notion of individual criminal responsibility for the commission of crimes under international law, even where national law does not prescribe a penalty for such actions.[30] The notion of a crime under international law was therefore different from, and not necessarily dependent upon, specific provisions of national criminal law.

Indeed, in oft-quoted wording from the Nuremberg Judgment, the Nuremberg Military Tribunal observed that individual criminal responsibility for the actions in respect of which it was imposing judgment and pronouncing sentence stemmed

27 Richard Overy, 'The Nuremberg trials: international law in the making', in Philippe Sands (ed.), *From Nuremberg to The Hague: The Future of International Criminal Justice* (2003), 1, p. 4.

28 The ILC was established following the adoption by the United Nations General Assembly of Resolution 174 (II) on the Establishment of an International Law Commission, 21 November 1947, which approved the Statute of the International Law Commission (ILC Statute). Article 1(1) of the ILC Statute provides that 'The International Law Commission shall have for its object the promotion of the progressive development of international law and its codification.'

29 United Nations General Assembly Resolution 95(I) on the International Law Recognized by the Charter of the Nürnberg Tribunal, 11 December 1946.

30 Principle II, 'Principles of International Law Recognized in the Charter of the Nürnberg Tribunal and in the Judgment of the Tribunal', adopted by the International Law Commission in its second session in 1950 <http://untreaty.un.org/ilc/texts/instruments/english/draft%20articles/7_1_1950.pdf> (accessed 26 November 2010).

from the commission of acts that represented a breach of those standards imposed at the international level:[31]

> That international law imposes duties and liabilities upon individuals as well as upon States has long been recognized ... Crimes against international law are committed by men, not by abstract entities, and only by punishing individuals who commit such crimes can the provisions of international law be enforced.

Undoubtedly, during the course of the various trials that ensued before these Military Tribunals, a number of difficult legal issues arose. This was not surprising, given that this was, up until this point, an untested form of criminal justice. It was, for example, asserted by the accused at Nuremberg that the law had been made 'on the run' to fit the actions of those brought before the Military Tribunals, and that their respective mandates offended fundamental principles relating to the rights of an accused. Although the establishment of these Military Tribunals represented a very significant advancement on previous methods of dealing with (international) crimes committed during hostilities, these assertions were not without some justification.[32]

Indeed, as the trials at the Nuremberg and Tokyo Military Tribunals demonstrated, the international regulation of international crimes is typically developed *in reaction to* rather than in anticipation of horrendous events. As a practical matter, this may sometimes necessitate the adaptation of principles to meet particular situations. This suggests that international criminal courts, including the more recently established mechanisms of international criminal governance, must find a way of working within the *nullum crimen sine lege* (legality) principle[33] whilst, at the same time, refining and elaborating upon 'by way of legal construction, *existing* rules'.[34]

---

31 'International Military Tribunal (Nuremberg) Judgment and Sentences' (1947) *American Journal of International Law*, 41: 172, 221.

32 For example, the act of waging an aggressive war had, up until that time, never been defined as a crime in international law. The defendants at the Nuremberg Military Tribunal trials argued that the *ex post facto* punishment of such 'new' crimes in the Nuremberg Military Tribunal Charter violated the *nullum crimen sine lege* principle, which, although not specified in the Nuremberg Charter, had by this time already emerged an overarching principle of many domestic jurisdictions. Although it must be noted that such assertions were not dealt with in an entirely conclusive or satisfactory manner by the Judges of the Nuremberg Military Tribunal, it was generally recognised that those crimes for which the defendants in Nuremberg and Tokyo were charged and convicted were actions that did, in fact, offend the values of the international community.

33 The legality principle is expressed in article 15(1) of the *International Covenant on Economic, Social and Cultural Rights*, 993 UNTS 3 (ICCPR), which is one of the principle international human rights instruments, in the following terms: 'No one shall be held guilty of any criminal offence on account of any act or omission which did not constitute a criminal offence, under national or international law, at the time when it was committed.'

34 Antonio Cassese, *International Criminal Law* (2003), p. 149 (emphasis in original).

While this may be a necessary *modus operandi* of the judicial mechanisms of international criminal governance, particularly given the very complex and unique factual situations with which they often deal, it does have its dangers, even the more so if the relevant international justice mechanism – as was the case with the Nuremberg and Tokyo Military Tribunals – were to have the power to impose a sentence of death.[35]

While there have, of course, been many subsequent criticisms of the Nuremberg and Tokyo Military Tribunal processes as simply representing 'victors' justice', this conception of certain 'international' crimes as being (by definition) a part of international law has not been contested and represents an important part of international (criminal) law, forming the basis upon which the evolution of international criminal governance has developed in more recent times. For example, over fifty years after the judgment of the Nuremberg Military Tribunal, Lord Browne-Wilkinson of the British House of Lords noted in the *Pinochet* case that 'Since the Nazi atrocities and the Nuremberg trials, international law has recognised a number of offences as being international crimes.'[36]

An Era of Impunity

Despite the (generally) positive steps made by the Nuremberg (in particular) and Tokyo Military Tribunals regarding the formulation of principles of international criminal law, it would take almost fifty years until the next formative stage in the development of international criminal governance was to emerge.

Prior to this, there had been some suggestions in the early 1950s that a permanent international criminal court should be established,[37] either as a separate institution, or as part of a treaty regime focused on particular crimes, but this did not eventuate. The 1948 Convention on the Prevention and Punishment of the Crime of Genocide (Genocide Convention)[38] provided as follows:[39]

---

35 The various international and internationalised Tribunals that have been established over the past two decades, including the ICC, do not have the power to impose the death penalty, with the most severe punishment being imprisonment for life: see Steven Freeland, 'No Longer Acceptable: The Exclusion of the Death Penalty under International Criminal Law' (2010) *Australian Journal of Human Rights*, 15(2): 1.

36 *R* v. *Bow Street Metropolitan Magistrate and others, Ex Parte* Pinochet Ugarte (Amnesty International and others intervening) (No 3) (1999) 2 All ER 897 (HL), 898. In fact, it is widely agreed that the international crime of *piracy jure gentium* had been recognised by the maritime states of the world 'since time immemorial': *Attorney-General of the Government of Israel* v *Eichmann* (1961) 36 ILR 5, paragraph 13. See also D.J. Harris, *Cases and Materials on International Law* (6th edn, 2004), p. 266.

37 James Crawford, 'The drafting of the Rome Statute', in Philippe Sands (ed), *From Nuremberg to The Hague: The Future of International Criminal Justice* (2003), p. 110.

38 78 UNTS 277 (Genocide Convention).

39 Genocide Convention, article 6.

> Persons charged with genocide or any of the other acts enumerated in article III shall be tried by a competent tribunal of the State in the territory of which the act was committed, or by such international penal tribunal as may have jurisdiction with respect to those Contracting Parties which shall have accepted its jurisdiction.

In the same resolution in which it approved the text of the Genocide Convention, the United Nations General Assembly expressed the view that, over time, an 'increasing need of an international judicial organ for the trial of certain crimes under international law' would develop.[40] Accordingly, it invited the ILC to 'study the desirability and possibility of establishing an international judicial organ for the trial of persons charged with genocide or other crimes over which jurisdiction will be conferred upon that organ by international conventions'.[41]

Acting on this invitation, the ILC quickly concluded that the establishment of an international court to try persons charged with genocide or other crimes of similar gravity was both desirable and possible. The United Nations General Assembly then established a committee to prepare proposals relating to the establishment of such a court.[42] However, it was only a relatively short period of time later that the United Nations General Assembly halted the drafting process.[43] The spectre of *Realpolitik* had emerged, with the onset of the Cold War making it impossible for the international community to find the common will to build upon the foundations laid by the Nuremberg and Tokyo Military Tribunal processes.

Instead, over the ensuing decades, an era of 'impunity for the perpetrators of these [international] crimes'[44] took hold, which would not be challenged to any significant degree until after the fall of the Berlin Wall in November 1989. During this period, atrocities took place in countries around the globe – including in the Soviet Union, Uganda, Nigeria, Argentina, Bangladesh, East Timor, Algeria, Cambodia and Iraq. However, these crimes were for all intents and purposes neither investigated, let alone punished, by a court of law.

---

40 United Nations General Assembly Resolution 260 (III) B on the Prevention and Punishment of the Crime of Genocide: Study by the International Law Commission of the Question of an International Criminal Jurisdiction, 9 December 1948, paragraph 2.

41 Ibid., paragraph 3.

42 United Nations General Assembly Resolution 489 (V) on International Criminal Jurisdiction, 12 December 1950, paragraph 1. The committee was initially comprised of representatives of 17 states – Australia, Brazil, China, Cuba, Denmark, Egypt, France, India, Iran, Israel, The Netherlands, Pakistan, Peru, Syria, the United Kingdom of Great Britain and Northern Ireland, the United States of America, and Uruguay.

43 See United Nations General Assembly Resolution 897 (IX) on the Draft Code of Offences Against the Peace and Security of Mankind, 4 December 1954, paragraph 3; United Nations General Assembly Resolution 898 (IX) on the International Criminal Jurisdiction, 14 December 1954, paragraph 2.

44 Rome Statute, preambular paragraph 5.

Indeed, it has been estimated that approximately 170 million people were killed during the period 1945–90,[45] with little if any accountability, at either the international or national level. In certain respects, it was as if the principles that had emerged from the Nuremberg Military Tribunal process, as well as the Genocide Convention, were treated as ends unto themselves – sitting on the shelf – with little tangible action to address the commission of such crimes in a practical sense.

There were only a few relatively minor steps taken in this regard by the international community during this lengthy period of (virtual) inaction. A treaty was finalised specifying that statutory limitations under national law were inappropriate and should not be applicable to war crimes and crimes against humanity, which were described as 'among the gravest crimes in international law'.[46] Yet, there was an almost total lack of political will by most countries to prosecute, within their respective national court systems, individuals suspected of committing such crimes over more than four decades.

The prosecution and subsequent conviction of Otto Adolf Eichmann by the Israeli District Court in 1961[47] (affirmed by the Israeli Supreme Court in the following year)[48] was one of the very few exceptions to this failure to act.

Another example (of sorts) of an attempt during this period to prosecute those alleged to have committed international crimes followed the fall of the Khmer Rouge regime in Cambodia. By most estimates, almost two million people, representing over 20 per cent of the total population of the country at the time, had died directly as a result of the four-year reign of terror between 1975 and 1979.[49] Following its invasion of Cambodia, the Vietnamese authorities established a revolutionary people's tribunal, which in 1979 tried, convicted and imposed a death sentence on Khmer Rouge leader Pol Pot and his deputy prime minister. However, this 'trial' and sentence had not been preceded by any semblance of due process, had been held *in absentia*, and was not recognised internationally as being credible. In any event, the accused were by that time already safely in Thailand, thus rendering futile any attempt to have them extradited back to Cambodia.

---

45 M. Cherif Bassiouni, 'Introduction to the Symposium: The Normative Framework of International Humanitarian Law: Overlaps, Gaps and Ambiguities' (1998) *Transnational Law and Contemporary Problems* 8: 199. See also Steven Freeland, 'Saddam trial underlines need to take tough stand on genocide', *Canberra Times*, 29 August 2006, p. 11.

46 Convention on the Non-Applicability of Statutory Limitations to War Crimes and Crimes against Humanity, 8 ILM 68, preambular paragraph 4.

47 *Attorney-General of the Government of Israel* v *Eichmann* (1961) 36 ILR 5. Eichmann was prosecuted under Israeli law (the 1951 Nazi and Nazi Collaborators (Punishment) Law) for war crimes, crimes against the Jewish people (the definition of which was modelled on the definition of genocide in the Genocide Convention) and crimes against humanity.

48 *Eichmann* v *Attorney-General of the Government of Israel* (1962) 36 ILR 277.

49 Yale University, 'Cambodian Genocide Program' <www.yale.edu/cgp> (accessed 26 August 2009).

Much later, in 1987, Klaus Barbie, who had been the head of the Gestapo in Lyons from November 1942 to August 1943 and was known as the 'Butcher of Lyons', was convicted by the Rhone *Cour d'assises* of 17 counts of crimes against humanity. His appeal was dismissed by the French Court of Cassation[50] and Barbie was sentenced to life imprisonment.

Apart from these isolated examples, however, there was a lack of credible action on the part of national jurisdictions to deal with the perpetrators of serious crimes and, coupled with the fact that there were also no mechanisms of international criminal governance, this lead to an acknowledgement by the United Nations General Assembly in 1970 that 'many war criminals and persons who have committed crimes against humanity are continuing to take refuge in the territories of certain States and are enjoying protection.'[51]

A New Era of International Criminal Governance – the 1990s and Beyond

It was not until the shackles of the Cold War were loosened in the early 1990s that the United Nations was able to play a more active role in addressing international crimes, albeit *after* the fact. Faced with the genocides in both Rwanda and in the former Yugoslavia – each of which took place 'under the watch of the [United Nations] Security Council and United Nations peacekeepers'[52] – the United Nations Security Council, acting under its powers pursuant to Chapter VII of the Charter of the United Nations,[53] established two *ad hoc* Tribunals (the ICTY and the ICTR)[54] to prosecute the perpetrators of serious crimes committed during those conflicts.

---

50 *Féderation National des Déportées et Internés Résistants et Patriots and Others* v. *Barbie* 100 ILR 330.

51 United Nations General Assembly Resolution 2712 (XXV) on the Question of the Punishment of War Criminals and of Persons who have Committed Crimes against Humanity, 9 December 1970, paragraph 1.

52 United Nations General Assembly, 'Implementing the responsibility to protect: Report of the Secretary-General' (12 January 2009) UN Doc A/63/677, paragraph 5.

53 1 UNTS 16; 59 Stat. 1031 (United Nations Charter). Chapter VII of the United Nations Charter (articles 39–51) gives the United Nations Security Council certain powers 'with respect to Threats to the Peace, Breaches of the Peace, and Acts of Aggression': United Nations Charter, chapter VII, title. This was the first time that these powers had been used to establish *ad hoc* international criminal Tribunals. In early cases before each of the *ad hoc* Tribunals, it had been argued that they were established unlawfully by the United Nations Security Council. In both cases, these claims were dismissed: see ICTY, Decision on Defence Motion for Interlocutory Appeal on Jurisdiction, *Prosecutor* v. *Duško Tadić*, Case No: IT-94-1, Appeals Chamber, 2 October 1995: ICTR, Decision on the Defence Motion on Jurisdiction, *Prosecutor* v. *Joseph Kanyabashi*, Case No: ICTR-96-15-T, Trial Chamber II, 18 June 1997.

54 See United Nations Security Council Resolutions 827 on Tribunal (Former Yugoslavia), 25 May 1993, and United Nations Security Council Resolution 955 on

The establishment of these *ad hoc* Tribunals was a significant and highly symbolic development. As noted above, it had been almost fifty years since the Nuremberg and Tokyo Military Tribunals had been created. Apart from the judgments of those two Military Tribunals and the rare national trial, there had been virtually no jurisprudence relating to the application of international law principles to the commission of international crimes. There was a clear recognition that such crimes existed in international law – however, there was, understandably, only limited expertise in the area of international criminal law. For all intents and purposes, there had been no 'practice' of international criminal law, and no exercise of international criminal governance, for two generations.

No doubt conscious of the arguments raised by the accused before the Nuremberg Military Tribunal in relation to the *nullum crimen sine lege* principle, the then secretary-general of the United Nations, Kofi Annan, in reporting on the establishment of the ICTY, expressed the widely held view that this new Tribunal would only be concerned with the prosecution of those crimes that were 'doubtless part of customary international law'.[55] Like the Nuremberg and Tokyo Military Tribunals, both of these *ad hoc* Tribunals were created and mandated by way of a Statute,[56] with the crimes within the jurisdiction of each Tribunal expressly specified,[57] as were their respective temporal and geographic jurisdictions.[58]

Establishment of an International Tribunal and Adoption of the Statute of the Tribunal, 8 November 1994, respectively.

55 United Nations Security Council, 'Report of the Secretary-General Pursuant to Paragraph 2 of Security Council Resolution 808' (3 May 1993), paragraphs 33–5.

56 These were the Statute of the International Tribunal for the Prosecution of Persons Responsible for Serious Violations of International Humanitarian Law Committed in the Territory of the Former Yugoslavia since 1991, 32 ILM 1159 (ICTY Statute) and the Statute of the International Criminal Tribunal for the Prosecution of Persons Responsible for Genocide and Other Serious Violations of International Humanitarian Law Committed in the Territory of Rwanda and Rwandan Citizens Responsible for Genocide and Other Such Violations Committed in the Territory of Neighbouring States, between 1 January 1994 and 31 December 1994, 33 ILM 1598 (ICTR Statute), respectively.

57 The crimes for which the ICTY has jurisdiction are grave breaches of the Geneva Conventions of 1949 (ICTY Statute, article 2), Violations of the laws or customs of war (ICTY Statute, article 3), Genocide (ICTY Statute, article 4) and Crimes against Humanity (ICTY Statute, article 5). The crimes for which the ICTR has jurisdiction are Genocide (ICTR Statute, article 2), Crimes against Humanity (ICTR Statute, article 3) and Violations of Article 3 Common to the Geneva Conventions and of Additional Protocol II (ICTR Statute, article 4).

58 The territorial jurisdiction of the ICTY is 'the territory of the former Socialist Federal Republic of Yugoslavia, including its land surface, airspace and territorial waters' and its temporal jurisdiction 'extend[s] to a period beginning on 1 January 1991': ICTY Statute, article 8. The territorial jurisdiction of the ICTR is 'the territory of Rwanda including its land surface and airspace as well as … the territory of neighbouring States in respect of serious violations of international humanitarian law committed by Rwandan

Even though the terms of the Statutes of the ICTY and ICTR vary in relation to some of the crimes within their respective jurisdiction – and even in some aspects of the definition of particular crimes[59] – they both reflect the acceptance of the international community as a whole that the actions that constitute these crimes constitute '[s]erious violations of International Humanitarian Law', for which those most responsible should be brought to account.[60] In other words, the very existence of these international crimes assumes the existence of globalised norms that regulate the behaviour of individuals.

In crafting their respective mandates, difficult decisions also had to be taken as to the scope of logistical issues such as location, staffing and financing for these *ad hoc* Tribunals,[61] as well as their procedural arrangements, which would, ultimately, represent an 'amalgam' of common law and civil law principles.[62] At the time that they were created, no one could be entirely sure how the first international criminal Tribunals to be established for five decades would fare and what would flow from their activities, and from the activities of any other subsequent international Tribunals. Indeed, there was some uncertainty as to how 'active' they would be at all.

Yet, since their establishment, the activities of these temporary mechanisms of international justice have grown, giving rise to a gradual but undeniable

---

citizens' and its temporal jurisdiction 'extend[s] to a period beginning on 1 January 1994 and ending on 31 December 1994': ICTR Statute, article 7.

59 The respective definitions of the crime of Crimes against Humanity in the ICTY and ICTR Statutes are different. However, with the provisions of the ICTR Statute and the Rome Statute (article 7(1)) in mind, the subsequent jurisprudence of the ICTY confirmed that it is necessary to prove *inter alia* that the actions took place within the context of a 'widespread or systematic attack against any civilian population' for the crime to have been committed: see, for example, ICTY, Judgement, *Prosecutor* v. *Tihomir Blaskic*, Case No: IT-95-14-T, Trial Chamber, 3 March 2000, paragraph 202.

60 See the preamble to both the ICTY Statute and the ICTR Statute.

61 Joel F. England, 'The Response of the United States to the International Criminal Court: Rejection, Ratification or Something Else?' (2001) *Arizona Journal of International and Comparative Law* 18(3): 941, 943.

62 James Podgers, 'The World Cries for Justice' (1996) *American Bar Association Journal* 52, 58, quoting Judge Gabrielle Kirk McDonald in the Decision on the Prosecutor's Motion Requesting Protective Measures for Victims and Witnesses, *Prosecutor* v *Duško Tadić*, Case No. IT-94-1, Trial Chamber, 10 August 1995, paragraph 22. This amalgam of principles has, at times, led to significant differences in the approach taken by some Judges from common law as opposed to those from civil law backgrounds, particularly in the early days of these Tribunals: see, for example, the Separate Opinion of Judge Stephen in the same case. For a discussion of the application of this amalgam of principles in the procedural practice of the *ad hoc* Tribunals, see Steven Freeland, 'Commentary on 'Decision on Prosecutor's Appeal on Admissibility of Evidence, *Prosecutor v Zlatko Aleksovski*', in André Klip and Göran Sluiter (eds), *Annotated Leading Cases of International Criminal Tribunals, Volume III, The International Criminal Tribunal for the Former Yugoslavia, 1997–1999* (2001), p. 260.

acceptance of their credibility in terms of dealing in practical terms with (some of) the issues resulting from the particular situations with which they were involved. As an indication of the extent to which it has been active, as of 26 October 2010, the ICTY had indicted 161 persons. Of these, 63 have been sentenced by the ICTY, 13 have been referred to national jurisdictions pursuant to Rule 11 *bis* of the ICTY Rules of Procedure and Evidence (RPE),[63] 12 have been acquitted, 36 have had their indictments withdrawn or are deceased, and there are 37 in relation to whom proceedings are still ongoing.[64]

Although not as prolific, the ICTR has also been increasingly active, having completed 50 cases (of which eight involved acquittals and another eight are currently on appeal), with another 24 cases in progress, two accused awaiting trial and two cases referred to national jurisdictions.[65] In 1998 – 50 years after the conclusion of the Genocide Convention – the ICTR handed down the first international conviction for genocide, which was imposed upon a leading figure in the Rwandan massacres of 1994.[66]

In addition, the Serious Crimes Panels for Timor-Leste has, as noted, completed its mandate, and the Special Court for Sierra Leone, the Extraordinary Chambers for Cambodia and the Special Tribunal for Lebanon are at various stages of their judicial operations.

Seen from this perspective, therefore, it might at first glance be assumed that the system of international criminal governance that has evolved since the early 1990s has been a 'success'. Yet, this may be an all-too-hasty assumption. For example, even though they have had relatively limited mandates, as noted earlier, the operation of the Serious Crimes Panels for Timor-Leste has left a number of unresolved issues, while the ICTY process has not alleviated many of the tensions that still remain in that region.

Moreover, given that the most significant mechanism of international justice that has been established is the ICC, the world's first permanent international criminal tribunal, it is important to consider how the operation and 'performance' of that specific justice mechanism should be considered as we move further in the development and refinement of this latest phase of the internationalisation of criminal governance. This chapter therefore turns to a discussion of the ICC.

---

63 Rule 11 *bis* (A) of the ICTY RPE provides as follows: '(A) After an indictment has been confirmed and prior to the commencement of trial, irrespective of whether or not the accused is in the custody of the Tribunal, the President may appoint a bench of three Permanent Judges selected from the Trial Chambers (hereinafter referred to as the "Referral Bench"), which solely and exclusively shall determine whether the case should be referred to the authorities of a State.'

64 ICTY, 'Key Figures of ICTY Cases' <http://www.icty.org/x/file/Cases/keyfigures/key_figures_101026_ en.pdf> (accessed 1 December 2010).

65 ICTR, 'Status of Cases' <http://69.94.11.53/default.htm> (accessed 1 December 2010).

66 ICTR, Judgement, *The Prosecutor* v. *Jean-Paul Akayesu*, Case No: ICTR-96-4-T, Trial Chamber I, 2 September 1998.

The International Criminal Court

Establishment

In December 1989, in response to a request by Trinidad and Tobago, the United Nations General Assembly asked the ILC to resume work on an international criminal court, with a jurisdiction that would specifically include drug trafficking.[67] The ILC subsequently completed its work on the draft statute for an international criminal court (ILC Draft Statute) and submitted it to the United Nations General Assembly in 1994.[68] Even though the final version of the Rome Statute differed quite significantly from the ILC Draft Statute,[69] in the words of the chairperson of the ILC Working Group that produced the draft, it 'got the diplomatic ball rolling again'.[70]

Following receipt of the ILC Draft Statute, the United Nations General Assembly established the Ad Hoc Committee on the Establishment of an International Criminal Court (Ad Hoc Committee), which met twice in 1995 and then reported back to the United Nations General Assembly. Having considered the Ad Hoc Committee's report, the United Nations General Assembly subsequently created the Preparatory Committee on the Establishment of an International Criminal Court (PrepCom), to prepare a widely acceptable consolidated draft text for submission to a diplomatic conference. The PrepCom, which began meeting in 1996, held its final session in March and April of 1998, at which time it completed the drafting of the text.

At its 52nd session, the United Nations General Assembly decided to convene the United Nations Diplomatic Conference of Plenipotentiaries on the Establishment of an International Criminal Court (1998 Rome Conference),

67 United Nations General Assembly Resolution 44/39 on the International Criminal Responsibility of Individuals and Entities Engaged in Illicit Trafficking in Narcotic Drugs across National Frontiers and Other Transnational Criminal Activities, 4 December 1989, paragraph 1.

68 Draft Statute for an International Criminal Court, Report of the International Law Commission on Its Forty-sixth session, United Nations General Assembly Official Records 49th Sess., Supp. No. 10, UN Doc A/49/10 (1994) (ILC Draft Statute).

69 It has been suggested by one commentator that the ILC Draft Statute was 'a common law orientated' document, and consequently required considerable amendment in order to accommodate the concern among civil lawyers that the Court would become an 'International Criminal *Common* Law Court': Gilbert Bitti, 'Two Bones of Contention Between Civil and Common Law: The Record of the Proceedings and the Treatment of a Concursus Delictorum', in Horst Fischer, Claus Kress and Sascha Rolf Lüder (eds), *International and National Prosecution of Crimes Under International Law: Current Developments* (2001), pp. 273–4 (emphasis added).

70 James Crawford, 'The drafting of the Rome Statute', in Philippe Sands (ed), *From Nuremberg to The Hague: The Future of International Criminal Justice* (2003), pp. 109, 110.

which was to be held from 15 June to 17 July 1998, 'with a view to finalizing and adopting a convention on the establishment of an international criminal court'.[71]

The 1998 Rome Conference was attended by delegations from over 160 states, 30 intergovernmental organisations and 230 non-governmental organisations. At the beginning of those four weeks in Rome, several complex questions remained to be agreed. As a result, the discussions during the 1998 Rome Conference were at times tortured and acrimonious, not the least because many of the states represented there had not participated in the Ad Hoc Committee or PrepCom discussions and were thus confronted with a detailed draft perhaps even for the first time.[72] Right up until the final vote at the 1998 Rome Conference, there remained a number of significant issues – particularly in relation to the extent of the Court's proposed jurisdiction and its relationship with the United Nations Security Council – with which some states had great difficulty. In the end, however, the 1998 Rome Conference agreed on the final terms of the Rome Statute, albeit not unanimously.[73]

As events at the 1998 Rome Conference and subsequently have illustrated, the establishment of the first permanent international criminal court was as political an event as it was significant in the evolution of international criminal justice. The negotiating states, as well as the other stakeholders at the 1998 Rome Conference, represented a multitude of differing views as to how the Court should be structured. There were significant divisions among the participating delegations in a number of important areas. The final terms of the Rome Statute were, in many respects, the result of an 'enduring tension inherent in multilateral negotiations between sovereignty and universality',[74] which by necessity required a 'solution' based upon political compromise.[75] Indeed, compromise was needed on all sides in order that the Rome Statute could be presented as a 'marketable' instrument

71 United Nations General Assembly Resolution 52/160 on the Establishment of an International Criminal Court, 15 December 1997, paragraph 3.

72 Elaina I. Kalivretakis, 'Are Nuclear Weapons Above the Law? A Look at the International Criminal Court and the Prohibited Weapons Category' (2001) *Emory International Law Review* 15: 683, 697–8.

73 Of those represented at the 1998 Rome Conference, 120 states voted to adopt the Rome Statute. There were 21 abstentions and seven states – China, Iraq, Israel, Libya, Qatar, Yemen and the United States of America – voted against the resolution.

74 Tim McCormack and Sue Robertson, 'Jurisdictional Aspects of the Rome Statute for the New International Criminal Court' (1999) *Melbourne University Law Review* 23: 635, 636.

75 As an example, a number of states had argued at Rome that the definition of war crimes should include a provision prohibiting the use of nuclear weapons. As the 1998 Rome Conference was drawing to a close, these states largely agreed to compromise on this point – with the result that such a provision was not included in the Rome Statute as finalised – since they were prepared to 'put the larger goal of achieving an international criminal court first': see Elaina I. Kalivretakis, 'Are Nuclear Weapons Above the Law? A Look at the International Criminal Court and the Prohibited Weapons Category' (2001) *Emory International Law Review* 15: 683, 702.

to the conference delegates. Such is the nature of multilateralism, which seeks to be broadly inclusive, rather than representing the prevailing views of one or two states above all others.

In the end, the conclusion of the Rome Statute, and the establishment four years later of the ICC, were considered by the international community to be a more important outcome than the (impossible) task of satisfying every concern of all of those involved in the negotiations that culminated in Rome. If anything, the importance of the principles represented by the aims of the Court has grown further since 1998. Indeed, the finalisation of the Rome Statute and its subsequent ratification (thus far) by 114 states, demonstrates a broader acceptance of the principle underlying the establishment of the ICC: the need for more effective enforcement of the universal norms of international criminal law.

Nature

As noted above, the ICC was established on 1 July 2002, following the ratification of the Rome Statute by 60 states.[76] The Court has been given the mandate to play a role when international crimes have (allegedly) been committed. As a permanent court, it differs from the *ad hoc* international criminal Tribunals. The ICTY and ICTR were set up as 'UN subsidiary organs'[77] in response to specific events and were always intended to have a limited life-span, as is indicated by the formulation of the Completion Strategy that each is currently operating under.[78]

By contrast, the ICC is 'a permanent institution',[79] established under a treaty and, as such, independent of the United Nations, although there is clearly an ongoing relationship between the two institutions on several key issues.[80] The Court has the

76 See Rome Statute, article 126(1).

77 Danesh Sarooshi, 'The Statute of the International Criminal Court' (1999) *International and Comparative Law Quarterly* 48: 387, 389.

78 See, for example, United Nations Security Council Resolution 1503 (28 August 2003) on the International Criminal Tribunal for the former Yugoslavia and International Criminal Tribunal for Rwanda, which refers in preambular paragraph 7 to the 'ICTY Completion Strategy' and in preambular paragraph 8 to the 'ICTR Completion Strategy'. Paragraph 3 of United Nations Security Council Resolution 1534 (26 March 2004) on the International Criminal Tribunal for the former Yugoslavia and International Criminal Tribunal for Rwanda emphasizes the 'importance' of each of the *ad hoc* Tribunals implementing their respective Completion Strategies and calls upon the Tribunals to 'plan and act accordingly'. However, it remains to be seen whether the *ad hoc* Tribunals will be able to adhere to the timetable specified in their respective Completion Strategies for the completion of their work.

79 Rome Statute, article 1.

80 There is a Negotiated Relationship Agreement between the International Criminal Court and the United Nations (4 October 2004) ICC Doc ICC-ASP/3/Res. 1, whose purpose is to 'define ... the terms on which the United Nations and the Court shall be brought into relationship' (article 1(1)). In addition, there are a number of provisions in the Rome

power to exercise its jurisdiction with respect to circumstances that may occur *in the future* – that is, at any time after the Rome Statute came into force.[81] Unless the Assembly of States Parties to the Rome Statute decides to completely alter the nature or focus of the Court, the ICC will remain in place for the long term and will have the potential to play a role in circumstances where 'the most serious crimes of concern to the international community as a whole' have been committed.[82]

In this sense, the ICC represents an important guardian of those values and norms that are accepted universally among the international community. As the then United Nations Secretary-General Kofi Annan put it, following the agreement of delegates at the 1998 Rome Conference to adopt the Rome Statute, the Court's creation is 'a gift of hope to future generations, and a giant step forward in the march towards universal human rights and the rule of law'.[83]

Not only is this important in and of itself; it also reaffirms the interrelationship between the maintenance of international peace and security – one of the principal purposes of the United Nations – and the respect for fundamental human rights. Indeed, the United Nations Security Council has acknowledged that 'peace and security, development and human rights are the pillars of the United Nations system and the foundations for collective security and well-being, and … in this regard … development, peace and security and human rights are interlinked and mutually reinforcing.'[84]

Jurisdiction

The Rome Statute provides that the following crimes, when committed after 1 July 2002,[85] fall within the jurisdiction of the ICC:

a. The crime of Genocide – when committed 'with intent to destroy, in whole or in part, a national, ethnical, racial or religious group, as such';[86]

Statute that formalise various aspects of the specific relationship between the Court and the United Nations Security Council: see, for example, Rome Statute, articles 13(b), 16, 53(2)(c), 53(3)(a), 87(5), 87(7) and 115(b).

81 It should be noted, however, that if a state becomes a State Party to the Rome Statute after 1 July 2002, the Court may exercise its jurisdiction only with respect to crimes committed after the entry into force of the Rome Statute for that state, unless that state has made a declaration as a non-State Party under article 12(3) of the Rome Statute: Rome Statute, article 11(2).

82 Rome Statute, preambular paragraph 4.

83 United Nations Website <www.un.org/News/facts/iccfact.htm> (accessed 28 November 2009).

84 United Nations Security Council Resolution 1674 on the Protection of Civilians in Armed Conflict, 28 April 2006, preambular paragraph 3.

85 As noted, this is subject to the terms of article 11(2) of the Rome Statute.

86 Rome Statute, article 6 chapeau.

b. Crimes against Humanity – when committed 'as part of a widespread or systematic attack directed against any civilian population, with knowledge of the attack';[87]
c. War Crimes – which usually involves a breach of 1949 Geneva Conventions[88] and/or the laws and customs of armed conflict, 'in particular when committed as part of a plan or policy or as part of a large-scale commission of such crimes'[89]
d. The Crime of Aggression[90] – although left undefined at the conclusion of the 1998 Rome Conference, a definition of the crime of Aggression has recently been agreed by the States Parties to the Rome Statute during the first Review Conference of the Rome Statute (Review Conference), which was held in Kampala, Uganda from 31 May to 11 June 2010. The definition is complex,[91] but a 'roadmap for activation'[92] of the jurisdiction of the ICC in relation to this crime has been set out, commencing on 1 January 2017.

Articles 12 and 13 of the Rome Statute specify the '[p]reconditions to the exercise of jurisdiction' and 'exercise of jurisdiction' by the Court respectively. In summary, the Court can exercise its jurisdiction in relation to these crimes in the following circumstances:

a. where an (alleged) crime has been committed on the territory of a State Party to the Rome Statute;[93]
b. where a national(s) of a State Party to the Rome Statute is alleged to have committed a crime;[94]
c. where a situation in which a crime(s) 'appears to have been committed' has been referred to the Prosecutor of the ICC by the United Nations

87 Rome Statute, article 7(1).

88 Geneva Convention for the Amelioration of the Condition of the Wounded and Sick in Armed Forces in the Field, 75 UNTS 31; Geneva Convention for the Amelioration of the Condition of the Wounded, Sick and Shipwrecked Members of Armed Forces at Sea, 75 UNTS 85; Geneva Convention Relative to the Treatment of Prisoners of War, 75 UNTS 135; Geneva Convention Relative to the Protection of Civilian Persons in Time of War, 75 UNTS 287.

89 Rome Statute, article 8(1).

90 Rome Statute, articles 5(1)(d) and 5(2).

91 See Resolution RC/Res. 6, adopted by consensus at the Review Conference on 11 June 2010 <http:// www.icc-cpi.int/iccdocs/asp_docs/Resolutions/RC-Res.6-ENG.pdf> (accessed 2 December 2010).

92 Coalition for the International Criminal Court, 'Report of the First Review Conference of the Rome Statute', Executive Summary <http://www.coalitionfortheicc.org/documents/RC_Report_finalweb.pdf> (accessed 2 December 2010).

93 Rome Statute, article 12(2)(a).

94 Rome Statute, article 12(2)(b).

Security Council acting under Chapter VII of the United Nations Charter;[95] or

d. where a non-State Party to the Rome Statute lodges a declaration with the Registrar of the ICC, accepting the jurisdiction of the Court with respect to the 'crime in question'.[96]

As noted above, the ICC is also subject to a specific *ratione temporis*, as set out in article 11 of the Rome Statute.[97]

A System of Complementarity – Shifting the Primary Responsibility to States

The jurisdiction of the Court is subject to the principle of 'complementarity' that has been established under the Rome Statute.[98] In essence, this means that primary responsibility for the prosecution of these crimes lies with states and that the ICC therefore operates as a 'court of last resort'. This in itself demonstrates a shift in emphasis from the culture of impunity that had existed before the 1990s, during which time it was evident that states were very reluctant to try their own nationals for war crimes, 'and even more [so] where crimes against humanity or genocide [we]re concerned'.[99]

Article 17 of the Rome Statute applies the complementarity principle in terms of the 'admissibility' of a case. A case is determined by the Court as being inadmissible *inter alia* where:[100]

---

95 Rome Statute, article 13(b).

96 Rome Statute, article 12(3). For a discussion of the declaration process by non-State Parties under article 12(3) of the Rome Statute, see Steven Freeland, 'How Open Should the Door Be? – Declarations by non-States Parties under Article 12(3) of the Rome Statute of the International Criminal Court' (2006) *Nordic Journal of International Law* 75(2): 211.

97 Article 11 of the Rome Statute provides as follows:

'1. The Court has jurisdiction only with respect to crimes committed after the entry into force of this Statute.

2. If a State becomes a Party to this Statute after its entry into force, the Court may exercise its jurisdiction only with respect to crimes committed after the entry into force of this Statute for that State, unless that State has made a declaration under article 12, paragraph 3.'

98 See Rome Statute, articles 17 and 18. For a discussion of the principle of 'complementarity' as it is applied in the Rome Statute, and some of the uncertainties that its implementation may give rise to, see Alexis Goh and Steven Freeland, 'Report on the Rome Statute and the International Criminal Court', in Gabriël A Moens and Rodophe Biffot (eds), *The Convergence of Legal Systems in the 21st Century – An Australian Approach* (2002), pp. 285, 290–96.

99 Philippe Sands, 'After Pinochet: the role of national courts', in Philippe Sands (ed), *From Nuremberg to The Hague: The Future of International Criminal Justice* (2003), pp. 68, 72.

100 Rome Statute, article 17(1).

a. The case is being investigated or prosecuted by a State which has jurisdiction over it, unless the State is unwilling or unable genuinely to carry out the investigation or prosecution;
b. The case has been investigated by a State which has jurisdiction over it and the State has decided not to prosecute the person concerned, unless the decision resulted from the unwillingness or inability of the State genuinely to prosecute;
c. ...
d. The case is not of sufficient gravity to justify further action by the Court.

This creates what has been described as a 'presumption in favour of prosecution in domestic courts',[101] given that it accords a priority to national jurisdiction. This is to be contrasted with the 'primacy' principle under which the *ad hoc* Tribunals operate.[102]

Article 17(2) specifies those circumstances in which the ICC may determine the 'unwillingness' of a State in a particular case. This may arise in the following situations:[103]

a. The proceedings were or are being undertaken or the national decision was made for the purpose of shielding the person concerned from criminal responsibility ... ;
b. ... an unjustified delay in the proceedings ... inconsistent with an intent to bring the person concerned to justice;
c. The proceedings were or are not being conducted independently or impartially, and ... are being conducted in a manner ... inconsistent with an intent to bring the person concerned to justice.

---

101 Danesh Sarooshi, 'The Statute of the International Criminal Court' (1999) *International and Comparative Law Quarterly* 48: 387, 395.

102 Article 9(1) of the ICTY Statute stipulates that the ICTY and national courts have 'concurrent jurisdiction'. However, article 9(2) expressly grants the ICTY 'primacy over national courts' and that, '[a]t any stage of the procedure, [it] may formally request national courts to defer' to its competence. The Appeals Chamber of the ICTY confirmed the legitimacy of its primacy in Decision on Defence Motion for Interlocutory Appeal on Jurisdiction, *Prosecutor* v *Duško Tadić*, Case No. IT-94-1, Appeals Chamber, 2 October 1995, paragraphs 49–64. Article 8(1) of the ICTR Statute also specifies that the ICTR and national courts have 'concurrent jurisdiction'. However, article 8(2) of the ICTR Statute is expressed in broader terms than its counterpart in the ICTY Statute, specifying that the ICTR has 'primacy over the national courts of *all States*' (emphasis added). It has been suggested that this wording in the ICTR Statute, which was drafted subsequent to the ICTY Statute, reflected a broader consensus at that time among the United Nations Security Council as to the concept of primacy: Bartram S. Brown, 'Primacy or Complementarity: Reconciling the Jurisdiction of National Courts and International Criminal Tribunals' (1998) *The Yale Journal of International Law* 23: 391, 402.

103 *Rome Statute*, article 17(2).

In assessing these circumstances, the Court is to have regard to 'the principles of due process recognized by international law'.[104] In determining a state's (in) ability in a particular case, the Court must consider whether 'due to a total or substantial collapse or unavailability of its national judicial system, the State is unable to obtain the accused or ... evidence or otherwise [is] unable to carry out its proceedings'.[105]

How to (Ultimately) Determine the Effectiveness of the ICC?

Any consideration of whether, and how, the ICC should ultimately be considered as 'effective' must therefore take account of the complementarity principles described above, together with the mandate and context within which it has been established. In this regard, it is important that the ongoing process of international criminal governance is based on experience and events as they unfold, as well as the aims of the international community and civil society in developing the various tools of international justice.

With regard to the ICC, the principal aims are articulated in the preamble of the Rome Statute as follows:[106]

> Affirming that the most serious crimes of concern to the international community as a whole must not go unpunished and that their effective prosecution must be ensured by taking measures at the national level and by enhancing international cooperation,
>
> Determined to put an end to impunity for the perpetrators of these crimes and thus to contribute to the prevention of such crimes:
>
> Recalling that it is the duty of every State to exercise its criminal jurisdiction over those responsible for international crimes ... .

Yet, the whole concept of international justice is itself a very complex issue. The ICC represents another (albeit significant) development in the ongoing evolution of this process of international justice. In reality, we are still in a relatively embryonic stage of understanding how the establishment of this permanent mechanism of international justice will, if at all, impact upon the actions and decisions of current and future political and military leaders. In addition, the ICC is still in its infancy as far as its judicial activities are concerned – there has not yet been a completed trial. Any assessment of its effect at this stage can therefore by necessity only be speculative in nature. The ICC faces many challenges and its ongoing activities

104 Ibid.

105 Ibid., article 17(3).

106 Ibid., preambular paragraphs 4, 5 and 6.

are, to some extent, also subject to the political priorities of the States Parties to the Rome Statute.

However, with these caveats in mind, this chapter now reflects on what may ultimately be four possible ways in which future analysts may seek to assess the ICC.

The End of All Armed Conflicts?

If success is to be regarded as a complete cessation of all wars, and an end to gross violations of human rights throughout the world, then it is obvious that the system of international criminal justice can never be effective. Warfare and violence appears to be an inherent part of the human psyche – indeed, there has never been a period in the recorded history of humankind that has seen a total absence of war. In the past two decades in particular, often due to pressure from civil society that itself has greater access to information as to the alleged commission of atrocities, many political leaders have called for action to stop the violations and prosecute the perpetrators – although sometimes such calls are disingenuous. Such calls for action have given momentum to the evolution of this latest phase of international criminal governance, leading to the development of the mechanisms of international justice as the 'solution' to the problem.

Viewed from this perspective, this places an impossible burden on international criminal justice. Although a system based on the rule of law and public, transparent and fair trials represents a very important component in addressing international crimes, the law cannot be left alone to cope with the problem. If ending all wars is the goal – and it should be, even though it may be unattainable – then what is required is an acknowledgement of the entire context of conflict. This involves an examination of the relevant social, cultural, geopolitical, economic, geographical, developmental and equity considerations, so as to properly deal with the circumstances that lead people to commit horrific acts of violence and rely on large-scale armed hostilities to resolve their disputes.

In this regard, mechanisms like the ICC, which implement the processes of international criminal governance, are not to be regarded as an alternative to armed conflict – rather, they are a (albeit very important) conduit by which those who violate fundamental norms are brought to judicial account. The system only operates *after* the killing, rape, torture and ethnic cleansing have taken place. It would therefore be naive and unrealistic to measure the effectiveness of international criminal justice only in terms of the cessation of war.

A Reduction of the Number of Armed Conflicts?

Should, at the very least, the establishment of a system of international criminal justice, spearheaded by the ICC, lead to a reduction in the overall number of armed conflicts? At first glance, this might be a realistic expectation, and perhaps an appropriate measure of success. However, once again, it is too simplistic. More and more armed conflicts – indeed, the majority of wars now being fought – are internal, as opposed to international, conflicts.[107] In this context, it appears that *more* rather than less war crimes are being perpetrated, even in the face of this evolving system of international criminal justice.

With some obvious exceptions, the nature of warfare has largely moved away from the traditional 'state versus state' conflict, which has historically been based on a reciprocal respect (more or less) for some of the fundamental principles of international humanitarian law. Internal conflicts, as well as the increasing involvement of 'non-state actors', complicate efforts to regulate the conduct of hostilities between combatants. This is due in part to the reluctance of states to agree to binding legal standards regulating what have traditionally been regarded as internal matters.

This is highlighted by the fact that, when the 1949 Geneva Conventions were 'upgraded' by the two 1977 Additional Protocols – one dealing with international armed conflict[108] and the other with conflicts of a 'non-international nature'[109] – what was striking was the enormous disparity in the range of rules that were specified. Whereas Additional Protocol I consists of over a hundred articles, some of them quite detailed and 'radical' (at least for the time), Additional Protocol II was far more modest (28 articles, of which only 18 were substantive in content). While, of course, the absolute number of provisions is not necessarily indicative of the content, it is clear to anyone familiar with both documents that there are many areas relating to internal armed conflicts that were simply not addressed in the relevant treaty norms.

In this regard, international lawyers increasingly rely on the rules of customary international law to 'fill in the gaps' in relation to this growing number of non-international conflicts.[110] In addition, of course, the Rome Statute does specify various crimes committed in non-international conflicts.[111] However, the historical reluctance of states to accord such conflicts with the same restrictions as 'traditional' wars has been a factor that has contributed to a greater number of atrocities being committed. The mechanisms of international criminal justice are now equipped

107 For an early and important discussion on the nature of internal, as compared with international conflicts, for the purposes of determining individual criminal responsibility for war crimes, see ICTY, Decision on Defence Motion for Interlocutory Appeal on Jurisdiction, *Prosecutor* v *Duško Tadić*, Case No: IT-94-1, Appeals Chamber, 2 October 1995.

108 Protocol I Additional to the Geneva Conventions of August 12, 1949, and relating to the Protection of Victims of International Armed Conflicts, 1125 UNTS 3, 16 ILM 1391 (Additional Protocol I).

109 Protocol II Additional to the Geneva Conventions of August 12, 1949, and relating to the Protection of Victims of Non-International Armed Conflicts, 1125 UNTS 609, 16 ILM 1442 (Additional Protocol II).

110 See, for example, Jean-Marie Henckaerts and Louise Doswald-Beck (eds), *Customary International Humanitarian Law* (Volume I: Rules, 2005).

111 For example, articles 7(2)(c)-(f) of the Rome Statute specifies particular war crimes that take place in 'armed conflicts not of an international character'.

to deal with at least some of these crimes – but once again, there continues to be a mindset and political will that stand in the way of greater effectiveness in this regard, at least in the short term.

A Large Number of Prosecutions by the ICC?

Would it perhaps be reasonable to determine the success of the ICC by the number of prosecutions that are initiated there? After all, isn't that what courts such as these have been set up to do within the framework of international criminal governance? The ICC has, for example, been established with the 'power to exercise jurisdiction over persons for the most serious crimes of international concern'.[112] What is the point of doing this if it does not proceed to prosecute anyone (and everyone?) who is suspected of having committed such crimes?

As logical as this argument may sound, it is, once again, unrealistic. It must be recalled that the mechanisms of international justice are, in general terms, intended to prosecute those 'most responsible' for the commission of such crimes. Of course, this has not always been the case, but virtually *any* trial before an International Court will be complex, detailed, lengthy and require large amounts of resources in terms of expertise, time and, ultimately, money. As a consequence, international criminal justice can only be, and always will be selective. It is simply not logistically possible to undertake a large number of international trials at the same time.

Indeed, the issue of finance remains a vital element in the operation of the ICC, which is required to submit a budget proposal each year to the Assembly of States Parties for the consideration of the Committee on Budget and Finance and the ultimate approval of States Parties to the Rome Statute.[113] As a part of this process, the Court continues to develop and refine its Strategic Plan, with '[t]he interaction between the Strategic Plan and the annual budgetary procedure [being] crucial for the credibility of the planning process'.[114]

All of these considerations give rise to a simple but fundamental question: 'how much international criminal justice are we prepared to pay for?' Seen in this context, it is impractical to expect that the system of international criminal governance will directly lead to the prosecution of all, or indeed most, of those people who are responsible for the commission of these crimes. This is not to say that there will be no trials – the experience of the *ad hoc* Tribunals largely

112 Rome Statute, article 1.

113 In relation to the 9th Assembly of States Parties to be held in New York in December 2010, see, for example, Assembly of States Parties, 'Report of the Committee on Budget and Finance on the work of its fifteenth session', 24 November 2010 <http://www.icc-cpi.int/iccdocs/asp_docs/ASP9/ICC-ASP-9-15-ENG.pdf> (accessed 2 December 2010).

114 Assembly of States Parties, 'Report of the Bureau on the strategic planning process of the International Criminal Court', 18 November 2010, paragraph 18 <http://www.icc-cpi.int/iccdocs/asp_docs/ASP9/ICC-ASP-9-32-ENG.pdf> (accessed 2 December 2010).

indicates that this is the case. Yet, the total number of prosecutions undertaken by the ICC should not be regarded as a correct measure of the effectiveness of the system, let alone the number of convictions.

Greater Accountability Within the Systems of National Criminal Governance?

While the system of complementarity is, by definition, a limiting factor on the ability of the Court to prosecute specific crimes, it has the consequence that all states have the primary responsibility – or perhaps viewed in another way, the primary 'opportunity' – to exercise their national criminal jurisdiction over those who have allegedly committed international crimes. Although there are, undoubtedly, still some uncertainties as to precisely how aspects of the complementarity principle may apply in practice, – we will simply have to wait to see how the ICC Judges interpret the relevant provisions in particular situations – the principle does represent a safeguard to a state that would otherwise be concerned that one of its nationals would face trial before the Court.

As an element of this complementarity process, we are gradually witnessing the 'upgrading' of national laws to accord with the principles contained in the Rome Statute. Of course, in some cases the primary motivation behind this is to ensure that the relevant state does not fall within the 'unable' criteria set out in article 17 of the Rome Statute. Nevertheless, one of the positive 'by-products' from the establishment of the Court is the incentive it provides for States Parties to implement appropriate domestic laws designed to enable their respective national courts to exercise jurisdiction in respect of any alleged act that constitutes an international crime within the mandate of the ICC. Even though various States Parties have yet to enact implementing legislation, as this international system of criminal justice further strengthens, governments will no longer be able to ignore the moral and legal imperative to recognise these crimes within their own national criminal justice systems.

For example, following ratification of the Rome Statute, the Australian Parliament enacted both the International Criminal Court Act 2002 and the International Criminal Court (Consequential Amendments) Act 2002 which, among other things, provided for cooperation between the Court and the Australian government and, more importantly, introduced the crimes defined in the Rome Statute into Australian domestic law. Other states have followed suit.[115]

For Australia, this legislation was both significant and symbolic, given that Parliament had previously failed to effectively implement the Genocide Convention

---

115 Another such state is New Zealand, which has implemented the Rome Statute into its domestic laws through the International Crimes and International Criminal Court Act 2000. This legislation is, in certain respects, significantly broader in scope than the Australian legislation: see Treasa Dunworth, 'The International Crimes and International Criminal Court Act 2000 (NZ): A Model for the Region?', in Neil Boister and Alberto Costi (eds), *Regionalising International Criminal Law in the Pacific* (2006), p. 145.

into domestic law, with the result that it had been very difficult to assert that a crime of genocide existed under Australian law.[116] As such, the ratification of the Rome Statute placed Australia in a position where it had to accept – albeit perhaps for pragmatic reasons – the inevitability that crimes such as genocide and crimes against humanity are and should be recognised as fundamental elements of its domestic criminal code.

Actions such as this do not impinge unacceptably on national sovereignty – instead the introduction of such domestic laws sends a signal to the international community that the relevant state is, and is seen to be, willing to accept its responsibilities to contribute in a positive way to the progress of international justice, as well as fulfilling its 'duty ... to exercise its [national] criminal jurisdiction over those responsible for international crimes'.[117]

The incorporation of these international crimes into domestic law will mean that greater pressure will exist for judicial accountability for perpetrators of war crimes to be initiated at the national level. This may, in many circumstances, bring with it benefits that the existing system of international criminal governance may not be able to provide – not only from a cost viewpoint, but perhaps also from a relevancy and 'access to justice' perspective, since the trials will therefore not take place many thousands of miles away from where victims and their families live.

Naturally, it is crucial that the domestic processes that are established in this regard are themselves public, transparent and fair. As if one needed reminding of the importance of this principle, it is appropriate to consider for a moment the trials of Saddam Hussein. The Supreme Iraqi Criminal Tribunal – a national court – that was established to hear the trials, lacked several fundamental protections to which the accused are entitled under international human rights principles. In addition, the trials before that court were marked by governmental interference (including the replacement of some Judges seen as being too lenient towards Saddam), the murder of several defence lawyers, the involvement of inexperienced Judges, chaotic scenes within the court room, allegations of bribery of and perjury by Prosecution witnesses, allegations of forgery of Prosecution evidence and allegations by the accused of torture.

As a result of the flawed process, an important opportunity was missed. The Saddam trial simply failed to promote reconciliation in Iraq. Instead, what it demonstrated was that, unlike the process that was actually implemented, if international or national criminal justice is to make an important contribution to peace, then it must respect the rule of law and ensure the rights of the accused, so as to limit any suggestions that it simply represents 'victors justice'.

However, if this acceptance of responsibility on the part of states is implemented in an appropriate manner, then the development of international criminal justice

116 See, for example, *Nulyarimma* v. *Thompson* (1999) 165 ALR 621, where the Full Court of the Federal Court held, by majority, that rules of customary international law making Genocide a crime were not part of Australian common law.

117 Rome Statute, preambular paragraph 6.

will have played a crucial role in moving us all towards the perhaps unattainable but still crucial goal of 'putting an end to impunity' for the perpetrators of such crimes. Somewhat ironically, therefore, perhaps the ultimate criteria that will be the most appropriate for assessing the effectiveness of the ICC, currently the most important of the mechanisms of international criminal governance, will be the extent to which international standards and norms of behaviour are protected and enforced at the *national* level. Of course, only time will tell.

Concluding Comments

The establishment of the permanent ICC represents a further and critical step forward in the evolution of international criminal governance. The Court has been given the jurisdiction to act in relation to several international crimes, each of which represents a gross violation of universal human rights norms. Although it is only one element in the overall matrix of enforcement mechanisms designed to ensure that these norms are respected and adhered to, the establishment of a permanent mechanism of international justice reflects a determination of the international community that those who bear the greatest responsibility for mass killings and other atrocities directed towards specific groups be made fully accountable in a transparent process, leaving no room for subsequent historical revision. While these are lofty – and perhaps even unattainable – goals, they are certainly worthy of every effort.

The momentum of this international process is also gradually being reflected in national law, with domestic trials for war crimes and crimes against humanity now taking place in countries ranging from Argentina to Bosnia to Senegal. Largely driven by the momentum created by the mechanisms and processes of international criminal governance, national governments can no longer ignore the moral imperative to recognise these crimes within their own legal systems.

Yet, there is still much to be done. We are currently witnessing the first genocide of the twenty-first century in the Darfur region of Sudan. It has been estimated by various human rights groups that the actions of the government-backed Janjaweed have already resulted in the deaths of more than 250,000 people and the internal displacement of a further two million.[118] The various crimes so far detailed by the Prosecutor of the ICC give us an indication of the scale and horror of the actions taking place almost on a daily basis.[119] As well as a number of other alleged perpetrators, the ICC has now issued arrest warrants against the current

118 Human Rights Watch, 'Entrenching Impunity: Government Responsibility for International Crimes in Darfur', December 2005 <http://hrw.org/reports/2005/darfur1205/> (accessed 3 March 2008).

119 ICC, Decision on the Prosecution Application under Article 58(7) of the Statute, *Prosecutor* v. *Ahmad Muhammad Harun and Ali Muhammad AlAbd-Al-Rahman*, Case No: ICC-02/05-01/07-01, Pre Trial Chamber I, 27 April 2007.

head of state of Sudan, President Omar Al Bashir,[120] for crimes against humanity, war crimes and genocide.[121] Thus far, however, no action has been taken to bring President Bashir before the ICC and, in fact, various States Parties appear to have violated their express obligations under the Rome Statute to cooperate with the Court on this issue.[122]

It is in this regard that, notwithstanding the development of a system of internationalised justice, states have crucial roles to play. The mechanisms of international criminal governance that have been established have no 'police force'. They are, to a large degree, entirely reliant on states to affect the arrest of indicted individuals so that they can be brought before the Court to face trial or, alternatively, as discussed above, to implement credible and appropriate prosecutions under their national criminal governance systems.

This ongoing development of the international criminal governance, involving as it does a variety of international and (increasingly) national justice mechanisms, requires that the principles of international criminal law and the protection of fundamental human rights norms are implemented consistently. The United Nations Security Council has recently noted that such mechanisms 'can promote not only individual responsibility for serious crimes, but also peace, truth, reconciliation and the rights of the victims'.[123]

If we are truly to achieve the realisation of these goals and move towards the end of impunity – an essential element 'if a society in conflict or recovering from conflict is to come to terms with past abuses committed against civilians affected by armed conflict and to prevent future such abuses'[124] – then it is necessary that international criminal governance structures properly reflect the importance of these sentiments. Failure to respect these ideals must not be tolerated, as this would represent a failure of the rule of law and thus undermine the very premise of existing and emerging legal obligations, such as the concept of the

120 For an analysis of the prosecution of Heads of State within the system of international criminal governance, see Steven Freeland, 'A Prosecution too far? Reflections on the Accountability of Heads of State under International Criminal Law' (2010) *Victoria University of Wellington Law Review* 41(2): 179.

121 ICC, 'Warrant of Arrest for Omar Hassan Ahmad Al Bashir, *The Prosecutor v. Omar Hassan Ahmad Al Bashir*, Case No: ICC-02/05-01/09, Pre Trial Chamber 1, 4 March 2009 <http://www.icc-cpi.int/iccdocs/doc/doc639078.pdf> (accessed 2 December 2010); ICC, 'Second Warrant of Arrest for Omar Hassan Ahmad Al Bashir, *The Prosecutor v. Omar Hassan Ahmad Al Bashir*, Case No: ICC-02/05-01/09, Pre Trial Chamber 1, 12 July 2010 <http://www.icc-cpi.int/iccdocs/doc/doc907140.pdf> (accessed 2 December 2010).

122 See, for example, ICC, 'Pre Trial Chamber I requests the cooperation of the Central African Republic to execute the warrants of arrest of Omar Al Bashir', Press Release, 1 December 2010 <http://www.icc-cpi.int/NR/exeres/8F0B6FF8-CF0C-45CE-9BE8-9B0770AB47D3.htm> (accessed 2 December 2010).

123 United Nations Security Council Resolution 1674 on the Protection of Civilians in Armed Conflict, 28 April 2006, paragraph 7.

124 Ibid.

'responsibility to protect' populations from genocide, war crimes, ethnic cleansing and crimes against humanity, which was endorsed by the 2005 World Summit[125] and subsequently reaffirmed by the United Nations Security Council.[126]

Furthermore, the United Nations continues to confirm that 'States [bear] the primary responsibility to protect and ensure the human rights of all individuals within their territories.'[127] Whilst the precise legal effect of such statements and emerging concepts may not be entirely clear at this point, they certainly strongly suggest that a culture of impunity is no longer acceptable.

Courts like the ICC have a vital role to play in this process, but their creation is not the panacea that will stop these atrocities from taking place. In the end, the effectiveness of international criminal governance will largely depend on the efforts of states. What is required is sincere and determined political will on the part of all states to respect the norms of international law, to listen to the calls of those under threat and to ensure that crimes such as these do not in fact occur or, if (unfortunately) they do, that proper and timely processes of accountability are initiated.

125 See United Nations General Assembly, '2005 World Summit Outcome', 15 September 2005, paragraphs 138–9 <http://www.who.int/hiv/universalaccess2010/worldsummit.pdf> (accessed 2 December 2010).

126 See, for example, United Nations Security Council Resolution 1674 on the Protection of Civilians in Armed Conflict, 28 April 2006, paragraph 4.

127 United Nations Security Council, 'In Presidential Statement, Security Council Reaffirms Commitment to Protection of Civilians in Armed Conflict, Adopts updated Aide Memoire on Issue', Press Release, 22 November 2010 <http://www.un.org/News/Press/docs/2010/sc10089.doc.htm> (accessed 3 December 2010).

Chapter 9

Governing Humanitarian Intervention: Time for Change

Michelle Sanson

Introduction

The past century has seen major developments in technology and science, but far less seismic shifts in global governance. States continue to cling to the paradigm of state sovereignty in an interstate system, while practical sovereignty is eroded in favour of a globalised world.[1] What prevails is a largely seventeenth-century notion that arose from the ashes of the Thirty Years War,[2] of disparate sovereign territories interacting on the twin basis of unfettered domestic control by each state and concomitant respect for the domestic control of other states within their territories. This simply does not work in the twenty-first century. Nowhere is this more evident than in the sporadic, uncoordinated nature of humanitarian intervention as a norm of international law. Humanitarian intervention reveals the inherent tension between the power of every state to govern within its territory and the right of every human being to protection, whether their state affords it to them or not.

The key argument put forth in this chapter is that a clear criterion is needed for governing humanitarian intervention. The chapter does not take the well-trod path of criticising the way humanitarian intervention is implemented[3] – not because the United Nations Security Council's actions over the past six decades have been in any way exemplary, but because it is too difficult, and therefore is at the present

1 Formal, *de jure* sovereignty remains, but practical, *de facto* sovereignty is being eroded, with significant areas already being largely beyond the control of a single state – take for instance, global financial stability, environment, health, terrorism and the acts of global companies. See Michelle Sanson *International Law and Global Governance* (London: Cameron May, 2008).

2 The Treaty of Westphalia 1688 divided territory in Europe between princes on the basis that each exercised governance in his own territory and respected the governance of other princes over their territory.

3 See, for example, Thomas G Weiss, 'The Illusion of UN Security Council Reform', *Washington Quarterly,* Autumn 2003: 147–161; Christian Reus-Smith, Marianne Hanson, Hilary Charlesworth and William Maley, *The Challenge of United Nations Reform* (2004), available at <http://ips.cap.anu.edu.au/ir/pubs/keynotes/documents/Keynotes-5.pdf> (accessed 14 September 2010).

time unrealistic, to reform the Security Council. The veto power of the permanent five members of the Security Council (the United States, United Kingdom, France, China and Russia)[4] extends to any amendment of the United Nations Charter, and it is unlikely to get all five permanent members to agree to any decision that reduces their power.[5] The degree of urgency and the need for certainty and predictability in international law with respect to humanitarian intervention is such that we cannot wait for Security Council reform.

Development of, and Justification for, Humanitarian Intervention

The norm of humanitarian intervention is relatively recent, having arisen gradually since the Second World War.[6] Across history, violent war has been a regular occurrence in most cultures.[7] There are references in the Christian Bible to 'God's word' being to kill a whole people including children and babies so that only the victorious people continue to live on the Earth.[8] For centuries, it was assumed that a conqueror could do in the conquered territory what it chose, including killing or enslaving an entire people. The murderous exercise of power remained unquestioned through to the early part of last century. For example, no issue was raised about the alleged massacre of 1.5 million Armenians by the Turks in 1915–17. It was only after the death of between seven and ten million people in the 1930s under Stalin, and eleven million people in the 1940s under Hitler, that mass killing was widely condemned.[9]

4 United Nations Charter, Article 27.

5 Article 108 of the United Nations Charter provides: 'Amendments to the present Charter shall come into force for all Members of the United Nations when they have been adopted by a vote of two thirds of the members of the General Assembly and ratified in accordance with their respective constitutional processes by two thirds of the Members of the United Nations, *including all the permanent members of the Security Council*' (emphasis added).

6 'Governments no longer have the right to mistreat their own people while hiding behind walls of sovereignty': G.A. Geyer, 'Arena of grand intentions', *Washington Times*, 17 July 1999, quoting a state leader at a dinner. The contrary view is expressed by Kratochwil, who considers the right to sovereignty is itself a right to do wrong: F. Kratochwil, *Rules, Norms and Decisions: On the Conditions of Practical and Legal Reasoning in International Relations and Domestic Affairs* (Cambridge: Cambridge University Press, 1989).

7 Peter Singer, *One World: the ethics of globalisation* (Melbourne: The Text Publishing Company, 2002), p. 97.

8 See the Old Testament, for example, Exodus 32:28; Numbers 21:34–5; Numbers 31:7–41.

9 According to Suter, the reason for the lack of formal complaints about Hitler's violations of Jewish human rights was that it was seen to be a domestic matter: Keith Suter, *Global Order and Global Disorder: Globalization and the Nation-State* (Westport, CT: Praeger Publishers, 2003), p. 22.

But moral condemnation proved insufficient to challenge the principle of non-intervention in sovereign affairs during the aftermath of the Second World War. The negotiations leading up to the creation of the United Nations to replace the beleaguered League of Nations[10] resulted in a charter that provided clearly for the territorial integrity of states. Article 2(4) of the United Nations Charter enshrines this: 'All Members shall refrain in their international relations from the threat or use of force against the territorial integrity or political independence of any state, or in any other manner inconsistent with the Purposes of the United Nations.'

As does Article 2(7):

> Nothing contained in the present Charter shall authorize the United Nations to intervene in matters which are essentially within the domestic jurisdiction of any state or shall require the Members to submit such matters to settlement under the present Charter; but this principle shall not prejudice the application of enforcement measures under Chapter VII.

Enforcement measures under Chapter VII are for international 'threats to peace, breaches of peace, and acts of aggression' and are a measure of last resort. Article 33(1) provides that the parties 'shall, first of all, seek a solution by negotiation, enquiry, mediation, conciliation, arbitration, judicial settlement, resort to regional agencies or arrangements, or other peaceful means of their own choice'. The power and responsibility for collective action rests with the Security Council, pursuant to Article 24(1) of the United Nations Charter:

> In order to ensure prompt and effective action by the United Nations, its Members confer on the Security Council primary responsibility for the maintenance of international peace and security, and agree that in carrying out its duties under this responsibility the Security Council acts on their behalf.

As will be seen in this chapter, the latter part of this provision has been largely ignored by Security Council members, who have instead seen their role as an extension of their individual domestic foreign policy. As such, the Security Council has acted on behalf of its own members more than on behalf of all UN members. More broadly, this absence of any entity bearing responsibility for action in the common good, be it to alleviate large-scale suffering or to ensure a sustainable planet for future generations, is a significant lacuna in our present international system.[11] When focusing specifically on the maintenance of international peace and security, the needs of particular groups in states without oil, minerals, diamonds,

10 Principal Suggestions concerning the Dumbarton Oaks Proposals, Appendix B to the Agenda of a Special Meeting of the General Council of the League of Nations Union on 5–6 April 1945, [10].

11 For further discussion on the inadequacies in international law and global governance, see Sanson, above n 1.

or hosted military facilities can take second place to groups in states where civil unrest could impact on the interests of a permanent member, or their companies operating in that jurisdiction.

The norm of non-intervention was carefully guarded for the first two decades of the United Nations experience, where even raising a state's internal affairs to be the subject of diplomatic discussion was considered a breach of non-intervention.[12] It is therefore unsurprising that nothing was done in the 1970s to stop the massacre of two million people in Cambodia by the Khmer Rouge.[13] Intervention by Vietnam without Security Council authorisation was frowned upon by other states at the time, and the Khmer Rouge continued to enjoy United Nations membership for some twenty years afterwards.[14] In the 1990s, a major shift in principle took place – in the face of gross human rights violations, often perpetrated by domestic government forces, the Security Council was increasingly called upon to intervene.

Intervention, by definition, takes place without the consent of the subject state. If the state was to consent, we would have humanitarian action/aid but not humanitarian intervention. Humanitarian action is incredibly important and has the potential to calm tensions and prevent the need for later intervention. It includes the work of non-government organisations, aid departments of various states, and agencies such as UNICEF. Each acts with the permission of the host state, who bears a responsibility to ensure they are able to carry out their work safely and effectively. Humanitarian action and aid is entirely consistent with the principle of state sovereignty. Humanitarian intervention, on the other hand, overrides a state's sovereignty through non-consensual incursion into the territory of the state. Under the United Nations system, intervention of any kind must be authorised by the Security Council pursuant to Chapter VII of the Charter. The only exception is legitimate acts of self-defence (and in more recent years, pre-emptive self-defence).

This definition of humanitarian intervention, of military acts for humanitarian purposes within a state's borders without the state's consent, is narrower than some definitions of humanitarian intervention that have been used. For example, the International Commission on Intervention and State Sovereignty, composed during the United Nations Millennium Assembly in 2000 and comprising 12 expert commissioners to develop international consensus on responding to massive violations of human rights and humanitarian law, used a broader definition, including not only military action but also economic sanctions, arms

---

12 Suter, above n. 9, p. 79, referring to Higgins' statement while at University of London.

13 Just as Hitler published his intentions in *Mein Kampf* well before acting upon them, Pol Pot openly declared that only three million of the existing seven million people living in Cambodia were needed in the agrarian society of the future Cambodia. Through the Khmer Rouge, Pol Pot succeeded in killing half of his desired goal.

14 It is only recently that a Special Tribunal for Cambodia has been established (2007).

embargoes, and diplomatic isolation.[15] However, these actions, whilst they may exert pressure on a state to behave differently, do not amount to intervention. Such techniques may successfully avert a humanitarian catastrophe, and are actions taken without state consent and for humanitarian purposes, but they do not amount to humanitarian intervention per se, because the territorial integrity of the relevant state is maintained.

Examples of humanitarian intervention with Security Council authorisation include France into Rwanda in 1994 (much too late) to intervene in the massacre of the Tutsis by the Hutus;[16] Italy into Albania in 1997 to intervene in the massacre of Kosovars;[17] the United Kingdom into Sierra Leone in 1997–2000 to end civil war in the diamond-rich nation,[18] and Australia into East Timor in 1999, in response to massacres by militia supported by the Indonesian Army.[19]

Additionally, on several occasions, there has been intervention by the United States or US-led NATO forces without Security Council authorisation: in 1991, in the massacre of the Kurds and Shiites in Northern Iraq; in 1992–95, in Bosnia and Herzegovina; in 1992–93, in Somalia, and in 1994 in Haiti. In the case of northern Iraq[20] and Somalia,[21] the Security Council resolutions were issued after

15 International Commission on Intervention and State Sovereignty (ICISS), *The Responsibility to Protect: Report of the International Commission on Intervention and State Sovereignty* (2001), pp. 29–31.

16 Security Council Resolution 925, 8 June 1994, came three months into the genocide, after 800,000 of the 1.2 million Tutsis in Rwanda had been massacred. It would appear that the main concern of the United Nations was its credibility, not wanting to risk another Somalia: see M. Barnett, 'The UN Security Council, Indifference, and Genocide in Rwanda', (1997) *Cultural Anthropology*, 12(4): 551, 553. The greatest shame with this genocide was that the peacekeeping forces that had been present at the start of the incident were not given the mandate to stop the genocide. See A. Des Forges, *Leave None to Tell the Story: Genocide in Rwanda*, Report of the Human Rights Watch, March 1999. Essentially the view taken was that they would have to leave, as peace keepers were there by consent, and then return as an intervening force. This meant abandoning thousands of helpless people who had sought shelter in UN-secured compounds, schools, hotels, and churches.

17 Security Council Resolution 1114, 19 June 1997.

18 Security Council Resolution 1132, 8 October 1997.

19 Security Council Resolution 1272, 25 October 1999.

20 Security Council Resolution 688, 5 April 1991.

21 Security Council Resolution 794, 3 December 1992. Wheeler has noted Somalia was less a case of intervening against the will of the ruling government, and more about intervening to restore law and order in a failed state, and as such it can be seen as part of the development of a responsibility by the Security Council to act in such situations: N.J. Wheeler, 'The Humanitarian Responsibilities of Sovereignty: Explaining the Development of a New Norm of Military Intervention for Humanitarian Purposes in International Society', in J.M. Welsh, *Humanitarian Intervention and International Relations* (Oxford: Oxford University Press, 2004), p. 36.

the intervention, thereby retrospectively legalising them.[22] The fact that there was no challenge by the United Nations membership[23] suggests that there was general acceptance that the Security Council had power to not only authorise humanitarian intervention,[24] but also to provide that authorisation retrospectively.

What then, was the basis of the United Nations Security Council's justification for authorising intervention in a state's territory for humanitarian purposes? After all, there is nothing specifically in the UN Charter to support it, and indeed, reading the Charter provisions in their ordinary meaning in the light of their context and purpose,[25] the clear message is that intervention is prohibited except for self-defence[26] or where in the Security Council's opinion the circumstances represent a threat to international peace and security. It is difficult to imagine humanitarian circumstances that take place wholly within one state, with no spillage of violence or people across the borders, which do not spill over its borders, could justify intervention in self-defence by a neighbouring state, and it may seem somewhat artificial to characterise these circumstances as a threat to international peace and security. Clearly, the language used in the Charter was directed towards collective security in a global system, as opposed to human security within a state.

The absence of express provision for humanitarian intervention has necessitated a dynamic interpretation of the Charter.[27] According to Roberts:

---

22 According to Wheeler, 'the moral and legal responsibility that falls on those who intervene without Council authority is to persuade the Council – and wider global opinion – that its action should be excused or tolerated on humanitarian grounds': Ibid. at p. 46. The fact that seven of the ten non-NATO states on the Security Council voted against a Russian resolution condemning NATO's action indicates that they were persuaded that NATO had discharged the burden of justifying the use of force on these grounds: Ibid. at p. 49. The challenge is that 'tracking the moment when a practice casts off its illegality and creates the conditions for its own validity is not simple': Simpson, above n. 7, p. 106.

23 There has however been academic challenge. For example, Nye has said that the erosion of state sovereignty may help advance human rights in repressive regimes by exposing them to international attention, but it also portends considerable disorder: J. Nye, 'Redefining the National Interest', *Foreign Affairs*, July-August 1999, 78: 30. See also Babic, who depicts humanitarian intervention as a kind of fanaticism aimed at imposing a particular 'value matrix' not only on a given state but eventually on the entire world: Burleigh Wilkins, 'Introduction' in Alexander Jokic, *Humanitarian Intervention: Moral and Philosophical Issues* (Calgary: Broadview Press, 2003), p. 11.

24 A. Roberts, 'The United Nations and Humanitarian Intervention', in Welsh, above n. 21,p. 84.

25 Vienna Convention on the Law of Treaties (1979), Article 31.

26 United Nations Charter, Article 51.

27 The alternative view is that doing so is a breach, not a dynamic interpretation, of the Charter. See Singer, 'At its face value, it would seem that the United Nations cannot set up procedures to authorize humanitarian intervention, because in doing so, it would be violating its own Charter': above n. 7, p. 110.

> What has been happening at the United Nations is a gradual and incremental change in the interpretation of the Charter rules and the United Nation's responsibilities, particularly as regards the balance between the rights of individual sovereign states and the rights of the community – whether the latter be defined as individual human beings or the entire community of states.[28]

The Security Council has two potential avenues under the Charter for justifying intervention. The first is through a broad interpretation of Articles 55 and 56, which provide:

> Article 55
>
> With a view to the creation of conditions of stability and well-being which are necessary for peaceful and friendly relations among nations based on respect for the principle of equal rights and self-determination of peoples, the United Nations shall promote: ... universal respect for, and observance of, human rights and fundamental freedoms for all ...
>
> Article 56
>
> All Members pledge themselves to take joint and separate action in co-operation with the Organization for the achievement of the purposes set forth in Article 55.

Arguably, the Security Council may authorise action under Article 56 to promote observance of human rights and fundamental freedoms under Article 55. Of course, not all human rights breaches warrant it – only the most egregious breaches can do so. These would be peremptory norms of international law, *jus cogens* and obligations *erga omnes*. These non-derogable norms apply to all states regardless of their consent, and include genocide, slavery, torture and piracy.

The second option involves construing a domestic violation of human rights as a threat to international peace and security, thereby sidestepping Article 2(7) and calling into play Chapter VII powers. Examples where the Security Council has characterised a domestic violation as a threat to international peace and security include intervention in northern Iraq in 1991 with reference to Iraq's repression of the Kurds;[29] in Somalia in 1992–93 with reference to civil strife perpetuated by local warloads,[30] and in Haiti in 1995, with reference to the overthrow of the democratically elected president, Jean-Bertrand Aristide.[31]

---

28 A. Roberts, 'The United Nations and Humanitarian Intervention', in Welsh, above n. 21, p. 97.

29 Security Council Resolution 688, 5 April 1991.

30 Security Council Resolution 794, 3 December 1992.

31 Security Council Resolution 975, 30 January 1995.

Characterising a domestic violation as a threat to international peace and security is rarely difficult, given that there is usually a steady flow of people out of a conflict zone into neighbouring states, or at least some impact that surpasses the relevant state's borders. An example, used by former United Nations Secretary General Kofi Annan, is the 1997 forest fires in Indonesia, which had been set deliberately by Indonesian plantation owners. In the face of inaction by Indonesian authorities and with a 'health-threatening haze' traversing the south-east region, 'ASEAN ministers felt no compunction about "interfering" in Indonesia's domestic affairs, because what it was doing clearly affected the lives of people in the other member states.'[32]

However, there is always the 'slippery slope' argument: if the international community endorses a breach of the territorial integrity in another state by reason of humanitarian intervention, what is there to stop an intervention in one's own territory, in relation to circumstances which are considered unacceptable by others but entirely acceptable and lawful in one's own culture? Ultimately, why should the views of the prevailing members of the Security Council trump the acts of a sovereign state in its own territory? Which fundamental principle is overriding, when in stark conflict with one another – non-interference in the internal affairs of a sovereign state, or protection of the human rights of a state's people?[33] To use Friedman's words, 'there is an obvious conflict between any concept of universal human rights and that sacred cow, national sovereignty.'[34] Or in the words of former United Nations Secretary General Kofi Annan: We confront a real dilemma. Few would disagree that both the defence of humanity and the defence of sovereignty are principles that must be supported. Alas, that does not tell us which principle should prevail when they are in conflict.

Humanitarian intervention is a sensitive issue, fraught with political difficulty and not susceptible to easy answers. But surely no legal principle – not even sovereignty – can ever shield crimes against humanity. Where such crimes occur and peaceful attempts to halt them have been exhausted, the Security Council has a moral duty to act on behalf of the international community. The fact that we cannot protect people everywhere is no reason for doing nothing when we can.

---

32 Kofi A. Annan, 'Global Values: The United Nations and the Rule of Law in the 21st Century', Singapore Lecture 14 February 2000, Institute of Southeast Asian Studies, p. 9.

33 See R. Müllerson, *Ordering Anarchy: International Law in International Society* (The Hague: Martinus Nijhoff Publishers, 2000), p. 367.

34 L.M. Friedman, 'Frontiers: National and Transnational Order', in K.H. Ladeur, *Public Governance in the Age of Globalization* (Aldershot: Ashgate, 2004), p. 45. See also Czernecki, who has described the tension between sovereignty and humanitarian intervention as 'the greatest conflict in the international realm': J. Czernecki, 'The United Nations Paradox: The Battle Between Humanitarian Intervention and State Sovereignty' (2003) *Duquesne Law Review*, 41: 391.

Armed intervention must always remain the option of last resort, but in the face of mass murder it is an option that cannot be relinquished.[35]

Perhaps the apparent conflict in the Charter between Article 2(7), which calls for non-intervention in domestic matters, and Articles 55 and 56, which promote action to protect human rights, can be resolved on the basis that the Article 2(7) right of sovereign states to non-intervention does not extend to a state committing or allowing crimes against humanity within its territory.[36] This draws upon international customary law to establish a universal jurisdiction over those who commit crimes against humanity, which the United Nations Charter does not, and cannot, displace.

Acceptance of this limitation to the ambit of Article 2(7) paves the way for a methodology for intervention, namely through the establishment of clear criterion for the (a) justification of intervening, and (b) justification of not intervening. We all would agree that grave violations of human rights (such as what we saw in Rwanda in 1994) would justify intervention, just as we would agree that failure by Australia to enforce a right to same-sex marriages would not justify intervention. But what lies between, and where should the line be drawn? Is it acceptable for Security Council members to simply decide on a case-by-case basis, placing humanitarian intervention within the realm of a mere discretion? Even if it were to be considered a discretion – which is debatable given that the delegation of authority by the international community must bring with it an obligation to act, and not merely a discretion – surely such discretion should be exercised within parameters.

The prevailing lack of a clear criterion explains the schizophrenic approach to humanitarian intervention by the Security Council over the past two decades. The price is currently being paid by the Sudanese, for example. It is a price that humanity cannot afford to pay, and in centuries to come, students of history will reflect upon the barbaric practices of the international community in the twentieth and twenty-first centuries in the same way that students of history today look back to trial by ordeal as an acceptable means of uncovering the truth. The hypocrisy and inherent unfairness of a system in which certain states, through no reason other than the fact they were the main victors in a world war, decide whether to leave vulnerable groups to fend for themselves, will be readily apparent. They will question, if we of the twenty-first century truly subscribed to the view that all human beings have equal rights, then why should we have allowed the suffering of people who happen to live in a country rich in natural resources or otherwise of geopolitical importance to one or more of the permanent five members of the

35 K.A. Annan, 'We the Peoples: The Role of the United Nations in the 21st Century', UN Doc A/54/2000 48.

36 The notion of what is a purely 'internal' affair has undergone a shift described by Claude as a 'domestication of international relations', whereby elements of intrastate relations are incorporated into the international system: I. Claude, *Swords into Plowshares: The Problems and Progress of International Organization* (New York: Random House, 1971), p. 17.

United Nations Security Council be given priority over the suffering of their brethren in countries lacking in resources attractive to Westerners?

Whether or not the Security Council, which is largely a political body where decisions are made not in accordance with the common good but in accordance with the geopolitical interests of its members,[37] is the correct body to apply the criterion to particular factual circumstances, is debatable. Perhaps an Advisory Opinion from the International Court of Justice, using an expedited procedure, would be preferable. After all, the question should be more a legal one and not merely a political one, particularly if we accept that the international community has a legal as opposed to moral obligation to protect the human rights of people everywhere.[38] This may reduce concerns about the true motivation being regime change or imperialism on the part of powerful nations, rather than purely humanitarian motivators. Assuming for the moment that the Security Council, with its present composition and powers, remains as the entity to authorise humanitarian intervention, the question is what criterion they should apply.

Towards a Clear Criterion for Humanitarian Intervention

A clear criterion would be primarily directed towards those who can decide whether to authorise humanitarian intervention, but it would also serve as a positive guide to states in their behaviour. After all, prevention is better than cure, and the best way to deter offenders is to provide a clear criterion as to what actions could jeopardise a state's territorial sovereignty.

The place to commence is the proposals by the International Commission on Intervention and State Sovereignty (ICISS). Their 2001 report covers not only humanitarian intervention (which they refer to as the responsibility to react), but also preventative efforts before the intervention, and rebuilding efforts afterwards, referred to as the responsibility to prevent, and rebuild, respectively.[39] The principles for military intervention, which is referred to as 'an exceptional and

---

37 As Wheeler has stated, the permanent five oppose or support humanitarian intervention for political or cultural reasons, leaving the fate of people whose human rights are being violated resting in the hands of the policy considerations of five states: see Wheeler, above n. 21, pp. 46 and 49. Note the difference between motive and intention – Security Council members may *intend* to resolve a humanitarian crisis but their *motive* may be their own benefit. See Burleigh Wilkins, 'Introduction' in Alexander Jokic, *Humanitarian Intervention: Moral and Philosophical Issues* (Calgary: Broadview Press, 2003).

38 According to Wheeler, the theory of state sovereignty as encompassing the rule of non-intervention has shifted from being conceived as an inherent right of states to one that carries with it concomitant responsibilities: N.J. Wheeler, 'The Humanitarian Responsibilities of Sovereignty: Explaining the Development of a New Norm of Military Intervention for Humanitarian Purposes in International Society', in Welsh, above n. 21, p. 37.

39 ICISS Report, above n 15, Chapters 3 to 5.

extraordinary measure' require 'just cause', namely serious and irreparable harm to human beings on a large scale, being done or imminently likely to occur.[40]

In addition to just cause, the ICISS refer to four 'precautionary principles'. The first is 'right intention': the primary purpose must be to avert or halt human suffering. The intention cannot be, for example, the alteration of the relevant state's borders, or overthrow of a present regime.[41] The ICISS indicates that collective or multilateral action is preferable to ensuring right intention; however, provided the intervention is endorsed by the Security Council, it should not matter if the intervening troops are from one state, as long as they are wearing United Nations insignia and act within the terms of the mandate.

The second precautionary principle is 'last resort', requiring that every diplomatic and non-military avenue be 'explored'. The ICISS appears to have been careful not to use the more common term in international law, whereby local remedies must be 'exhausted', because in some instances there will simply not be time to exhaust all other options. Therefore, it is enough that there be 'reasonable grounds for believing that, in all the circumstances, if the measure had been attempted it would not have succeeded'.[42]

Third is 'proportional means', namely the minimum action necessary to achieve the humanitarian objective. This encompasses the scale of the military operation, its intensity and duration. Fourth is 'reasonable prospects' (of success), which is controversial unless what is 'reasonable' is set out with some clarity. The challenge is the automatic inference of relativity of action to consequences – reasonable prospects of success in the light of the cost and likely casualties on the side of the interveners. The ICISS did not specifically refer to this aspect under its discussion of 'reasonable prospects' although it does mention earlier in the report that 'force protection for the intervening force must never have priority over the resolve to accomplish the mission'.[43]

It is difficult to argue with the content of these principles – but the choice of the term 'precautionary principle' is somewhat unexpected, given that it usually applies where there is a lack of consensus as to whether a particular action is creating harm, such as, for example, in relation to scientific consensus around climate change,[44] or the use of genetically modified organisms.[45] Here, the ICISS is setting out the requirements for justifiable intervention. Perhaps the ICISS uses the term in its lay meaning, being prudence or care.

The use of 'precautionary principle' in this instance is regrettable, because the term could actually have specific operation in this area – particularly in situations

40 Ibid., p. XII.

41 Ibid., p. 35.

42 Ibid., p. 36.

43 Ibid., p. 67.

44 See the Rio Declaration on Environment and Development (1992), Principle 15.

45 See *European Communities – Measures Concerning Meat and Meat Products (Hormones)* DS26.

where there is uncertain information on large-scale loss of human life, and the Security Council may authorise intervention as a precautionary measure. This could have been used, for example, with Zimbabwe in recent years, where the refusal to allow entry and free movement of foreign journalists greatly reduced the capacity to report on the true extent of the situation. It remains to be seen what exactly has been done to the people of Zimbabwe, most likely when President Mugabe passes.

The principles only address the circumstances in which humanitarian intervention can be justified – they do not address the circumstances in which inaction cannot be justified.[46] Typically, setting out criteria for action would be to impose upper limits on the actors' discretion. They would be suitable where, for example, there is a risk that the authorised entity may exceed its mandate otherwise. To date, however, there have been no issues about the need to limit the Security Council's otherwise untrammelled power to intervene – it has largely erred on the side of non-intervention, and has not to date sought to use the power to intervene too readily in the domestic affairs of other states. Yet where there is a general reluctance to intervene, it is necessary to set out criteria for inaction, to impose lower limits on the actors' discretion. There needs to be criteria which obliges the Security Council to act, particularly in circumstances where it otherwise would not due to a lack of individual economic or political interests to protect.

In what circumstances, then, can non-intervention be unjustifiable? This should be the topic for reconstituting the ICISS, a decade along the path from its previous report. Undoubtedly what may still be considered justifiable non-intervention in 2011 may be considered a vital necessity in 2050. Therefore the ICISS should meet each decade to review developments in the field of humanitarian law and adjust the criteria accordingly. The process, as with the original report, should entail detailed assessment and lengthy consultation with stakeholders. However, to further show what is envisaged, three examples are provided of circumstances in which, in the author's opinion, non-intervention is unjustified.

First, where the relevant state not only lacks the ability to respond adequately to the humanitarian problem in its state, but is actively fuelling it through financial or military support, or through intentional acquiescence, there is little recourse for those suffering harm, apart from fighting in self-defence. It is rarely the case that vulnerable, targeted groups have the resources and training to fight against the power and resources of government forces.[47] If diplomatic efforts fail to pressure

46 In a similar vein, John Stuart Mill said that philosophers should decide on a rule or criterion by which domestic intervention is justified, but also should decide on a criterion by which refraining from intervention is justified. See Singer, above n. 7, p. 104.

47 See, for example, the attempts by the Caprivi people in north-east Namibia, who had been discriminated against since colonial power Britain gave the Caprivians' land to Germany in return for Zanzibar in the late 19th century. Following the failure of the new government after independence to accord the Caprivians independence, as promised when the Caprivians were asked to join the independence struggle, secession efforts by a

the state to investigate and quell the action, or stop supporting it, then non-intervention cannot be justified. There is no need to wait years, as has happened with the situation in Sudan. The issuance by the International Criminal Court of an arrest warrant for Bashir,[48] while he is an ongoing head of state, is largely meaningless if he can continue to behave in the same manner, providing only that he avoids jurisdictions party to the Rome Statute.

Secondly, often in eroding domestic situations, states will allow international aid organisations to enter their borders and assist people with food, clothing and shelter, usually internally displaced persons in makeshift camps. If international aid organisations are expelled or their assistance efforts are significantly hampered by government action (including government control and excessive delay in movement of people and supplies), and the relevant country's weather and natural resources are such that people will be unable to obtain adequate shelter and food for themselves, then non-intervention is not justifiable. It is not necessary to wait until there is large-scale loss of life through denial of basic necessities of life – provided the state is unwilling to provide the resources, the people are otherwise unable to access them, and the state has refused humanitarian aid agencies, the necessary ingredients are there. If nothing more, this criterion will prompt states to ensure they remain accessible to aid agencies.

Third, non-intervention by reason of the exercise of veto power where the actions causing the humanitarian catastrophe are alleged to have been orchestrated or materially supported by one of the permanent five Security Council members cannot be justified. The relevant Security Council member should be excluded from the decision-making process, in the same way decision makers across governments and judiciaries discharge themselves in the event of a conflict of interest.[49] Until recently, there have been abstentions or non-appearances by Russia and China, who are ideologically opposed to intervention but prefer not to openly exercise their veto power.[50] This remained the approach in relation to the Libyan intervention in March 2011,[51] but concerns regarding intervention forces

---

small handful of Caprivians in 1995 resulted in a mobilisation of the whole state's military resources.

48 Warrant of Arrest for Omar Hassan Ahmad Al Bashir. No. ICC-02/05-01/09. 1/8 (4 March 2009).

49 Although Article 27(3) of the United Nations Charter already provides for abstention from voting where a dispute involves a Security Council member, this covers only the 'pacific settlement of disputes' between states.

50 See, for example, China's abstention on Security Council Resolution 1333, on 19 December 2000. It imposed wide measures against Taliban authorities in Afghanistan and called on them to stop providing sanctuary and training camps for international terrorists. See also Russia, China and France's abstention on Security Council Resolution 1284 on 17 December 1999. It established an inspection commission to verify Iraq's compliance regarding weapons of mass destruction.

51 Security Council Resolution 1973, 17 March 2011.

over-stepping their mandate in Libya resulted in their double veto of a proposed resolution for Syria in October.[52]

Of course, excluding the exercise of the veto power in situations where the alleged humanitarian abuses are taking place in the territory of the permanent five members of the Security Council is dangerously close, if not within, the topic of Security Council reform, which is beyond the scope of this chapter. Suffice it to say that the veto power, if exercised to prevent humanitarian intervention into a state's own territory, effectively places those five states beyond the law, being immune from legal intervention in their territory, and there being no alternative course provided in international law for legalised use of force. Take, for example, the unauthorised intervention by the United States into Iraq on the ostensible basis of finding weapons of mass destruction. Little could be done in terms of sanctions against this illegal conduct, owing to the veto power of the United States. As such, the rule of law did not apply. Shue has described this as 'a pivotal fault in their conception of sovereignty'.[53]

Although the ICISS has no power to effect reform in the area of humanitarian intervention, its 2001 report was endorsed at the 2005 World Summit, including endorsement of the 'Responsibility to Protect' (known by the acronyms RTP and R2P). The Security Council has also reaffirmed these provisions.[54] There was also broad agreement between states to set up a new Human Rights Council, which was established by the General Assembly in 2006.[55] However, although the mandate of the Human Rights Council includes to 'address situations of violations of human rights, including gross and systematic violations, and make recommendations thereon', the recommendations are to the General Assembly, seeing the Human Rights Council is a subsidiary organ of that body and not the Security Council. There needs to be an appropriate body under the Security Council to maintain a watching brief on human rights abuses and regularly advise the Security Council on their current status, using agreed criteria and diagnosing situations as either (a) no intervention can be justified, (b) intervention can be justified, and (c) non-intervention cannot be justified.

---

52 On 4 October 2011 China and Russia both vetoed a resolution in relation to Syria. Russian Federation UN Ambassador Vitaly Churkin stated: 'The situation in Syria cannot be considered in the Council separately from the Libyan experience': Security Council Report No. S/PV.6627, p. 4, http://www.securitycouncilreport.org/atf/cf/%7B65BFCF9B-6D27-4E9C-8CD3-CF6E4FF96FF9%7D/Golan%20Heights%20S%20PV%206627.pdf.

53 H. Shue, 'Limiting Sovereignty', in Welsh, above n. 21, p. 20.

54 Security Council Resolution 1674, 28 April 2006, 'Reaffirm[ed] the provisions of paragraphs 138 and 139 of the 2005 World Summit Outcome Document regarding the responsibility to protect populations from genocide, war crimes, ethnic cleansing and crimes against humanity'.

55 General Assembly Resolution 60/251, 3 April 2006.

Concluding Remarks

No changes in the machinery of international law and global governance come quickly. Wherever states consider the international system as a forum for the pursuit of domestic foreign policy objectives, little progress is made on initiatives for creating global public goods. This is borne out clearly in the governance paralysis in the area of humanitarian intervention as discussed in this chapter. One can only imagine that, when the locus of power shifts further in the direction of the populous developing nations of China and India, powers in decline such as the United States and United Kingdom will regret not using their former power to establish more democratic and accountable processes for global governance. In the area of humanitarian intervention, let us hope that it does not take another Hitler or Stalin to prompt true law reform.

Index

For Product Safety Concerns and Information please contact our EU representative GPSR@taylorandfrancis.com
Taylor & Francis Verlag GmbH, Kaufingerstraße 24, 80331 München, Germany

www.ingramcontent.com/pod-product-compliance
Ingram Content Group UK Ltd.
Pitfield, Milton Keynes, MK11 3LW, UK
UKHW010957180926
475701UK00004B/418

* 9 7 8 1 1 3 8 2 4 9 3 3 2 *